Problem Solving

Second Edition

Problem Solving

in

Microeconomics

Second Edition

A Study Guide for
Eaton and Eaton: Microeconomics
Second Edition

Nancy T. Gallini
University of Toronto

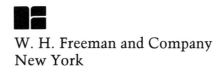

W. H. Freeman and Company
New York

Library of Congress Cataloging-in Publication Data

Gallini, Nancy Theresa.
    Problem-solving in microeconomics: a study guide for Eaton and
Eaton: Microeconomics/Nancy T. Gallini. — 2nd ed.
        p.   cm.
    ISBN 0-7167-2174-0
    1. Microeconomics.   2. Microeconomics — Problems, exercises, etc.
I. Eaton, Buford Curtis, 1943 –   Microeconomics.
HB172.G35   1991
338.5 — dc20   90-43088
                                                                    CIP

Printed in the United States of America

1 2 3 4 5 6 7 8 9 0   H   9 9 8 7 6 5 4 3 2 1

CONTENTS

PREFACE

Problem Solving in Microeconomics, Second Edition, offers a comprehensive review of the concepts taught in intermediate microeconomics courses. This study guide is designed to complement *Microeconomics*, Second Edition, by B. Curtis Eaton and Diane F. Eaton. Both books teach students how to think as economists do; hence, the emphasis is on economic applications. *Problem Solving in Microeconomics* uses real-world applications to help students understand economics. Students learn basic economic principles, not through rote memorization but through problem solving, which will enable them to develop an intuition for economic theory.

To make economics accessible to all students of intermediate microeconomics, each chapter includes several problems of varying length and difficulty. In addition, a chapter summary, case studies, key words, multiple-choice questions, and true-false questions prepare the student for the applied problems by reviewing and testing the student's basic understanding of the economic theory developed in the chapter. New problems have been added to this second edition to make economics more understandable and intriguing to the student.

Detailed answers to all the problems are included at the end of each chapter. These answers show students how to approach economic problems and give them an opportunity to check their understanding of the material.

Problem Solving in Microeconomics offers five ways for students to review and test their understanding of economics:

A chapter summary outlines the important concepts. Students should read the summary carefully and return to their textbook when they do not recall a particular concept, before working through the problems.

Key words, listed after the summary, enable students to check the main concepts in the chapter quickly.

Case studies present students with interesting real-world applications of one or more fundamental economic concepts covered in the chapter. Because economic intuition may be needed to work through a case study, it may help some students to do the exercises before working through the case study.

Multiple-choice and true-false questions test students' knowledge and understanding of economic theory, the primary tool required for economic applications.

Short and long problems enable students to apply economic knowledge to a variety of everyday situations. Those who work through these problems can feel very confident that they understand the material in the chapters.

The questions and problems in each section are usually presented in order of increasing difficulty. The more difficult problems are marked with an asterisk. Students are strongly encouraged to work through and answer these, but should attempt to work through and answer the less difficult problems first to build their confidence and intuition.

I am grateful to the many instructors at the University of Toronto who have contributed problems to my intermediate microeconomics tests over the past several years, which have been revised and are now part of this book. In particular, I wish to thank Al Berry, Don Campbell, John Ham, Sue Horton, Mike Krashinsky, Ron Saunders, George Slasor, Dan Trefler, Roger Ware, and Ralph Winter. I also appreciate Jerry Butters, Ed Lazear, and Edgar Olson for their creative contributions to this book and Devon Garvie and Gary Koop for their careful proofreading of the first edition. Special thanks go to all those individuals on the publishing side who contributed so much time and effort to the first edition of the study guide, especially Scott Amerman, Gary Carlson, and Jim Dodd. Gary Carlson and Diana Siemens deserve special thanks for their direction and helpful suggestions in improving the study guide for the second edition. I am particularly grateful to Nancy Harbin, who did a superb job of revising the study guide to correspond to Eaton and Eaton's second edition of *Microeconomics*, providing new problems that appear in the second edition, and making the study guide more understandable to students. Finally, I am indebted to Curtis and Diane Eaton for their careful reading of the study guide and for their creative approach to economics.

Nancy T. Gallini
October 1990

Problem Solving in Microeconomics

Second Edition

1

DOING MICROECONOMICS: A WORKING METHODOLOGY

Chapter Summary

Economic Models

The exciting and fascinating study of **economic theory** — a systematic attempt to make sense of the economic world — begins with an observation. For example, Why do we often find two or three supermarkets located next to one another? You may think the answer is obvious: Firms cluster in particular locations because that's where the customers are. Looking at your answer more closely, we see that this is not simply fact, but a tentative **theory,** or **model.** You used **deductive reasoning** by starting with a set of assumptions from which a conclusion can be reached: Firms want to earn profits, and customers are located in a certain area and do not like to travel far to buy goods. The conclusion is a **prediction** that can be tested by observing clustering behavior by firms in various population centers.

Now that you can construct simple economic models, let's build a formal model of this clustering phenomenon. To build an **economic model,** we abstract from the real world; that is, we reduce the multitude of real-world complexities of the problem to a set of **essential elements** that approximate reality. This is exactly what **assumptions** do.

The first task, then, is to determine which assumptions must be made for our economic model. Since we're asking a question about how firms locate, we clearly need to say something about (1) the geographical locations, (2) the firms and the kinds of products they sell, (3) the customers, and (4) what motivates the buyers and sellers. The most simplifying assumptions we can make (and that Harold Hotelling[1] made in his paper) are as follows: (1) The geographical area is a line of unit length. (2) The firms sell identical products at a constant price P and cost C, where $P > C$. (3) Consumers are uniformly distributed along the line and buy 1 unit at a fixed price P plus travel costs, which increase with distance traveled. (4) Buyers and sellers are motivated by self-interest: Producers want to maximize profits, and consumers want to travel the shortest distance.

Predictions from Models

From this well-defined economic model, we can state some predictions. First, a firm will choose a location adjacent to its rival on the side with the

---

[1] Harold Hotelling (1929), ''Stability and Competition,'' *Economic Journal,* **39:** 41–57.

largest market. Second, in **equilibrium,** the firms will locate next to each other in the center of the market. Both conclusions or predictions are directly deduced from the four assumptions.

Model Evaluation

What makes a good model? **Simplicity** is a desirable quality of any model. A simple model often provides the best insight into a problem without cluttering the issue with unnecessary detail. Simple models are also the most **fruitful** because their conclusions can often be applied to a wide range of economic phenomena. For example, the Hotelling model not only can explain how firms choose their locations, but also can explain why firms offer the same quality in products, why different airlines have the same schedules, and why political parties have similar platforms. The results of a model should be **robust;** that is, the predictions of the model should stand up well to changes in the underlying assumptions of the model. The conclusions of the Hotelling model are not robust with respect to the assumption of the geographical market or the number of firms, but they are robust with respect to the assumption of uniform density.

The primary reason for building economic models is to get predictions about the real economic world. Economic models can therefore be **evaluated** by their ability to reflect reality. We can never actually prove that a theory is true; we can only provide evidence that contradicts the theory. Even then we must be careful: Economics is a social science in which experiments can rarely be controlled or repeated. Nevertheless, the economic theorist should make serious attempts to test the predictive ability of models with real-world evidence. **Econometrics** is a branch of economics devoted to the empirical testing of theoretical models.

Normative Versus Positive Economics

The equilibrium to the Hotelling problem represents the **market solution:** that is, the solution based on **self-interested** behavior. To find this equilibrium, we had to complete an exercise in **positive economics.** We asked an "if, then" ques-

tion: *If* firms are profit maximizers and consumers are located on a line, *then* where will the two firms locate? To answer this question, we made reference to objective **facts.** Suppose instead that we want to ask whether this market solution is **desirable** by some criteria. In this case, we ask a "should" question: Where *should* firms locate? Questions such as these lie in the domain of **normative economics** because they involve ethical or value judgments. We often attempt to rank the desirability of different social states by appealing to the underlying value judgment that the well-being of the individual members of society is of primary importance.

For example, in the Hotelling problem, one sensible social objective is to minimize the travel costs of consumers. Under this objective, we find that firms *should* locate at $\frac{1}{4}$ and $\frac{3}{4}$. In this solution, no customer is farther than $\frac{1}{4}$ from the nearest store. This solution yields a positive implication of the theory: Transport costs in the market equilibrium exceed the minimum possible transport costs.

Pareto Criterion and Cost-Benefit Analysis

To answer normative questions, we often implement the **Pareto criterion** for comparing economic states. Under the Pareto criterion, state 1 is said to be better than state 2 if everyone is as well off and at least one person is better off in state 1. Alternatively, state 1 is said to be **Pareto-preferred** to state 2. Unfortunately, the Pareto criterion may be too restrictive for making some policy decisions because it is unable to rank social states under some circumstances. An alternative approach for ranking states is **cost-benefit analysis.** Under this scheme, social states are ranked according to net social benefits: that is, social benefits less social costs. State 1 is said to be better than state 2 according to cost-benefit analysis if the net social benefits are larger in state 1.

Many economic questions can be answered with a well-defined body of economic theory. This theory is the essence of the following chapters. More importantly, you will learn how to *use* economic theory to answer a wealth of fascinating economic puzzles.

Key Words

Assumptions
Cost-benefit analysis
Deduction
Econometrics
Economic theory or
  model
Equilibrium
Market solution
Model evaluation:
  Fruitfulness

Robustness
Simplicity
Pareto criterion
Pareto-improving
Positive versus
  normative eco-
  nomics
Predictions
Self-interest

Case Study: Competing with the Government

In Canada, Petrocan was once a government-owned oil company that competed in the market with the major private oil companies and the independent producers. The government's intention in operating Petrocan may have been to collect oil revenues, to undertake risky exploration activities that would not be undertaken by private companies, and to suppress some of the market power of the major oil companies.

Petrocan, like the major oil companies, owned several gasoline stations throughout Canada. In this case study, we examine decisions made by the oil companies on the location of their gasoline stations. We consider three situations. In all situations, we make the following assumptions.

Two gasoline companies want to choose the location for their gasoline stations that will maximize their respective benefits. One firm is a private firm (for example, Shell), and the other firm is Petrocan. The objectives of the two firms are different: Shell wants to maximize profits, and Petrocan wants to choose a location to minimize travel costs to the consumer. Assume that consumers are uniformly distributed along a line of unit length and that each consumer purchases 1 unit (10 gallons) of gasoline at regular intervals at a fixed price P. Travel costs to the gasoline station increase with the distance to the gasoline station.

A Given Petrocan's objective of minimizing travel costs, where will Petrocan want to locate, given a particular location of Shell?

B Suppose that each firm initially chooses a location for its station that maximizes its benefits, given the location of its rival. Will there be an equilibrium? Why or why not?

C Now suppose that Petrocan knows the profit-maximizing objective of Shell. That is, Petrocan knows that wherever it locates, Shell will move next to it, on the side with the larger market area. Petrocan moves first in choosing its location; Shell observes Petrocan's choice and then makes its location decision. Will there be an equilibrium in this situation? If so, what will it look like?

D Finally, suppose that Shell is the first mover. That is, Shell chooses the location that maximizes profits, given Petrocan's reaction to the location choice. Petrocan follows after observing Shell's locational decision. Will there be an equilibrium in this situation? If so, what will it look like?

E In which situation are both firms (and by the nature of Petrocan's objective, the consumers) better off or at least no worse off compared with the other situations? How do you explain this surprising result?

Exercises

Multiple-Choice

Choose the correct answer to each question. There is only one correct answer to each question.

To answer questions 1 to 4, refer to Figure 1.1.

We consider a variation of the Hotelling model in which consumers' tastes for music are uniformly distributed along the music line in the figure. Each of two record companies produces only one type of music at a constant price per unit. Consumers incur a cost from not being able to purchase their most desired music, and that cost increases with the difference between the purchased music and the desired type.

FIGURE 1.1

1 Which of the following two types of music (described by location) will minimize the total cost to consumers?

    a 1 and 9

    b 2 and 8

    c 3 and 7

    d 4 and 6

    e None of the above

2 Given a private-property institution and the assumptions just listed, which two music types will be produced by the two firms in equilibrium?

    a Both at 3

    b Both at 5

    c Both at 8

    d One at 3 and the other at 7

    e One at 1 and the other at 9

3 Suppose that a third firm enters the market. Then which of the following describes the equilibrium locations of the three firms?

    a The new firm will locate at 3, and the other firms will not change their locations.

    b The new firm will locate at 7, and the other firms will not change their locations.

    c The three firms will locate at 2.75, 5, and 7.25 in equilibrium.

    d The three firms will locate at 1, 5, and 9 in equilibrium.

    e An equilibrium does not exist.

4 Suppose the assumption that individuals are uniformly distributed along the music line is changed. Instead, assume that two-thirds of the customers live to the left of 5 and one-third live to the right of 5. Then which of the following statements is true?

    a The result that the two firms will locate next to each other is no longer true.

    b The two firms will locate at 5.

    c The two firms will locate next to each other somewhere to the left of 5.

    d The two firms will locate next to each other somewhere to the right of 5.

    e None of the above.

5 Which represents a positive economic statement?

    a An increase in a sales tax on automobiles leads to a decrease in the number of new-car purchases.

    b All countries should engage in free trade because it is efficient.

    c If a minimum wage is increased, some individuals will become unemployed.

    d All the above.

    e Only **a** and **c**.

6 Which is the normative statement?

    a We should redistribute income from the rich to the poor.

    b Since the market is efficient, we should allow it to work without government intervention.

    c Since all society is against discrimination, policies should be imposed to combat it.

    d All the above.

    e Only **a** and **c**.

7 Among other characteristics, an economic model is a good one if it

    a Is based on assumptions that accurately describe all the complexities of the economic world

    b Makes different predictions when assumptions of the model are changed

    c Yields predictions that are supported by empirical testing

    d Can be applied to a narrow set of economic observations

    e None of the above

8 An allocation of resources is Pareto-efficient if

    a The distribution of income is equitable.

    b There is no reallocation of resources that will make some people better off without making some people worse off.

    c Total profits in the economy are maximized.

    d Only **b** and **c**.

    e None of the above.

9 An allocation of resources A is Pareto-improving to an allocation B if

    a Some people are better off, and no one is worse off under allocation A compared with allocation B.

    b The net social benefit of moving to state A is positive.

    c The distribution of income is equitable.

    d The sum of the gains of those made better off exceeds the sum of the losses of those made worse off in moving to allocation A.

    e None of the above.

10 Using cost-benefit analysis, in which of the following cases would allocation A be chosen over allocation B?

a Some people are better off, and no one is worse off under allocation A compared with allocation B.

b Net social benefits under allocation A are larger than net social benefits under allocation B.

c The sum of the gains of those made better off exceeds the sum of the losses of those made worse off in moving to allocation A.

d All the above.

e None of the above.

True-False

11 The assumption of self-interested behavior rules out charitable actions.

12 The answers to normative questions in economics lie within a set of values and are not the result of a logical economic model.

13 Logically drawing conclusions from a set of assumptions involves deductive reasoning.

14 The results of a model are also predictions of the model.

15 Models built on a set of assumptions that do not explicitly describe details of reality cannot be very useful.

16 All Pareto-efficient allocations of resources are Pareto improvements over Pareto-inefficient allocations.

17 Since the social planner's solution to the location problem represents a Pareto-efficient allocation of resources, it logically follows that we should adopt this solution over the market solution.

18 For every Pareto-inefficient allocation of resources, there exists a reallocation for which some people could be made better off and no one made worse off.

19 A set of locations of two firms along a line is an equilibrium if and only if each firm gets one-half of the industry profits, regardless of the production costs of the two firms.

Problems

20 The assumption of self-interest is not relevant to planned economies where prices are not determined by market forces. Discuss.

21 Two stores locate along a street between a residential area and the downtown area of some city. Every day, people from the residential area pass both stores on their way to work and on their way home from work. How does this behavior of the potential customers affect the results of the Hotelling model?

22 The social planner's solution of the Hotelling locational problem is a Pareto-efficient allocation of resources, whereas the market solution is Pareto-inefficient. Nevertheless, the planned solution does not represent a *Pareto improvement* over the market solution. Suggest a way in which everyone could be made better off in moving from the market to the planned solution.

23 Since positive economics does not provide answers to normative questions, positive economic theory is of little use in resolving important real-world policy issues. Comment.

24 Show that the Hotelling model is not robust to the number of firms by showing that an equilibrium does not exist when there are three firms.

25 Consider the Hotelling model but change the assumption of geographical area from a line to a circle. Assume that individuals are uniformly distributed along the circle (the suburbs) and that the downtown, industrial area of the city is in the center of the circle, as shown in Figure 1.2. Sup-

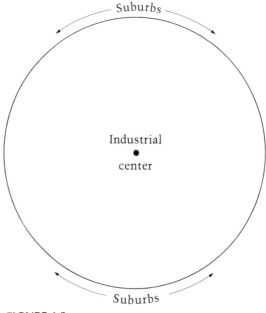

FIGURE 1.2

pose that two firms can locate their stores anywhere along the circumference of the circle or inside the circle. Individuals can travel along the circle or in a straight line to the industrial center. (They cannot travel in a straight line between two points on the circumference of the circle.) Determine the market equilibrium set of locations.

Answers to Chapter 1

Case Study

A Given Shell's location, Petrocan will want to locate on the side with more customers. That is, suppose Shell located at A, where $A > \frac{1}{2}$; then Petrocan would want to locate in the interval $(0, A)$. If $A < \frac{1}{2}$, Petrocan would want to locate in $(A, 1)$. If $A = \frac{1}{2}$, then Petrocan would be indifferent between locating on either side of Shell. Since customers are distributed uniformly, it follows that Petrocan will locate as follows:

If $A > \frac{1}{2}$, Petrocan will locate at $A/3$.
If $A = \frac{1}{2}$, Petrocan will locate at either $\frac{1}{6}$ or $\frac{5}{6}$.
If $A < \frac{1}{2}$, Petrocan will locate at $\frac{2}{3} + A/3$.

These location rules are illustrated in Figure A1.1a, b, and c, respectively. Shell's and Petrocan's locations are denoted by A and B, respectively. The vertical lines delineate market boundaries.

B No. Shell will always want to locate right beside Petrocan, but Petrocan will always want to locate as described in Part **A**. If one chooses a location that maximizes its benefits given the other's location, the rival firm will always have an incentive to move.

C Yes. Petrocan will locate at $\frac{1}{2}$, and Shell will locate right next to it.

D Yes. Shell will locate at $\frac{1}{2}$ and Petrocan at $\frac{1}{6}$ or $\frac{5}{6}$.

E Both firms are better off in part **D**. By not having the first move, Petrocan makes both Shell and customers better off. This follows from the different objectives of the two firms.

Multiple-Choice

1 c	2 b	3 e	4 c	5 e
6 d	7 c	8 b	9 a	10 d

True-False

11 F	12 T	13 T	14 T	15 F
16 F	17 F	18 T	19 F	

Problems

20 Even in planned economies in which prices are determined by some centralized authority, the notion of self-interest is relevant. In setting the prices at which goods are traded, the central authority must recognize that individuals will act on those prices in a way that best achieves some objective; that is, they will act out of self-interest.

21 If all individuals pass by both stores on their way to and from work, then the travel costs of buying from the two stores are equal for everyone. Individuals will patronize the two stores equally. Then if individuals randomly choose one of the stores, each store will get half the customers, as in the Hotelling model; however, there will be no incentive for the stores to locate next to each other.

FIGURE A1.1

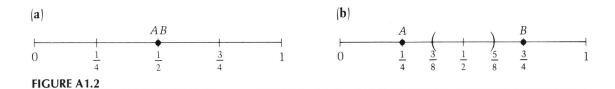

FIGURE A1.2

22 Figure A1.2a shows the equilibrium in which firms A and B locate at $\frac{1}{2}$, or point AB. Figure A1.2b shows the planned solution in which firm A locates at $\frac{1}{4}$, or point A, and firm B locates at $\frac{3}{4}$, or point B. In moving from Figure A1.2a to A1.2b, the individuals in the interval $(\frac{3}{8}, \frac{5}{8})$ are harmed because they have farther to travel, whereas everyone else is made better off. If side payments were possible, individuals in the intervals $(0, \frac{3}{8})$ and $(\frac{5}{8}, 1)$ could bribe the harmed individuals to accept the move with an amount of money that would leave the harmed individuals at least as well off as in the private solution in Figure A1.2a. If individuals are distributed uniformly, then the losses to those in the interval $(\frac{3}{8}, \frac{5}{8})$ are smaller than the gains to winners in $(0, \frac{3}{8})$ and $(\frac{5}{8}, 1)$. Since the gains exceed the losses, bribery is possible.

23 Although answers to normative questions lie within a set of values and are not the result of a logical economic model, economists can analyze policies by using positive economic theory to predict whether normative goals will be achieved with the policies. For example, to say "we should get rid of discrimination" is a normative statement. The economist's expertise is not to argue the validity of the statement; since the statement is based on value judgments and a set of moral ethics, it is neither true nor false. However, given that a value judgment is accepted (through democratic vote or successful lobbying), economists can analyze policies such as "equal pay for work of equal value" and quotas to determine whether, as a result of implementing those policies, the goal of reducing discrimination will be achieved.

24 Place the three firms A, B, and C anywhere along a line of unit length and show that each firm will always have the incentive to relocate, given its rivals' locations. For example, initially give the firms equal market shares; that is, place firm A at $\frac{1}{6}$, firm B at $\frac{1}{2}$, and firm C at $\frac{5}{6}$. Clearly, each firm will have the incentive to move right next to its closest rival. For example, firm A will move to the left $\frac{1}{2}$. But then firm B will want to "jump" over firm A and relocate just to the left of it. This will continue until it pays the next mover to relocate just to the left of firm C. But then firm C will want to move, and so on.

25 In equilibrium, the two firms A and B will locate side by side in the center of the circle. To see this, suppose that the firms initially locate along the circumference of the circle: for example, at A' and B' in Figure A1.3. At these locations, each firm receives half the market, as shown by the arrows in the diagram. If firm A moved to the center, it would capture some of firm B's customers. For example, take the customer at D. That individual would have to travel r (the radius of the circle) to get to the center, whereas to get to B', the customer would have to travel $2\pi r/4$ (one-fourth of the circumference), which is approximately $1.5r$. Firm B will want to recapture that customer by moving next to point A in the center. If both firms are in the center, neither can profit by changing its location alone.

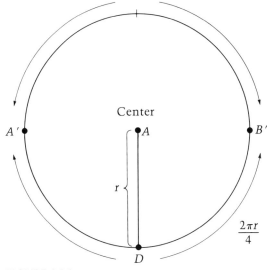

FIGURE A1.3

2

THE ECONOMY AND ECONOMICS

Chapter Summary

Defining Economics

Economics is the study of the allocation of scarce resources to the production of alternative goods. **Scarcity** is a fundamental concept in economics: If a resource is not scarce, then there is no "economic problem" because everyone can have as much as they desire. Moreover, **alternative** or **competing uses** for the resource are necessary to define an interesting economic question. If there is only one use for the resource, then the allocation solution is simple. In the real world, most resources are scarce, and many competing uses of resources can be defined. The problem of allocating resources to their end uses is complex. Our focus is on the principles that govern resource allocation in a **market economy**.

Building Blocks of an Economy

What does an economy look like? An economy is composed of at least four essential features. First, **a resource endowment** describes all the resources available in the economy. Second, the economy must have a **technology** that produces goods from these resources. Together, the resource endowment and the technology describe the economy's **production possibilities set** — all combinations of goods that the economy could produce.

In economics, we are interested in how these goods are distributed among individuals in the economy; that is, we are interested in the **economic state** actually attained in the economy.

To determine the social state achieved in the economy, we need the third building block: **individual preferences**. Given an individual's ordering of all bundles of goods and services from the most to the least preferred, we can predict the consumer's behavior under the assumption that individuals choose actions that yield the *most preferred* bundle in their **preference ordering**.

Finally, an economy is made up of **institutions** that provide the "rules of the game" being played by all individuals in the economy. Institutions can be anything from antitrust laws for corporations to the informal practice of leaving a rental deposit on a pair of cross-country skis. The common feature of all institutions is that they regulate economic activity, and together they determine which social state will actually be achieved. Unlike the first three building blocks, which are relatively immutable, institutional changes occur whenever there are changes in underlying policies and laws, particularly with respect to those that govern property rights in society.

Positive economics is concerned with three questions: *What* goods will be produced? *How* will these goods be produced? *For whom* will these goods be produced? Given the institutional setting of **common property, private property,** or some alternative arrangement, our goal is to **predict** the social state achieved by the economy. Indeed, **comparative institutional analysis** involves the comparison of social states attained under various institutional arrangements. Normative economics, however, *compares* the alternative economic states to determine the most preferred from a social point of view. On discovery of this social state, we may want to return to positive economic tools to determine which institutions will direct the economy to this most-preferred state.

Basic Concepts of a Market Economy

The benchmark model used throughout this text is that of the pure market economy with its institutions of private property and its minor role for government. A market economy can be described with a **circular-flow diagram.** Individuals own resources and supply their labor and other resources to firms, the demanders of these resources. The firms produce goods from these resources and supply the goods to individuals, the demanders of the goods. In **equilibrium,** a price and a quantity can be determined in every resource and goods market.

Partial equilibrium analysis involves the determination of price and quantity in one or some markets, holding *all other prices and quantities constant.* The important tools used in partial equilibrium analysis are demand and supply curves. A **demand curve** describes the quantities of a good that all individuals are willing to buy at any given price. Generally, demand curves are negatively sloped. A **supply curve** indicates the quantities that firms are willing to supply at any given price. Generally, supply curves are positively sloped. Equilibrium price and quantity are defined by the intersection of the two curves.

The price of a good is only one of many **determinants** of the demand and supply of the good. For example, an increase in the price of a **complement** (or **substitute**) will shift the demand curve down (up), resulting in a lower (higher) equilibrium price and quantity. An increase in the price of an input used in the production of the good will shift the supply to the left, resulting in a higher equilibrium price and lower quantity. These are **comparative statics exercises.**

In **general equilibrium analysis,** on the other hand, *all* prices and quantities in *all* markets are determined simultaneously. It is fair to say that equilibrium analysis is dominant in economics. We should remember that equilibrium doesn't involve **exogenous** variables (those that are determined outside the model) but rather **endogenous** variables (those that are determined within the model). A **Nash equilibrium** results when the endogenous variables are determined by the decisions of individual agents, and no individual agent can improve its position by changing its actions. Similarly, a **competitive market equilibrium** results when prices (as determined by the collective actions of all agents) are such that no agent can improve its position by changing its decisions.

We now begin the intriguing study of **microeconomics.**

Key Words

Alternatives	Institutions
Circular-flow diagram	Market economy
Comparative statics	Microeconomics
Comparative institutional analysis	Nash equilibrium
Competitive market equilibrium	Partial equilibrium analysis
Demand curve	Preferences
Economics	Production possibilities set
Economic (social) state	Resource endowment
Endogenous	Scarcity
Exogenous	Supply curve
General equilibrium analysis	Technology

Case Studies

I. Property Rights on Clean Air and Water

Acid rain has become a serious problem in southern Ontario in Canada and in the midwestern and eastern United States. The accumulation of industrial pollution has resulted in a deterioration of many freshwater lakes and rivers in these regions and a steady decline in the number of fish inhabiting these waters. In response to this pollution problem, a joint U.S.–Canadian commission was formed in 1985. The recommendation of the commission called for voluntary controls on the pollution emissions from industrial plants.

A Is the pollution problem an interesting *economic* problem? Why or why not?

B Describe the current institutions governing the right to clean air and water and explain how these institutions have directed resources toward a social state with a serious pollution problem.

C Suggest an alternative institutional arrangement that would direct resources toward a social state with a cleaner environment. What policies might be instituted to achieve this social state? Comment on the expected effectiveness of the policy proposed by the joint U.S.–Canadian commission.

II. Depleting the Antarctic Fin Whales

Because of serious overfishing by the Antarctic whaling industry, fewer than 5000 blue whales remained by 1965, one-thirteenth of the original population. In response to this rapid depletion, the International Whaling Commission prohibited the capture of blue whales from 1965 onward. The whaling industry responded to this restriction by exploiting the smaller Antarctic fin whale; eventually, annual quotas were placed on the fin whale.

A Has the allocation of resources to the whaling industry been Pareto-efficient? Why or why not?

B How might a Pareto-efficient allocation of resources be achieved in this industry?

Exercises

Multiple-Choice

Choose the correct answer to each of the following questions. There is only one correct answer to each question.

1 Which of the following is *not* an important feature of an economy?

a Institutions.
b Individual preferences.
c The technology that produces goods from resources.
d Resource endowments.
e All the above are important features of an economy.

2 A resource allocation problem is interesting from an economics point of view if
a There is an unlimited amount of the resource available.
b The resource is limited in supply.
c There are many alternative uses for the resource.
d Both **a** and **c**.
e Both **b** and **c**.

3 Which of the following represents a partial equilibrium exercise?
a The effect of a tobacco tax on the equilibrium price of cigarettes is analyzed, given prices and quantities of other goods.
b The effect of the minimum-wage legislation on unemployment and inflation in the economy is examined.
c The effects of removing import quotas from automobiles on all markets are examined.
d All the above.
e None of the above.

4 An economic state describes
a The allocation of resources to the production of goods
b The profits made by all firms in the society
c The allocation of goods to individuals
d The quantities of resources supplied by individuals
e None of the above

5 Which of the following could result in an increase in the demand curve for bread?
a An increase in the price of flour
b An increase in the price of jam
c A decrease in income
d A decrease in the price of peanut butter
e None of the above

6 Which of the following could result in a decrease in the equilibrium price of cereal products?
a An increase in the price of eggs
b Good weather for agricultural products

c A decrease in the price of milk

d An increase in income

e None of the above

True-False

7 A production possibilities frontier gives all combinations of inputs that the economy can use in its production of goods.

8 Determination of the social state that is "best" for society is a problem in positive economics.

9 The equilibrium price in a market is determined by the intersection of demand and supply.

10 An increase in the price of a complement to good X will shift the demand for X upward, increasing equilibrium price and quantity.

11 A tax placed on firms for every unit product in the market for X will shift the supply to the left, resulting in a higher equilibrium price and lower quantity.

12 Partial equilibrium analysis involves examination of the market for one good (or a few goods), holding prices and quantities in other markets constant.

Problems

13 Assume that the market for carrots is perfectly competitive. Using diagrams, determine the impact on the short-run equilibrium price and quantity in the carrot market for each of the following:

    a The bean crop is a bumper crop.

    b A price ceiling is set below the equilibrium price of carrots.

    c A per-unit subsidy is given to carrot producers.

    d The price of fertilizer increases.

14 A student in a microeconomics course enjoys leisure activities — playing squash, reading, and skiing. She wants to determine how much of the two goods, leisure (measured in hours) and economic knowledge (measured in pages of economics books), she can produce in 1 day by using the two resources of time and economics books. If she reads 50 pages of economics material in 1 hour, what will her daily production possibilities set look like?

15 What is the difference between partial equilibrium analysis and general equilibrium analysis? How might partial equilibrium analysis be useful in making policy decisions?

16 Give an example of how institutions can affect the economic state achieved by the economy. Show how positive economics can be useful in directing the economy toward a desirable social state through institutional change.

17 The following data are the market supply and demand schedules for shoelaces, which are products in a competitive market.

Price ($)	Quantity Demanded	Quantity Supplied
1	500,000	100,000
2	400,000	200,000
3	300,000	300,000
4	200,000	400,000
5	100,000	500,000

    a Graphically construct the supply and demand schedules and determine the equilibrium price and quantity.

    b Suppose that a tax of $1 per shoelace is imposed on the producers. What will be the new equilibrium price paid by consumers and the quantity of shoelaces demanded after the tax has been imposed? What will be the price the producers *receive* after the tax has been imposed? Would your answers change if the tax were imposed on the consumers instead of the producers? Explain.

    c Derive the algebraic equations of the demand and supply schedules and check the answer you reached in **a** using these equations.

Answers to Chapter 2

Case Studies

I A Yes, because it is a problem of allocating scarce resources toward competing ends.

I B Both air and the water in lakes are examples of *common property*; as a result, current institutional arrangements do not protect either from pollution. In the absence of private-property rights on clean air and fresh water, users do not have to internalize the costs of pollution to others. Hence, the use of clean air and fresh water (and the level of pollution) will not be Pareto-efficient.

I C A tax on pollution could be imposed. Alternatively, property rights could be assigned that would require polluters to pay for the right to pollute (or be bribed not to pollute, depending on how the property rights are assigned). This is analyzed in more detail in Chapter 17. Voluntary controls, as recommended by the U.S.–Canadian Commission, are not likely to be effective.

II A No. Whales are a common-property resource; whalers will choose the number of whales to harvest that maximizes their utility. Since a whaler does not receive the full benefits next year from reducing this year's harvest, he or she will allocate too many resources toward harvesting the whales today.

II B This problem might be resolved by setting quotas on the harvest per whaler, as in the case of the blue whale. However, policymakers should consider the effect this will have on other species of whales.

Multiple-Choice

1 e　　2 e　　3 a　　4 c　　5 d　　6 b

True-False

7 F　　8 F　　9 T　　10 F　　11 T　　12 T

Problems

13 a The supply curve for beans shifts to the right, decreasing the equilibrium price and increasing the equilibrium quantity. Since beans and carrots are substitutes, the demand for carrots will fall, decreasing equilibrium price and quantity as shown in Figure A2.1a.

b At the price ceiling p_1, the quantity demanded y_d exceeds the quantity supplied y_s, as shown in Figure A2.1b. The excess demand that results at price p_1 implies that not all consumers will be satisfied. The situation may result in the introduction of a rationing scheme.

c A per-unit subsidy causes a parallel shift in the supply curve of carrots to the right, resulting in a lower equilibrium price and a higher quantity of carrots, as shown in Figure A2.1c.

d An increase in the price of fertilizer shifts the supply curve to the *left*, resulting in the *opposite* effect on equilibrium price and quantity than that shown in Figure A2.1c.

14 As shown in Figure A2.2, the student can "produce" 24 hours of leisure and 0 economic knowledge or 1200 pages of economic knowledge and 0 leisure hours or any combination of leisure and economic knowledge in the shaded region. Since the cost (in terms of leisure hours) of producing another unit of economic knowledge is constant, the production possibilities curve is a straight line.

15 Partial equilibrium analysis is the study of one (or a few) market(s) by holding the prices and

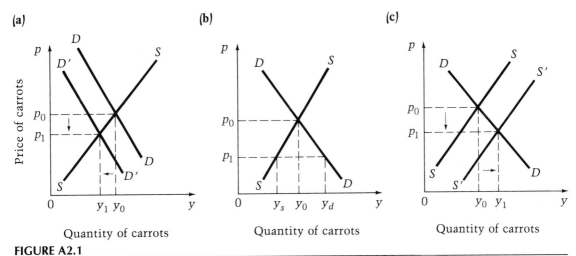

(a) (b) (c)

FIGURE A2.1

FIGURE A2.2

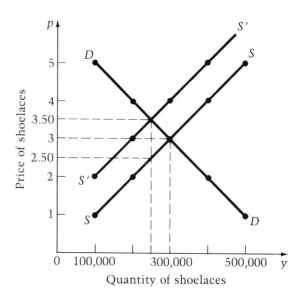

FIGURE A2.3

quantities of all the other goods constant. In general equilibrium analysis, all the prices and quantities in all markets are determined simultaneously. Partial equilibrium analysis is especially useful when a government wants to measure the *direct* impact of a policy on a particular market — for example, a tax on gasoline purchases — by holding constant the cost of public transportation.

16 An institution of common property in which anyone could have access to another individual's invention would result in a social state in which there would be little incentive to invest in research and development. Suppose that a social state in which more innovation takes place were desirable. Then, positive economics could determine whether institutions such as patent policy, intended to protect inventors' rights, would direct resources toward the desirable social state. For example, the following questions could be answered. What effect would patent protection have on the rate of technological advance? What effect would patent protection have on the prices and quantities of goods produced from an innovation?

17 a The demand and supply curves are illustrated in Figure A2.3. The equilibrium price of shoelaces is $3; the equilibrium quantity is 300,000.

b As illustrated in Figure A2.3, a $1 tax will shift the supply curve upward by $1 at every quantity. The new price paid by consumers will be $3.50; the equilibrium quantity will be 250,000. The producers receive $2.50. If the tax were imposed on consumers, the demand curve would shift down by $1 at every quantity, resulting in the same answers.

c The demand curve is found by the point–slope formula. Using the points (y, p) of $(500,000, 1)$ and $(100,000, 5)$, the equation for y_d is found as follows.

$$\frac{y_d - 500,000}{p - 1} = \frac{500,000 - 100,000}{1 - 5}$$
$$y_d - 500,000 = -100,000(p - 1)$$
$$y_d = 600,000 - 100,000p$$

Similarly, the supply curve is given by

$$y_s = 100,000p$$

Quantities demanded and supplied are equated to get

$$600,000 - 100,000p = 100,000p$$
$$p = 3$$

Substituting $p = 3$ into either the demand or supply curve gives

$$y = 600,000 - 100,000(3) = 300,000$$

3

A THEORY OF SELF-INTEREST: SELF-INTEREST, PREFERENCES, AND UTILITY FUNCTIONS

Chapter Summary

Concept of Self-Interest

In this chapter, we begin our study of the consumer. The most fundamental assumption about the consumer in economic models is a psychological one: Consumers are motivated by **self-interest**. Individuals have **preferences** about goods whether the goods are hamburgers and french fries, charitable donations, or Jaguar XK-Es. We assume that the choices consumers make regarding goods, subject to their budget constraints, result from self-interested behavior. As economists, our task is to figure out how to analyze consumers' choices, given this assumption.

For the notion of self-interest to make any sense, it must be the case that individuals can order bundles of goods that range from most preferred to least preferred so they can choose their favorite bundle within the limits of their budget constraints. Hence, to analyze consumer choices, we need to define a **preference ordering**. That is, given all possible **consumption bundles** of all goods, we need to be able to rank those bundles from most preferred to least preferred. This

ranking is possible only if the consumer has well-defined preferences. For example, if a consumer chooses consumption bundles in an erratic fashion, then the economist can say very little about that person's choices. Hence, our first task is to identify a set of **assumptions** about individual preferences that allows us to construct a ranking. Next—and this is where the utility function comes in—we want to describe that preference ordering by a mathematical function, a utility function, so that we can use the techniques of constrained maximization to analyze the consumer problem.

Consumer Assumptions

The first axiom of consumer choice is the **completeness assumption:** An individual must be able to compare *any and all* consumption bundles. If the individual cannot compare two bundles, the economist will certainly have difficulty predicting the individual's choice. The second axiom is that the consumer is allowed to make only one of the following three statements when comparing two bundles B_1 and B_2: B_1 is **preferred** to B_2

$(B_1 \ \mathbf{P} \ B_2)$, B_2 is preferred to B_1 $(B_2 \ \mathbf{P} \ B_1)$, or the individual is **indifferent** between the two bundles $(B_1 \ \mathbf{I} \ B_2)$. This is the **two-term consistency assumption**. Third, if an individual prefers bundle B_1 to B_2 (or is indifferent between them) and prefers B_2 to a third bundle B_3 (or is indifferent between them), then it must be the case that the consumer prefers B_1 or is indifferent to B_3; that is, preferences must satisfy the **transitivity assumption**. These three assumptions ensure that preferences are consistent and that a preference ordering exists.

Utility Functions and Indifference Curves

To be able to analyze consumer choice by using constrained maximization techniques, we need to define a **utility function** over this preference ordering; that is, we assign a number to each bundle, reflecting the most preferred to the least preferred, and assign the same number to bundles for which an individual is indifferent. All bundles for which the individual is indifferent can be illustrated by an **indifference curve**. To ensure that these indifference curves are true curves and not single points, we need the **continuity assumption**. This is a necessary condition for representing a preference ordering by a utility function; it says that a continuous indifference curve can be drawn through every consumption bundle. Another assumption that is useful but not necessary is the **nonsatiation assumption**. This assumption simply says "More is preferred to less" and makes the indifference curves nonpositively sloped.

Given these assumptions, a utility function exists. In fact, an individual's preference ordering can be represented by many different utility functions. To see this, imagine finding a utility function and then multiplying all the **utility numbers** by 2. The preference ordering would be preserved. This implies that the actual number assigned is of *no significance.* Utility numbers are **ordinal** not **cardinal** and, therefore, *cannot* be interpreted as a measure of "happiness" or "satisfaction." Furthermore, comparisons of individuals cannot be made by looking at utility numbers.

Marginal Rate of Substitution

By using indifference curves, we can identify the *rate* at which a consumer is willing to trade one good, good 2, for another, good 1, without changing the level of utility. We can call this rate the **marginal rate of substitution** MRS(x_1, x_2), and it is equal to the slope of the indifference curve multiplied by -1. If we make an "assumption of convenience" that indifference curves are **convex**, then MRS(x_1, x_2), if it is well defined, declines as one moves down the indifference curve. This assumption of **diminishing marginal rate of substitution** is a common, but certainly not necessary, assumption of consumer theory. A final assumption of convenience, the **smoothness of indifference curves**, ensures that MRS(x_1, x_2) is well defined.

Although we usually use the example of a consumption bundle that contains two goods — say, goods 1 and 2 — the arguments presented in this summary carry over to a world in which there are many goods. In such a world, a consumption bundle is simply a bundle $(x_1, \ldots x_n)$ such that there are no negative quantities of any given good. To ensure that preferences are consistent and that they can be ordered, we rely on the same three assumptions as before. Continuity now requires that the **no-worse-than set** and the **no-better-than set** be closed. To find the marginal rate of substitution between two goods in the many-goods case, simply fix the quantities of all other goods.

Key Words

Cardinal	No-worse-than set
Completeness assumption	Nonsatiety assumption
Consumption bundles	Ordinal
Continuity assumption	Preference ordering
Convexity	Preferences
Indifference curves	Self-interest
Marginal rate of substitution	Transitivity
No-better-than set	Two-term consistency
	Utility function
	Utility numbers

Case Study: Intransitivities of Youth

In an interesting paper by Arnold A. Weinstein (1968),[1] the results of the following were reported. Individuals were asked to make pairwise comparisons among 10 bundles, each being valued at approximately $3 (1968 dollars). Among the bundles were $3 in cash, a print of El Greco's "View of Toledo," a pair of white tennis shoes, two glasses of vanilla malted milk per day for 10 days, the three most recent Beatles records, and so on.

The purpose of the experiment was to test whether the individuals had transitive preferences. The percentage of transitive responses for children (9–12 years), teenagers (14–18 years), and adults were, respectively, 79%, 86%, and 93.5%.

A How would you explain the result that younger people have more intransitivities than adults? Do you agree with the author's conclusions that this result "lends some support to the political and economic restrictions placed upon the youth of our society" (p. 311)?

_____
[1] Arnold A. Weinstein (1968), "Transitivity of Preferences: A Comparison Among Age Groups," *Journal of Political Economy*, **76**: 307–311.

B Given the results from this study, do you think that transitivity is a restrictive assumption of consumer behavior? Why or why not?

C Discuss the restrictiveness of the assumptions of completeness, nonsatiety, and convexity.

Exercises

Multiple-Choice

Choose the correct answer to each of the following questions. There is only one correct answer to each question.

1 Which of the following is *not* a necessary assumption for the existence of a utility function?

    a Consumers are able to rank all conceivable bundles of goods.

    b If a consumer prefers bundle B_1 to bundle B_2 and bundle B_2 to bundle B_3, he must prefer bundle B_1 to bundle B_3.

    c Consumers prefer more to less.

    d Preferences must be continuous.

    e All of the above assumptions are necessary for a utility function to exist.

2 Consider the following sets of indifference curves in Figure 3.1 for two individuals, Ronnie

(a)

(b)

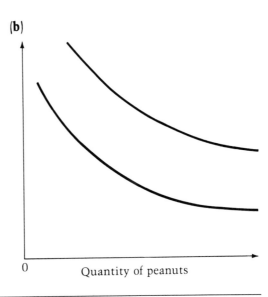

FIGURE 3.1

and Jimmy. Although both individuals prefer more of each good to less of the good, Ronnie prefers jelly beans to peanuts considerably more than Jimmy does. Which of the following is true?

a Ronnie is more likely to have the indifference curves in Figure 3.1*a*, whereas Jimmy's indifference curves are more likely to be those in Figure 3.1*b*.

b Jimmy is more likely to have indifference curves given in Figure 3.1*a* whereas Ronnie's indifference curves are more likely to be those in Figure 3.1*b*.

c Jimmy will have neither set of indifference curves; his indifference curves will be positively sloped.

d Ronnie will have neither set of indifference curves; his indifference curves will be positively sloped.

e None of the above.

3 A certain individual claims that she likes to eat a peanut butter sandwich only with a glass of milk, and she likes to drink a glass of milk only if she has a peanut butter sandwich to eat. If she is given more than one peanut butter sandwich per glass of milk, she throws it away, and vice versa.

a Her indifference curves between peanut butter and milk are straight lines.

b Her preferences violate the assumption of transitivity.

c Her indifference curves are right angles.

d Her indifference curves violate the assumptions of consumer choice because they intersect.

e None of the above.

4 The absolute value of the indifference curve at any point represents

a The amount of one good the individual is willing to give up to get some of the other good for some increase in utility

b The total amount of money spent on that bundle

c The ratio of prices of the two goods

d The rate at which the individual will trade off one good for another, holding utility constant

e None of the above

5 For the indifference curves in Figure 3.2,

a $MRS(x_1, x_2)$ is diminishing.

b Good 1 but not good 2 is a desirable good.

c Good 2 but not good 1 is a desirable good.

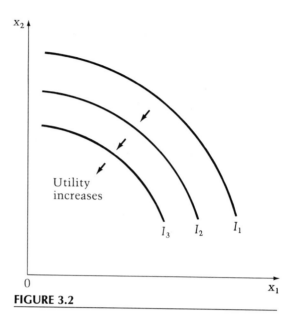

FIGURE 3.2

d Neither good 1 nor good 2 is desirable.

e None of the above.

6 Three commodity bundles, each consisting of two commodities good 1 and good 2, are listed in the accompanying table.

Bundle	Amount of Good 1	Amount of Good 2
A	2	3
B	1	3
C	2	2

Suppose that an individual ranks the bundles as follows: *A* is preferred to *B*, *C* is preferred to *A*, *B* and *C* are indifferent. Then the individual's preference ordering

a Violates the assumption of nonsatiety

b Violates the assumption of transitivity

c Violates the assumption of completeness

d Is consistent with all the assumptions of consumer behavior

e Both **a** and **b**

7 Which of the following statements about indifference curves is incorrect?

a Each point on the indifference curve represents a different combination of quantities of the two goods.

b All points on the indifference curve are equally preferred by the consumer.

c Some bundles of goods on an indifference curve may not be affordable.

d An infinite number of indifference curves go through every point in goods space.

e All the above statements are correct.

8 For the utility function $U = (x_1 + x_2)/5$, the indifference curves

a Are given by straight lines
b Exhibit diminishing MRS(x_1, x_2)
c Are positively sloped
d Violate the assumption of more is preferred to less
e None of the above

*9 Which of the following utility functions describe the same preference ordering over goods 1 and 2 as $U(x_1, x_2) = x_1x_2$?

a $V(x_1, x_2) = (x_1 - 5)(x_2 - 5)$
b $V(x_1, x_2) = (x_1/5)(x_2/5)$
c $V(x_1, x_2) = (x_1 + 5)(x_2 + 5)$
d Both **b** and **c**
e None of the above

True-False

10 An indifference curve is defined as a set of bundles that a consumer with a given income can afford, and among which she or he is indifferent.

11 More is preferred to less means that if the *total* number of goods in bundle A exceeds the *total* quantity in B, then A is preferred to B.

12 The assumptions of completeness, two-term consistency, transitivity, and continuity are necessary for constructing a utility function over a set of preferences.

13 The utility function $V(x_1, x_2) = 5[U(x_1, x_2)]/2 + 7$ represents the same preference ordering as the utility function $U(x_1, x_2)$.

14 A diminishing marginal rate of substitution implies that an individual requires increasing amounts of one good as he gives up more and more of the other good to remain at the same utility level.

15 More is preferred to less implies that two bundles with different amounts of either good 1 or 2 and the same amount of the other good cannot be on the same indifference curve.

16 Since utility is ordinal, not cardinal, interpersonal comparisons cannot be made.

17 The marginal rate of substitution for indifference curves: $x_1 + x_2 = c$ is diminishing.

18 The indifference curve between garbage and ice cream would be positively sloped.

Short Problems

19 Suppose the consumer has the indifference curves illustrated in Figure 3.3. Which of the assumptions about indifference curves do the curves violate?

20 Suppose Eleanor consumes two goods: economics books and food. Although Eleanor enjoys economics, she gets satiated beyond 100 books per month. Eleanor can give away any extra books that she acquires over 100 to her friends. (Assume that she doesn't get additional utility from giving the books away.) What do Eleanor's indifference curves look like?

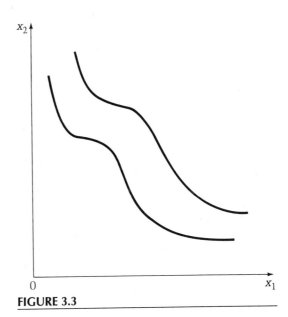

FIGURE 3.3

21 Show that the assumption of nonsatiety implies that indifference curves have a nonpositive slope.

22 What is the relationship between utility functions and indifference curves?

*23 Consider the following preference ordering: An individual consumes two goods, good 1 and good 2. Bundle $A = (x_1^A, x_2^A)$ is preferred to bundle $B = (x_1^B, x_2^B)$ if $x_1^A > x_1^B$ regardless of the amount of good 2 in each bundle. If $x_1^A = x_1^B$, then bundle A is preferred to bundle B if $x_2^A > x_2^B$. These preferences are call *lexicographic*. Give an intuitive explanation of why a utility function cannot be defined over preferences that are lexicographic. (*Hint*: Recall that the construction of a utility function requires every bundle to be assigned a number, with higher numbers given to "more-preferred" bundles and the same number given to all "indifferent" bundles.)

Long Problems

24 Consider the following bundles of bottles of beer (b) and bags of peanuts (p).

> A: (7, 3)   B: (5, 4)   C: (12, 1)
> D: (1, 9)   E: (6, 6)

Suppose an individual has the following preference ordering:

$$E \ P \ D \ P \ C \ P \ A \ P \ B$$

Find a utility function that describes the individual's preferences. Can you find more than one utility function? Explain.

25 Four university students have been asked to assign utility numbers to five bundles of good 1 and good 2, with more-preferred bundles getting higher numbers (see accompanying table). These utility numbers will help us find a representation for each student's utility function, U_1 to U_4. Unfortunately, only one of the university students has taken a course in microeconomics, so only one of the four utility functions is consistent with the assumptions of consumer preferences. Which is it? Can you explain why the other functions are inconsistent? *Hint*: Plot the bundles in the $x_1 x_2$ space.

Bundle	Amount of Good 1	Amount of Good 2	U_1	U_2	U_3	U_4
A	2	2	2	2	1	6
B	2	5	4	5	3	10
C	4	6	6	6	5	10
D	5	4	6	5	3	6
E	6	1	4	5	5	3

26 Measure bottles of beer on the horizontal axis and bags of popcorn on the vertical axis. Draw indifference curves for the following preferences, and then explain whether these indifference curves satisfy the assumptions of consumer choice. For those indifference curves that do not, explain why.

a Tom likes to drink beer or eat popcorn equally well.

b Rama likes a bottle of beer only with a bag of popcorn.

c The more beer the better, no matter how much popcorn Alejandro has, but if he can't have more beer, he prefers to have more popcorn.

d Let a bundle (b, p) represent the quantities of beer and popcorn, respectively. Beth is indifferent between $(2, 3)$ and $(3, 1)$. She is also indifferent between $(2, 3)$ and $(4, 2)$. But she would rather have $(4, 2)$ than $(3, 1)$.

e Motozo likes beer and popcorn, but three beers knock him out for the night, and he gets sick on four bags of popcorn.

*27 Show that a utility function can be constructed if one is given the assumptions of completeness, two-term consistency, transitivity, continuity, and nonsatiety.

*28 An individual's preferences can be represented by indifference curves $x_1 x_2 = c$, where c is some nonnegative constant. Bundles on an indifference curve identified by a particular c are preferred to those bundles on indifference curves identified by a lower c. (For example, all bundles on $x_1 x_2 = 10$ are preferred to all bundles on $x_1 x_2 = 2$.) Given the method for constructing a utility function outlined in the previous exercise, construct a utility function that represents these preferences.

*29 a Suppose the utility function $U(x_1, x_2) = x_1 x_2$ describes Mary's preference ordering. Derive the indifference curves for this preference ordering and show that the indifference curves have the property of diminishing marginal rate of substitution.

b Suppose that Fred has a utility function given by $V(x_1, x_2) = x_1 x_2 + 25$. Derive and illustrate the indifference curves for this preference ordering.

c The fact that Mary's utility function assigns a lower number to every bundle than Fred's utility function implies that Fred must enjoy consuming all bundles of goods more than Mary does. True, false, uncertain. Explain.

Answers to Chapter 3

Case Study

A Older people may have more experience with the products or with making decisions.

B If the results of this study are accurate, then transitivity is a restrictive assumption. A theory of consumer behavior, based on transitivity, risks being incorrect a fairly high percentage of the time.

C Completeness is not restrictive; it simply requires that people can compare bundles. Nonsatiety is more restrictive because individuals are likely to become satiated with most goods. Locally, however, it is not restrictive. For example, there may be some point at which I will get no additional utility from more money; however, at present I am nowhere near that point. Convexity is a restrictive assumption. It says that individuals prefer a mixture of good 1 and good 2 to bundles that have only good 1 or only good 2 in them. There is no psychological reason why this should be so. However, if commodities are defined broadly, convexity makes more sense; for example, most individuals would prefer a combination of food and clothes to only food or clothing.

Multiple-Choice

1 c	2 b	3 c	4 d	5 d
6 e	7 d	8 a	*9 b	

True-False

10 F	11 F	12 T	13 T	14 T
15 T	16 T	17 F	18 T	

Short Problems

19 Strict convexity

20 The indifference curves are shown in Figure A3.1. Eleanor's indifference curves are flat beyond 100 books because she gets neither more nor less utility from more than 100 economic books.

21 Consider point A in Figure A3.2. Given nonsatiety, all points to the northeast of A are preferred bundles because they have more of *both* goods in them; all points to the southwest of A are less-preferred bundles because they have less of *both* goods in them; hence, the indifference curve must pass through the shaded regions.

22 Given a utility function $U(x_1, x_2)$, an indifference curve is defined by $u^0 = U(x_1, x_2)$; that is, an indifference curve is all combinations of good 1 and good 2 that yield the same utility u^0.

*23 Suppose that preferences are lexicographic. Then the set of bundles that is preferred to A in

FIGURE A3.1

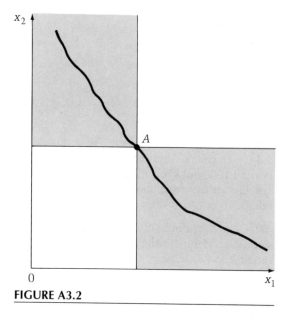

FIGURE A3.2

Figure A3.3 consists of all bundles to the right of A, including the solid line above A. Let the utility number for A be x_2^A and assign the number x_2 to each of the preferred bundles (x_1^A, x_2), $x_2 > x_2^A$. After these utility numbers are assigned, all the real numbers larger than x_2^A are used up. All bundles with more x_1 than x_1^A are preferred to all the bundles on the solid line and, therefore, must be assigned larger numbers. However, there are no numbers left to assign to these bundles; hence, a utility function cannot be constructed.

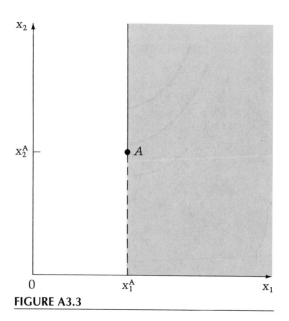

FIGURE A3.3

Long Problems

24 $U = 2b + 3p$. To see that this utility function describes the preference ordering, show that

$$U_E > U_D > U_C > U_A > U_B$$
$$U_E = (2)(6) + (3)(6) = 30$$
$$U_D = (2)(1) + (3)(9) = 29$$
$$U_C = (2)(12) + (3)(1) = 27$$
$$U_A = (2)(7) + (3)(3) = 23$$
$$U_B = (2)(5) + (3)(4) = 22$$

Any increasing monotonic transformation also represents the preference ordering. For example, any utility function $V(b, p)$ given by $v(b, p) = c[U(b, p)] + d$, where c and d are parameters, describes the same preference ordering.

25 Student 1 with utility function U_1 must study economics because no assumptions are violated, as shown in Figure A3.4a. Student 2 has concave rather than convex preferences, as shown in Figure A3.4b. Student 3's indifference curves (in Figure A3.4c) intersect and, therefore, violate transitivity. Student 4 (see Figure A3.4d) violates the assumption of nonsatiation (that is, that more is preferred to less) and so has positively sloped indifference curves.

26 The indifference curves are illustrated in Figure A3.5 for each case. The indifference curves in Figure A3.5a are for perfect substitutes. The preferences represented by these indifference curves can be ordered and represented by a utility function; however, they do not satisfy the assumption of strict convexity.

   The indifference curves in Figure A3.5b represent two complements. These preferences can be represented by a utility function; however, they do not satisfy nonsatiety or strict convexity.

   In Figure A3.5c are lexicographic preferences that violate the assumption of continuity. Preferences can be ordered, but no utility function can be constructed to represent these preferences.

   In Figure A3.5d, transitivity is violated, and no well-behaved preference ordering can be constructed. In Figure A3.5e, "more is preferred to less" is violated; these preferences can be represented by a utility function.

***27** If preferences are complete, reflexive, transitive, and continuous, and nonsatiety holds, then there exists a continuous utility function

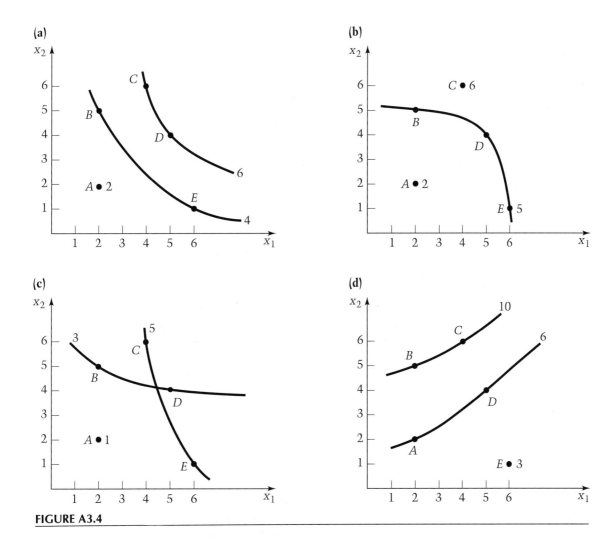

(a)

(b)

(c)

(d)

FIGURE A3.4

---

that represents those preferences. Define a utility function $U( ) = U(x_1, \ldots, x_n)$ such that

    a It assigns a number to all bundles

    b If B_1 **P** B_2, then $U(B_1) > U(B_2)$, and if B_1 **I** B_2, then $U(B_1) = U(B_2)$

By completeness, the individual is able to make comparisons of all bundles. Consider first those bundles on the 45° line in Figure A3.6. Assign a utility number x_1 to each bundle; that is, $U(B) = x_1$, where $B = (x_1, x_2)$. By nonsatiety, higher bundles on the 45° line are preferred to lower bundles; for example, B^2 **P** B^1, and by our rule for assigning utility numbers, the more preferred bundles are assigned higher numbers. This satisfies part **b** of the definition of a utility function for these bundles. Do all bundles get assigned a number (part **a** of the definition)? Consider a

bundle B^3 not on the 45° line. By continuity, indifference curves are smooth, and by the rule of more-is-preferred-to-less, they are negatively sloped. Then, the indifference curve through B^3 intersects the 45° line at a point, call it B^1. Since B^3 is indifferent to B^1, B^3 is assigned the utility number x_1^1.

    Last, we must show that all bundles off the 45° line will be assigned a number that correctly describes the individual's preferences; that is, part **b** of the definition of a utility function is satisfied for all bundles. Consider two bundles B^3 and B^4. By our earlier argument, there is a bundle on the 45° line that is indifferent to B^3, which we called B^1, and one that is indifferent to B^4, call it B^2. Both B^2 and B^4 are assigned utility number x_1^2; both B^1 and B^3 are assigned x_1^1. Recall that $x_1^2 > x_1^1$.

FIGURE A3.5

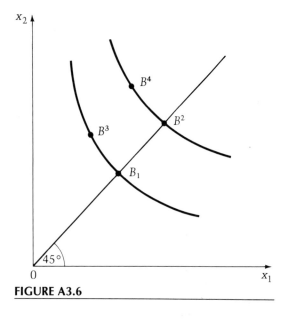

FIGURE A3.6

This assignment of utility numbers will be correct if B^4 **P** B^3. Since B^4 **I** B^2, B^2 **P** B^1, and B^1 **I** B^3, then, by transitivity, B^4 **P** B^3.

*28 Indifference curves are given by $x_1x_2 = c$. Consider the intersection of $x_1x_2 = c$ and the ray $x_2 = x_1$. (Note that the indifference curves are symmetric around the ray $x_2 = x_1$. The intersection occurs at $(\sqrt{c}, \sqrt{c})$. Assign the utility number $x_1 = \sqrt{c}$ to points on the curve $x_1x_2 = c$. Examples of the utility number assignment to bundles on various indifference curves are given in the table.

Utility Number	Bundles on
1	$x_1x_2 = 1$
$\sqrt{2}$	$x_1x_2 = 2$
$\sqrt{3}$	$x_1x_2 = 3$
$\sqrt{c}$	$x_1x_2 = c$

*29 a The indifference curves associated with Mary's preference ordering are $u^0 = x_1 x_2$. The slope of indifference curves is found by the formula

$$\Delta u^0 = x_2\, \Delta x_1 + x_1\, \Delta x_2$$

where $\Delta u^0 = 0$ (u^0 is constant along any given indifference curve.)

This implies that

$$x_1\, \Delta x_2 = -x_2\, \Delta x_1$$

$$\frac{\Delta x_2}{\Delta x_1} = \frac{-x_2}{x_1} \quad \text{and} \quad \text{MRS} = \frac{x_2}{x_1}$$

Note that as x_1 increases and x_2 falls, the MRS decreases.

b The indifference curves for utility levels 27, 28, and 29 are plotted in Figure A3.7.

c False. Utility is ordinal, not cardinal; hence, interpersonal comparisons cannot be made.

FIGURE A3.7

4

GETTING AND SPENDING:
THE PROBLEM OF
ECONOMIC CHOICE

Chapter Summary

Consumer's Choice Problem

As consumers, we are all involved in the complex task of making choices among competing goods, given constraints on our time, income, and human resources. To study an individual's static consumption decision in any given period of time, we must make several assumptions. First, we assume that the consumer has perfect knowledge of all prices in the economy. Next, we assume that the consumer has an income of M dollars to spend on the n consumption goods. Finally, we assume that the consumer has preferences that satisfy the assumptions of consumer theory laid out in the previous chapter. Given these assumptions, the consumer's choice problem becomes one of choosing quantities of the n consumption goods, the **endogenous variables,** in such a way that utility is maximized subject to the individual's **budget constraint.**

Properties of Demand Functions

The solution to this constrained maximization problem, the **utility-maximizing consumption bundle,** forms a system of **demand functions.** These functions tell us the quantities demanded of the consumption goods as a function of the **exogenous variables** of prices and income. Demand functions have two important properties. First, they are **homogeneous of degree zero.** If the quantities of all the exogenous variables change by the same factor, the quantity demanded of the good in question does not change. Second, **Engel's aggregation law** must hold. The sum of prices times quantities demanded must add up to total expenditures.

Graphical Analysis of Utility Maximization

The solution to the utility-maximization problem can be characterized by one of two possibilities. If indifference curves are smooth, then an **interior solution** (one in which positive quantities of both goods are consumed) occurs where the **marginal rate of substitution** of good 2 for good 1 equals the ratio of the price of good 1 to the price of good 2, and all the consumer's budget is spent. Alternatively, an interior solution can be characterized as the point of tangency, where the slope of the indifference curve equals the slope of the budget constraint. This solution implies that the amount of good 2 that the individual is willing to trade for a unit of good 1 is equal to the **opportunity cost** of good 2; that is, the amount that the consumer must trade in the market. A **corner solution** occurs when the consumer buys all of one good and none of the other. This latter good is referred to as an **inessential good**.

Comparative Statics Exercises

Now that we've solved the consumer's choice problem, we want to examine the effect of changes in the exogenous variables on the quantity demanded; that is, we want to do some **comparative statics**.

Income Changes — Consider a change in income, holding constant all other variables (prices). This simple exercise yields our first taxonomy: If consumption increases with increases in income, then the good is a **normal good**; if consumption falls with increases in income, it is an **inferior good**. If we were to draw a line through the various utility-maximizing bundles as income increases, it would form the **income-consumption path**. An **Engel curve** can also be drawn to show the relationship between income and quantity demanded.

Changes in the Own Price: Income and Substitution Effects — A change in the own price of a good is a bit more complicated because it can be decomposed into a **substitution** and an **income effect**. For example, an increase in the price of good 1 results in a substitution from good 1 to good 2, simply because the relative prices have changed in favor of good 2. This substitution effect is nonpositive. Moreover, the price increase implies a decline in **real income**; and so less or more good 1 will be consumed, depending on good 1 being a **normal** or **inferior** good, respectively.

If a good is an inferior good, the substitution and income effects work in opposite directions. For an unusual type of inferior good called a **Giffen good**, the income effect actually outweighs the substitution effect; hence, an increase in the price of the good may elicit an increase in the quantity demanded. The Irish potato famine is explained by the Giffen paradox: An increase in the price of potatoes made the consumers so poor that they could afford only potatoes in their diet!

It is possible to separate the income and substitution effects in the following manner: After a change in the price of a good, give the consumer enough **compensatory income** to enable her to remain on the original indifference curve. This isolates the substitution effect, which is always negative. Hence, the **compensated demand curve**, which reflects only the substitution effect, is always sloped downward. The income effect is isolated by taking away this compensatory income but allowing prices to remain at their new levels. This latter effect, as explained, can be either positive or negative.

Changes in the Price of Another Good — When the price of another good, good 2, changes, the response in the consumption of good 1 depends on the relationship between the two goods. The second taxonomy: If an increase in the price of good 2 elicits an increase in the consumption of good 1, then good 2 and good 1 are **substitutes**; if the quantity demanded of good 1 falls in response to the increase in the price of good 2, the two goods are **complements**.

Income and Price Elasticities

To measure these various effects of price and income changes on the quantity demanded of good 1, we need a unitless measure — one that doesn't change if we measure prices in dollars or British pounds or quantities in bushels or tons. The economic measure of responsiveness is called **elasticity**, which is the percentage change in quantity demanded with the percentage change in some economic variable (income, price of good 2, or price of good 1). Returning to our income taxonomy, the **income elasticity of demand** is positive if a good is normal and negative if it is inferior. For the second taxonomy: The **cross-price elasticity of demand** is positive if the goods are substitutes and negative if the goods are complements.

For our last, but most important, elasticity measure and third taxonomy: The **price elasticity**, which measures the demand response to changes in the good's own price, is negative except for Giffen goods. To make things easier, we talk about the absolute value of this elasticity. When the price elasticity of demand is greater than 1, the good is said to be **price-elastic**; when it is less than 1, it is a **price-inelastic** good. As the names suggest, an elastic good is relatively more responsive to price changes than an inelastic good. Moreover, when the good is price inelastic (elastic), the **price consumption line** is positively (negatively) sloped, and total expenditures decrease (increase) for decreases in the price of the good.

Composite Commodity

To provide a graphical analysis of the consumer's problem, it is useful to define a **composite commodity** good 2, which is simply the expenditure on all other goods. Using **Hick's composite commodity theorem**, we can reduce the complicated choice problem to one of a choice involving the quantity of some good, say good 1, and the quantity of good 2.

Key Words

Budget constraint
Comparative statics
Compensatory income
Compensated demand
    curve
Complements
Composite commod-
    ity
Convexity
Corner solution
Cross-price elasticity
Demand functions
Endogenous variables
Engel curve
Engel's aggregation
    law
Essential good
Exogenous variables
Giffen good
Hick's composite
    commodity theorem

Homogeneous of
    degree zero
Income-consumption
    path
Income elasticity
Inessential good
Inferior goods
Interior solution
Marginal rate of
    substitution
Normal goods
Opportunity cost
Price-consumption
    line
Price elasticity
Substitutes
Substitution and
    income effects
Utility-maximizing
    consumption bundle

Case Study: Rationing Gasoline in Canada[1]

The oil embargo in 1973 brought an unexpected shortage in the world oil supply. Although Canada was importing oil, it had reserves sufficient to satisfy domestic demand for at least a decade. However, because it was cheaper to import oil from Venezuela than to transport it from the oil-rich west to eastern Canada, oil production in Canada was reserved to fill the demand in western Canada and the western United States. As a result of this "comfortable" position in the world oil market, Canadian policy kept oil prices well below world prices for much of the 1970s. The inefficiency of this policy was finally recognized in the early 1980s, when the per-capita consumption of oil in Canada was the highest in the world.

One conservation policy that was discussed was a two-tier pricing policy that would work as follows. Each individual would be given a certain number of ration tickets, say 100, every month. Each ticket would allow the purchase of one gallon of gasoline at $0.75 (1980 prices). If an individual wanted to purchase more than 100 gallons of gasoline per month, he or she would have to pay $2 per gallon. Tickets could not be transferred between individuals nor between months. The price of gasoline at the time that this policy was discussed was $1.25 per gallon.

A What would an individual's budget constraint for gasoline and all other goods under the two-tier price system look like, given a monthly income of $M = \$500$?

B On an indifference curve diagram, show an individual who consumes less gasoline under this policy than if the price were uniform at $1.25 per gallon. Is it possible for an individual (with a $500 income) to consume more gasoline under this two-tier scheme? Illustrate this situation.

Consider an alternative rationing scheme. Instead of charging two prices for gasoline, suppose that, as before, 100 nontransferrable ration tickets are given to each driver per month. However, under this scheme, the individual must pay 1 ration ticket and $1.25 (the current price) for each gallon of gasoline. No more than 100 gallons of gasoline can be purchased per month.

C Using an indifference curve diagram, show an individual with a monthly income of $500 who is unaffected by this second rationing scheme relative to the nonrationing situation.

D On another diagram, show the case of an individual (with a $500 income) who experiences a decline in utility from this scheme relative to the initial situation.

E Given your analyses in **A** to **D**, which policy do you think is the more effective in conserving gasoline? Explain.

Exercises

Multiple-Choice

Choose the correct answer to each question. There is only one correct answer to each question.

1 An individual with an MRS of milkshakes for hamburgers equal to $\frac{1}{3}$ is maximizing utility if
  a The price of a hamburger is three times that of a milkshake.
  b The price of a hamburger equals that of a milkshake.
  c The price of a hamburger is $\frac{1}{3}$ the price of a milkshake.

  d She trades three milkshakes for a hamburger.
  e None of the above.

2 An individual is currently maximizing his utility subject to his monthly budget constraint at point A in Figure 4.1. The government wants to ration goods 1 and 2 and to achieve this by giving each consumer 10 ration tickets per month. In addition to money, the individual must pay 1 ration ticket per unit of good 1 and $2\frac{1}{2}$ ration tickets per unit of good 2. The individual must now consume
  a Less of good 1 than given by bundle A
  b Less of good 2 than at bundle A
  c More of both goods
  d The same as bundle A
  e Cannot say without more information

3 In Figure 4.2, which of the following is true?
  a The price of brie per pound is two-thirds the price of baguettes per dozen.
  b The price of brie per pound is 1.5 times the price of baguettes per dozen.
  c The individual will consume 1.5 times more baguettes than brie.
  d The individual will consume 1.5 times more brie than baguettes.
  e None of the above.

FIGURE 4.1

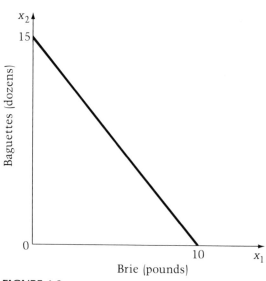

Brie (pounds)

FIGURE 4.2

4 A consumer consumes only two goods, good 1 and good 2. The marginal rate of substitution of good 2 for good 1 at any point (x_1, x_2) is x_2/x_1. Suppose that income $M = \$260$, $p_1 = \$2$, $p_2 = \$3$, and the consumer is consuming 40 units of good 1 and 60 units of good 2. Which of the following is true?

a The consumer is maximizing utility subject to her income.

b The consumer could increase utility by increasing her consumption of good 1 and decreasing her consumption of good 2.

c The consumer could increase her utility by increasing her consumption of good 2 and decreasing her consumption of good 1.

d The consumer should increase her consumption of both goods because she is not spending all the income.

e None of the above.

5 An increase in income results in

a An upward shift in the demand curve for an inferior good

b An upward shift in the demand curve for a normal good

c No change in demand because price will rise and offset any possible increase in the quantity demanded brought about by the income increase

d A movement along the demand curve

e Both **a** and **b**

6 A movement along the demand curve for a good must occur

a When the buyer's income increases

b When the prices of other goods change

c When the buyer's tastes change

d When the price of the good decreases

e None of the above

7 If all prices and incomes increase by 10%, homogeneity of degree zero implies that

a Quantity demanded of all goods will rise by 10%.

b Quantity demanded of all goods will fall by 10%.

c Quantity demanded of all goods will not change.

d Total expenditures on all goods will be less than income.

e Total expenditures on all goods will exceed income.

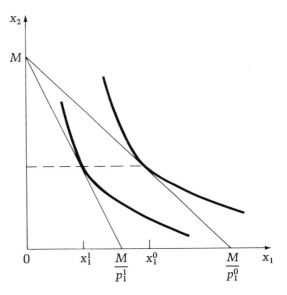

Number of squash balls

FIGURE 4.3

Refer to Figure 4.3 to answer questions 8 and 9.

8 When the price of squash balls is p_1^0, José purchases x_1^0 squash balls as shown in Figure 4.3. When the price rises to p_1^1, he purchases x_1^1 balls. Which of the following is true?

a Squash balls are an inferior good but not a Giffen good.

b Squash balls are a normal good.

c Squash balls are a Giffen good.

d The income elasticity of demand for squash balls equals 1 because consumption of good 2 stayed the same.

e I cannot tell if it is normal, inferior, or a Giffen good because a price change, not a change in income, brought about a change in the purchase of squash balls.

9 José's price elasticity of demand for squash balls (in absolute value) is

a 0

b Between 0 and 1

c 1

d Greater than 1

e None of the above

10 The price elasticity of demand (in absolute value) at point A in Figure 4.4 is

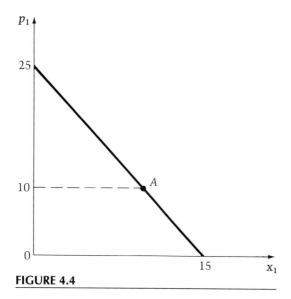

FIGURE 4.4

a $\frac{1}{3}$.
b $\frac{2}{5}$.
c $\frac{2}{3}$.
d $\frac{3}{2}$.
e There is not enough information to tell.

11 An individual's demand curve for peaches is

$$x_1 = 10 - 3p + 0.5M$$

where x_1 is the quantity of peaches measured in 10-bushel units, p is the price per bushel in dollars, and M is the consumer's income in thousands of dollars. An individual consumes 20 bushels when the price is $5 per bushel and his income is $10,000. At these values, the price elasticity of demand equals

a -3
b $-(5/2) \div 3$
c $-(5/2) \times 3$
d $-(5/20) \times 3$
e None of the above

12 For the demand curve in Exercise 11, the income elasticity at the given values is

a 0.5
b $(10/2) \times 0.5$
c $(10,000/20) \times 0.5$
d $(10/2) \div 0.5$
e None of the above

13 Suppose that an individual consumes only one brand of beer, brand 1, at the prevailing prices. If the price of brand 2 falls sufficiently, however, the individual would switch brands and consume only brand 2. The indifference curves between brands 1 and 2 are described by which diagram in Figure 4.5?

a a
b b
c c
d d
e None of the above

True-False

14 Since the real price of automobiles has increased but the quantity demanded has also increased over recent years, the demand curve for automobiles must be positively sloped.

15 The demand curve $x_1 = 5M(p_2/p_1)^{1/2}$ is homogeneous of degree zero in prices and income.

16 All inferior goods are Giffen goods.

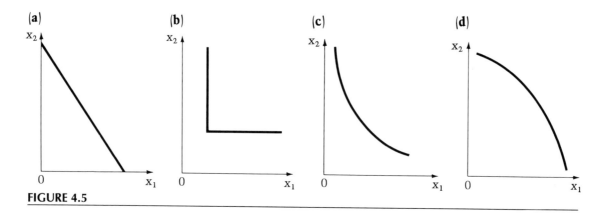

(a) (b) (c) (d)

FIGURE 4.5

17 All Giffen goods are inferior goods.

18 If the income elasticity of a good is negative, the demand curve of that good must be negatively sloped.

19 If, at the utility-maximizing bundle of good 1 and good 2, the MRS of good 2 for good 1 is greater than p_1/p_2, then good 1 is an inessential good.

20 Suppose that an individual consumes only two goods, good 1 and good 2. If the price of good 1 rises, with all else constant, and the price elasticity of demand for good 1 is -0.7, then the quantity of good 2 will increase.

21 If an individual's income is the same before and after an excise tax is imposed on good 1 and the demand for good 1 is elastic, the excise tax will lead to an increase in spending on other consumer goods.

22 Since a decrease in the price of 1 unit along a linear demand curve will result in an increase in the quantity demanded by a constant amount, the price elasticity is constant for all quantities along a linear demand curve.

23 If the cross-price elasticity between goods 1 and 2 is positive, then the indifference curves must be those given in Figure 4.6.

24 Let good 1 be the good on the horizontal axis, and let the quantity of the composite commodity be on the vertical axis. Then, if the (absolute value of the) price elasticity of demand for good 1 is less than 1, the price-consumption line is negatively sloped.

25 Along a consumer's budget line, money income is constant.

26 A commodity bundle lying below a consumer's budget line must be inferior to all bundles lying on the budget line.

27 Assume that a certain individual consumes only goods 1 and 2. If the prices of good 1 and good 2 double and his income doubles, then the quantities demanded for goods 1 and 2 will not change.

*28 If a decline in the prices of agricultural products results in a reduction in the *consumption* of these goods by many farmers, then these products must be inferior goods.

Short Problems

29 Suppose the consumer equilibrium is achieved along an indifference curve with a slope $(\Delta x_2/\Delta x_1)$ equal to $-200/x_1^2$. If the consumer's income is $60 and $p_1 = \$6$ and $p_2 = \$3$, what are the equilibrium quantities demanded of good 1 and good 2?

30 What two conditions must be satisfied for an individual to maximize his utility subject to his budget constraint?

31 The data in the accompanying table are gasoline prices and quantities of new cars sold in Nova Scotia, Canada (in 1971 dollars).

Year	Price (dollars per gallon)	Quantity Sold (millions of gallons)
1970	0.508	176.4
1974	0.659	229.5
1979	1.073	264.5

These data indicate that between 1970 and 1974 and between 1974 and 1979 there was a positive relationship between price and quantity demanded. Does this imply that the demand for gasoline is positively sloped?

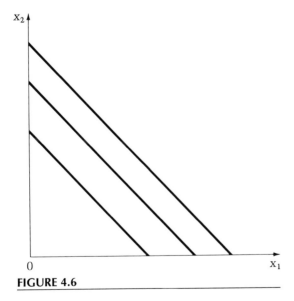

x_2

0 x_1

FIGURE 4.6

32 At the utility-maximizing bundle, a consumer spends all her income on good 1 and none on good 2. Illustrate this bundle on a diagram and show the maximum price of good 2 at which the individual would be willing to purchase some good 2.

33 Robinson Crusoe lives on an island in the middle of Lake Michigan. He consumes only air and water. Crusoe's preferences are characterized by diminishing MRS of air for water up to 50 cubic meters of air. Beyond 50 cubic meters of air, Crusoe is not willing to give up additional water to get more air. Furthermore, air is a free good; that is, it has a zero price. However, a price of $1 per gallon of fresh lake water must be paid to the state of Michigan. Given that Crusoe has an income of $100 per year from social security benefits, use a diagram to determine the optimal combination of air and water that will maximize Crusoe's utility subject to his income constraint.

34 Figure 4.7 shows two Engel curves. Which one refers to a normal good and which one to an inferior good? Explain.

35 Mr. Max E. Miser lives in a world of beer and peanuts. When Max's nominal income increased from 1984 to 1985, he increased his consumption of both peanuts and beer. However, Max claims that peanuts are an inferior good. If Max's preferences have not changed and peanuts are indeed an inferior good, then what must have happened to the relative price of peanuts to beer? Show the substitution and income effects for peanuts for the price change you propose.

36 Giuseppi owns a vineyard in northern Italy. He provides food and shelter for the grape growers, who make the wine and pay Giuseppi a fixed amount of wine. The workers' rent is Giuseppi's only source of income. Giuseppi consumes some of the wine and sells the rest for income to purchase a second good, good 2, the composite commodity. Suppose that the price of wine p_w rises. Will Giuseppi consume less wine? Explain, using diagrams.

37 The income (point) elasticity of demand for bread is 1.0 and the own price (point) elasticity is -0.4. The price of bread is $2, and income is $100. If price rises to $3, what level of income would leave the quantity demanded approximately unchanged?

38 Assume that a family consumes the combination of salt and "all other goods" described by point A in Figure 4.8. Show an example of the new utility-maximizing bundle if the price of salt decreases and salt is a price-inelastic good.

39 Compare the price elasticities of demand *at every price* for the two demand curves

FIGURE 4.7

Quantity of salt

FIGURE 4.8

$$x_1 = 450 - p_1$$

$$x_1 = 150 - \frac{p_1}{3}$$

Explain your answer by illustrating the two demand curves.

40 In empirical studies, the demand curve is often specified to be linear. For example, $x_1 = a - bp_1 + cp_2 + dM$, where x_1 is the quantity demanded of good 1, p_1 is the price of good 1, p_2 is the price of good 2, M is the income, and $a, b, c,$ and d are parameters. How might income and prices be defined to ensure that the demand curve is homogeneous of degree zero?

Long Problems

41 The Smith family had a total income of $15,000 in 1987. Of this amount, its expenditures for certain foods were

Fish	$2500
Bread	800
Cereal	500
Milk	700

In 1988, the family's income increased to $20,000 and its expenditures on the above items were

Fish	$3500
Bread	500
Cereal	700
Milk	950

a What assumptions must be made to calculate the income elasticity of demand for any of the food products using the given information?
b Having made these assumptions, calculate the Smith's income elasticity of demand for each of the items listed.
c Is the income elasticity you calculated necessarily the same for all income levels? Why or why not?

42 Suppose that the demand for pencils by a representative consumer is given by

$$x = 19.4 + 0.4M - 8p + 2p_f$$

where x is quantity demanded of pencils, M is income in thousands of dollars, p is price of pencils in dollars, and p_f is price of fountain pens in dollars. Suppose that the values of these variables for the consumer are

$$x = 25$$
$$M = 20$$
$$p = \$0.80$$
$$p_f = \$2$$

a Calculate the own-price elasticity, cross-price elasticity, and income elasticity of demand for pencils, given this information.
b Suppose that an increase in the price of ink refills results in a 20% increase in the cost of using a fountain pen. What will be the percentage increase in the quantity demanded of pencils?

43 Draw on separate diagrams the substitution and income effects of an increase in the price of good 1 for each of the following cases.
a Good 1 is a normal good.
b Good 1 is an inferior good but not a Giffen good.
c Good 1 is a Giffen good.

44 Suppose that an individual's utility function is given by

$$U = x_1 x_2$$

where x_1 is his own consumption (in dollars) and x_2 is his charitable contributions (in dollars). The marginal rate of substitution of good 2 for good 1 is x_2/x_1. Assume that the individual's income is $45,000 per year.
a Illustrate the optimal choice of the individual's own consumption and charitable contributions. Calculate the optimal consumption bundle.
b Suppose that the government puts a tax of 50% on own consumption but charitable contributions are tax-free. Illustrate the new optimum in this case.

45 We offer three explanations for the decline in the average family size in the United States. Illustrate the explanations with an indifference curve diagram for "children" and the composite commodity good 2.
a Children have become more expensive.
b People's tastes for large families have changed.
c Children are an inferior good.

(a)   **(b)**   **(c)**

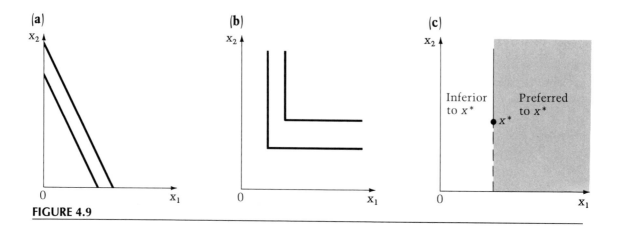

FIGURE 4.9

46 An individual's income is $1000 per week. Her preferences over goods 1 and 2 can be described by convex indifference curves. The price of good 2 is $1. Using an indifference curve diagram, derive the individual's demand curve for good 1. To derive the demand curve, find three points on the demand curve at which the price p_1 of good 1 is $2.50, $5, and $10. Make the following assumptions: The demand curve is linear, the point of unitary elasticity is at a price of $5, and the individual maximizes her utility subject to her budget constraint. Make sure your diagram reflects the information given.

47 Figure 4.9 shows sets of "indifference curves" representing preferences that violate one (or more) of the assumptions of consumer choice. In Exercise **26** of Chapter 3, you identified the assumption(s) violated in each case. In this exercise, you are to determine the effect that these nonstandard indifference curves have on the demand curves. For each set of preferences, superimpose a budget constraint on the indifference curve map and find the utility-maximizing bundle of good 1 and good 2. Then let the price of good 1 change to generate points on the demand curve for good 1. Do the preferences represented in the figure imply downward-sloping demand curves? Explain.

*48 Suppose that a consumer has the indifference curves illustrated in Figure 4.10.

  a Draw a budget constraint and find the consumer's utility-maximizing bundle of goods.

  b Is there any portion of the indifference curve that the consumer will never be on? Explain.

  c If the indifference curves were made convex (for example, if a line segment were to join points A and B on indifference curve I), then what would be the individual's utility-maximizing bundle of goods? When might this lead to incorrect predictions?

Answers to Chapter 4

Case Study

A The budget constraint under the rationing scheme is shown in Figure A4.1. The intercept on

FIGURE 4.10

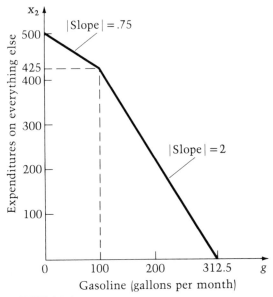

FIGURE A4.1

the good 2 axis is $500, which is the maximum expenditure on good 2 (if gasoline consumption equals zero). On the g axis, the intercept is 312.5, which is the maximum number of gallons that can be purchased if $x_2 = 0$. To show this, consider the number of gallons above 100 that can be

afforded at a price of $2. The amount of money spent on the first 100 gallons with the ration tickets is ($0.75)(100) = $75. The additional gallons that can be afforded are (500 − 75)/2 = 212.5; hence, 100 + 212.5 = 312.5. At $g = 100$, the budget constraint is kinked; the slope is flatter for $g \leq 100$ than for $g > 100$ to reflect the lower price of gasoline ($0.75 versus $2). At $g = 100$, $425 remains to be spent on good 2.

B The prerationing budgetline is given by AB in Figure A4.2. The individual who consumes less is shown in Figure A4.2a. The individual reduces gasoline consumption from g_0 to g_1. The individual who consumes more is shown in Figure A4.2b. This individual increases gasoline consumption from g_0 to g_1 as a result of the scheme.

C An individual who is unaffected by the second rationing scheme is shown in Figure A4.3.

D The utility of the individual shown in Figure A4.4 falls as a result of the second rationing scheme. Point C is not available because the consumer is not allowed to purchase more than 100 gallons.

E The strict rationing regime (the second scheme) will be more *effective* in conserving gasoline. No one will ever be induced to consume

FIGURE A4.2

FIGURE A4.3

more gasoline as a result of it. However, this rationing scheme is not necessarily more efficient in that it may result in a larger loss in utility.

Multiple Choice

1 c	2 b	3 b	4 b	5 b	6 d	7 c
8 b	9 c	10 c	11 c	12 b	13 a	

FIGURE A4.4

True-False

14 F	15 F	16 F	17 T	18 F
19 F	20 F	21 T	22 F	23 F
24 F	25 T	26 F	27 T	*28 F

Short Problems

29 The ratio of the price of good 1 to the price of good 2 is $\$6/\$3 = 2$. Setting the ratio of prices equal to the MRS gives

$$\frac{200}{x_1^2} = 2$$

and so

$$x_1 = 10$$

This value of good 1 is substituted into the budget constraint to get the utility-maximizing value of good 2.

$$60 = (6)(10) + 3y$$
$$x_2 = 0$$

30 a $\text{MRS}(x_1^*, x_2^*) = \dfrac{p_1}{p_2}$
  b $M = p_1 x_1^* + p_2 x_2^*$

31 No. Other variables may have changed. For example, the price of public transportation may have increased, shifting the demand curve for automobile travel to the right. An increase in population may have shifted the demand curve. If a movement from cities to the suburbs occurred, distances to work may have increased, shifting the demand curve for gasoline to the right.

32 The maximum price of good 2 for which some good 2 will be purchased (given the price of good 1) is p_2' shown in Figure A4.5. At p_2', $\text{MRS}(\bar{x}_1, 0) = p_1/p_2'$; that is, the price of good 1 relative to the price of good 2 equals the marginal rate of substitution evaluated at $x_1 = \bar{x}_1$ and $x_2 = 0$. For any higher price of good 2, $x_2 = 0$; for a price of good 2 lower than p_2', a positive amount of good 2 will be demanded.

33 The budget line is a straight line as shown in Figure A4.6. Air is a free good, so the maximum that can be bought is $\$100/0 = \infty$. Robinson is indifferent between bundles on AB; he consumes 100 cubic meters of water and 50 or more cubic meters of air.

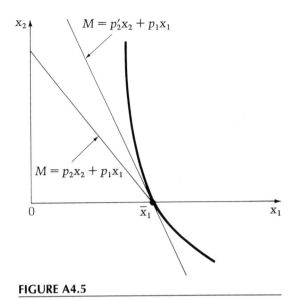

FIGURE A4.5

34 In Figure 4.7, I refers to an inferior good because it shows a negative relationship between income and quantity demanded; II refers to a normal good because it shows a positive relationship between income and good 1.

35 The price of peanuts relative to the price of beer must have fallen. The increase in income is shown by a parallel shift of the budget line from AB to CD in Figure A4.7. The consumption of

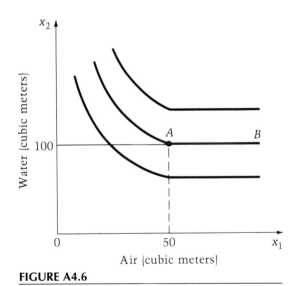

FIGURE A4.6

peanuts fell from x_1^0 to x_1^1 due to this income increase because peanuts are inferior. Since Max consumes more peanuts, the price must have dropped. The price decrease pivots the budget line CD to CE. The consumption increases to x_1^2. The substitution and income effects are shown for the price decrease. From x_1^1 to x_1^3 is the substitution effect; from x_1^3 to x_1^2 is the income effect. Note that peanuts are shown to be an inferior good by the income effect. As the problem states, the consumption of peanuts increases from x_1^0 to x_1^2 as a result of both an income increase and a price decrease.

36 Not necessarily. Wine is a source of income. When the price of wine increases, the maximum amount of wine that Giuseppi can consume remains at $\overline{w}$ (because he is paid in *quantity* of food by the workers). However, Giuseppi can sell all the food and earn $p_w'\overline{w}$ to spend on everything else. Giuseppi is shown in Figure A4.8 to consume more wine as a result of this increase in income.

37 The information can be substituted into the definitions of the price and income elasticities to answer the question. That is, substitute $M = 100$ into the income elasticity and set it equal to 1 to get

$$\left(\frac{\Delta x}{x}\right)\left(\frac{100}{\Delta M}\right) = 1 \qquad (1)$$

FIGURE A4.7

Bottles of beer

Bags of peanuts

FIGURE A4.8

FIGURE A4.9

Now substitute $\Delta p = 1$ and $p = 2$ into the price elasticity to get

$$\left(\frac{\Delta x}{x}\right)\left(\frac{2}{1}\right) = -0.4 \qquad (2)$$

Solve for $\Delta x/x$ from the price elasticity expression in equation (2) to get

$$\frac{\Delta x}{x} = -0.2$$

That is, as a result of the price increase of 50%, x falls by 20%. But we want to determine the percentage change in M ($\Delta M/M$) such that x goes back to its original level. Substitute $\Delta x/x = 0.2$ into the income elasticity expression in equation (1) to get ΔM:

$$\frac{0.2 \times 100}{\Delta M} = 1$$

and so

$$\Delta M = 20$$

Hence, M must increase \$20 to \$120 to keep x at the same level when price rises from \$2 to \$3.

38 Salt is shown to have a price-inelastic demand curve in Figure A4.9 by the upward-sloping price consumption curve.

39 Rewriting the demand curves with price as the dependent variable gives

$$p_1 = 450 - x_1 \qquad \text{and} \qquad p_1 = 450 - 3x_1$$

Note that the second demand curve is an "iso-elastic shift" of the first demand curve; both demand curves have the same price intercept but different slopes. The price elasticities for the two demand curves are the same at every price. The demand curves are illustrated in Figure A4.10.

40 Prices and income could be defined relative to the price of one of the goods or in terms of the price of a composite good. For example, let the prices and income be defined relative to the price of good 1. Then, the new demand is

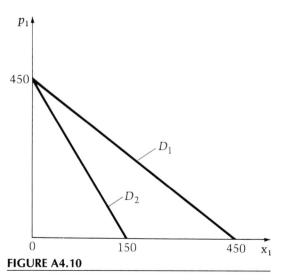

FIGURE A4.10

$$x_1 = a' + b'\frac{p_2}{p_1} + c'\frac{M}{p_1}$$

where a', b', and c' indicate that the parameters of this equation are not the same as in the original equation. Often, all prices and income are defined relative to the consumer price index (CPI), which gives the cost of a basket of goods today relative to the cost of that same basket of goods in a previous year.

Long Problems

41 a All prices must be held constant.

b Fish
$$\frac{(3500 - 2500)\ 17,500}{(20,000 - 15,000)\ 3000}$$
$$= \frac{1000 \times 175}{5000 \times 30} = 1.17$$

Bread $\dfrac{(500 - 800)\ 17,500}{5000 \times 650}$
$$= \frac{-3 \times 175}{5 \times 65} = -1.62$$

Cereal $\dfrac{(700 - 500)\ 17,500}{5000 \times 600}$
$$= \frac{2 \times 175}{5 \times 60} = 1.17$$

Milk $\dfrac{(950 - 700)\ 17,500}{5000 \times 825}$
$$= \frac{25 \times 175}{5 \times 825} = 1.06$$

Note that the elasticities are the "arc elasticities"; that is, they are calculated between two points (x_1^1, M_1) and (x_1^2, M_2). The formula used is
$$\frac{(x_1^2 - x_1^1)(M_1 + M_2)/2}{(M_2 - M_1)(x_1^1 + x_1^2)/2}$$

Expenditures on the goods rather than the quantities can be used in the calculations because prices are assumed to be constant.

c No. As the household's income rises, the income elasticities may change. For example, for larger increases in income, cereal products may be replaced by more expensive products.

42 a
$$e_p = -8\left(\frac{0.8}{25}\right) = -0.256$$
$$e_f = 2\left(\frac{2}{25}\right) = 0.16$$
$$e_M = 0.4\left(\frac{20}{25}\right) = 0.32$$

b Since $\% \Delta x / \% \Delta p_f = 0.16$, then for $\% \Delta p_f = 20$, $\% \Delta x = 0.16 \times 20 = 3.2$. That is, a 20% increase in the cost of using a fountain pen increases pencil use by 3.2%.

43 In all the cases shown in Figure A4.11, the substitution effect is from x_1^A to x_1^C and the income effect is from x_1^C to x_1^B.

44 a The utility-maximizing consumption bundle is where MRS $= p_1/p_2$. Since consumption is in dollars, the price of a unit of good 1 or good 2 is $1; therefore, the price ratio is 1/1. Then,

FIGURE A4.11

FIGURE A4.12

FIGURE A4.13

$$\frac{x_2}{x_1} = 1 \quad \text{or} \quad x_2 = x_1$$

Substituting this relationship into the budget constraint gives

$$\$45{,}000 = x_1 + x_2$$
$$\$45{,}000 = 2x_1$$

or

$$x_1 = x_2 = \$22{,}500$$

The utility-maximizing solution is illustrated in Figure A4.12.

b The effect of the tax is to increase the price of good 1 to 1.5. Therefore, the budget line pivots inward, as shown in Figure A4.13. The

new optimum is given by point B. Now the utility-maximizing solution occurs where

$$\frac{x_2}{x_1} = \frac{1.5}{1}$$
$$x_2 = 1.5x_1$$

Substituting this relationship into the budget constraint gives

$$45{,}000 = x_1(1.5) + x_2$$
$$45{,}000 = 2x_1(1.5)$$

or

$$x_1 = 15{,}000 \quad \text{and} \quad x_2 = 22{,}500$$

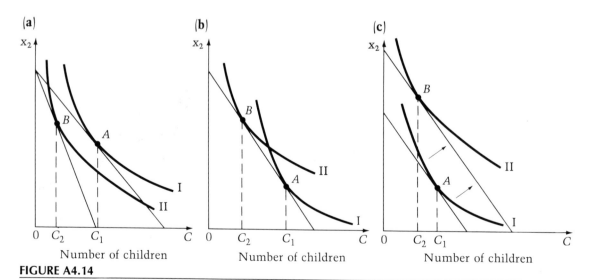

FIGURE A4.14

45 a If children are more expensive, the "price" of children is higher, pivoting the budget line inward as shown in Figure A4.14*a*.

b If tastes changed away from large families, then the indifference curves become flatter (indifference curve II in Figure A4.14*b*) because households are less willing to give up large amounts of good 2 for large families.

c If children are an inferior good, then an increase in real income will reduce the number of children in families as shown in Figure A4.14*c*.

46 The maximum values of good 1 that can be consumed at prices \$2.50, \$5, and \$10 are 400, 200, and 100, respectively. The utility-maximizing bundles of good 1 and good 2, constrained by the individual's income, are denoted by *A*, *B*, and

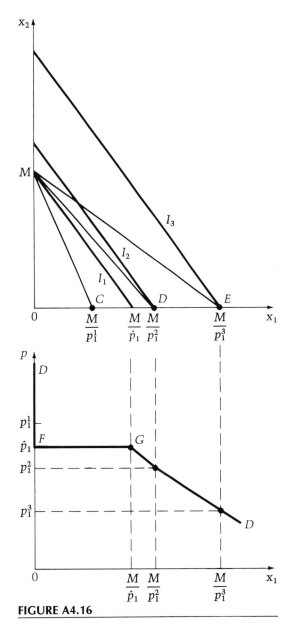

FIGURE A4.15

FIGURE A4.16

C, respectively. The demand curve for good 1 is shown to be linear in Figure A4.15. For high prices, the demand is price elastic, as indicated by the negatively sloped price-consumption curve (PC); for low prices, the demand is price inelastic, as indicated by the positively sloped PC; the point of unitary elasticity is at $p_1 = \$5$. Since the point of unitary elasticity is at the midpoint of a linear demand, the intercept of the demand curve must be at $p_1 = \$10$.

47 The indifference curves in Figures 4.9a, b, and c represent perfect substitutes, perfect complements, and lexicographic preferences, respectively. To find the demand curves in each case, denote income by M, let the price of good 2 be \$1, and let the price of good 1 (p_1) be p_1^1, p_1^2, and p_1^3,

where $p_1^1 > p_1^2 > p_1^3$. The three budget lines corresponding to these prices are denoted in Figure A4.16 and A4.17 by MC, MD, and ME, respectively.

Consider the case of *perfect substitutes* in Figure A4.16. For a price of good 1 equal to p_1^1, utility is maximized where $x_1 = 0$. For a lower price p_1^2, the consumer switches from good 2 to good 1 and consumes M/p_1^2. For lower prices, $x_2 = 0$ and $x_1 = M/p_1$. The demand curve for good 1 is discontinuous at $\hat{p}_1$. For prices higher than $\hat{p}_1$, $x_1 = 0$; for lower prices, x_1 increases with decreases in p_1.

Next consider the case of perfect complements in Figure A4.17a. The utility-maximizing bundle is given by the corners of the indifference curves at F, G, and H; that is, since good 1 and

(a)

(b)

FIGURE A4.17

(a)

(b)

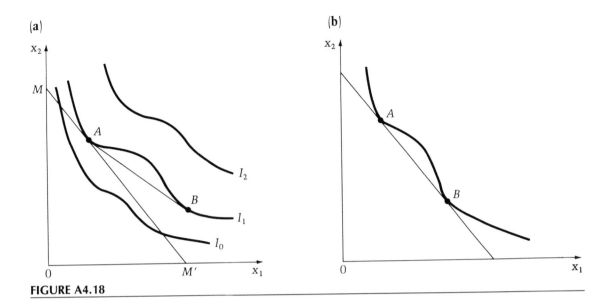

FIGURE A4.18

good 2 are perfect complements, the two goods are always consumed in the same ratio. The demand curve for good 1 is negatively sloped as shown.

Finally, consider the case of lexicographic preferences. In this case, the consumer prefers any bundle with more good 1; hence, given an income M, utility is maximized by consuming $x_2 = 0$ and $x_1 = M/p_1$ at points C, D, and E in Figure A4.17b. Again, the demand curve for good 1 is negatively sloped.

48 a Given the budget line MM', the individual maximizes utility by choosing point A in Figure A4.18a.

b The consumer will never choose a bundle on the nonconvex portion of the indifference curve; for example, from A to B in Figure A4.18a. If she did, the consumer would be *minimizing* utility subject to the budget constraint.

c If the indifference curves are made convex by drawing a line from point A to B in the diagram in Figure A4.18a, the utility-maximizing bundle will not change. This can lead to problems when the budget line is coincident with the line joining points A and B, as shown in Figure A4.18b. In this case, the prediction of the theory would be that the individual is indifferent among all points between A and B when, in fact, she would choose only A or B.

5

VICARIOUS PROBLEM SOLVING: APPLICATIONS OF THE THEORY OF CHOICE

Chapter Summary

Many intriguing puzzles about the consumer are explored in this chapter. Among the many questions asked are the following. If the government wants to subsidize low-income families, which payment scheme would be more efficient: lump-sum payments, payments-in-kind, or per-unit subsidies? What is the profit-maximizing pricing scheme for consumer durables? How can the waste from the tragedy of the commons be transformed into surplus or profits? How do consumers choose between work and leisure? How can the welfare of an individual be measured in a changing economic environment?

Lump Sum Versus Excise Taxes

When the government wants to collect taxes, it can chose to levy a fixed, **lump-sum tax** per individual, or it can impose an **excise tax** on every unit of a particular good purchased. Given that the aim of the government is to collect some specific revenue, the consumer would prefer that a lump-sum tax be used because it leaves the consumer at a higher level of utility. Alternatively, if the individual's utility level is held constant, the government can collect more revenue by using a lump-sum tax. This same result also holds for

comparing lump-sum subsidies and per-unit subsidies or cash payments and payments-in-kind.

Compensating Variation, Equivalent Variation, and Consumer Surplus

To measure the benefits to consumers from a change in a policy, such as a price decrease for good 1, three measures have been proposed. **Compensating variation** is the maximum amount of money that an individual is willing to pay to consume good 1 at the lower price. **Equivalent variation** is the minimum amount of compensation required to induce an individual to forfeit the opportunity of purchasing good 1 at the lower price. Although these measures are accurate benefit measures, their calculation requires knowledge of consumers' preferences. For this reason, **consumer surplus,** the area under the demand curve between the original price and the new lower price, is a practical measure that is commonly used. In the absence of an income effect, that is, when indifference curves are "vertically parallel," the three measures are identical.

Two-Part Tariffs

The result that a lump-sum charge allows the individual to maintain a higher level of utility for a given revenue suggests an optimal **two-part pricing scheme** in the case of **consumer capital goods.** These are items such as personal computers, refrigerators, and plane trips, which are of indirect value in and of themselves but which are used to produce a valued good or service. When a consumer capital good requires a complementary good, such as entry into squash clubs and court time or cameras and film, then a profit-maximizing firm selling these products will charge the marginal cost of producing the complementary good for that good and will charge the **reservation price** for the consumer capital good. The reservation price is the maximum price that makes the individual indifferent between buying the product and doing without it. Similarly, for constant profits of the firm, the consumer would prefer this pricing arrangement to one in which the firm extracts some profit from the complementary good.

Time and Wealth

When we examined the problem of the consumer in Chapter 4, we took the consumer's income as given. But where did that income come from? This question brings us to the choice problem between income and leisure, or time spent working and time spent doing other things. This problem can be reduced to one in which a consumer maximizes utility between income and leisure, subject to an income–time constraint; that is, the income earned and the income forgone in leisure must equal the "full wealth" or total potential wealth that could be earned. The solution to this problem is the **supply curve** of labor for an individual.

Many consumption goods require time as well as money. For example, concert tickets cost money and take time to use and eating a meal costs money and time to enjoy. When analyzing problems with such goods, we must consider the **full price** of the good, that is, the money price plus the **opportunity cost** of time spent consuming that good.

Tragedy of the Commons

The importance of introducing time into the consumer problem is most evident in the **tragedy of the commons.** In this problem, there is a limited supply of a good that is "everybody's property," such as clean air, forest lands, fish, and racquetball courts. Time and effort are wasted in attempts to get some of the good. Perhaps the money price is low — it may even be zero in the case of university racquetball court facilities — but the opportunity cost of the time spent standing in line for hours can be extremely large. Thus, the first-come, first-served method of allocation involves a real resource cost in the form of wasted time. Institutional methods of allocation can avoid this problem. For example, suppose that a money price equivalent to the value of time spent in lineups was charged for the common property good. This would reduce the excess demand for the good and at the same time eliminate the wastage of valuable time.

Index Numbers

Although we cannot observe individuals' indifference curves, we can sometimes infer changes in a consumer's welfare between two periods by simply observing the consumer's purchases and the market data in those periods. The procedure goes like this. If yesterday's bundle can be afforded today but is not chosen and today's bundle was not affordable yesterday, then you must be better off today. This implies that the **Paasche quantity index** must exceed 1 for the consumer to be better off today. Alternatively, if today's bundle was affordable yesterday but was not chosen and yesterday's bundle is not affordable today, then one must be worse off today. This is the same as saying that the **Laspeyres quantity index** must be less than 1 for yesterday's welfare to be higher.

An individual's change in welfare can also be measured with price and income indexes. In particular, if the **Laspeyres price index** is less than the **income index** (today's income divided by yesterday's income), then the consumer is better off today. If the **Paasche price index** is greater than the income index, then the individual is worse off today compared with yesterday.

Intertemporal Choice

The final topic of the chapter deals with **intertemporal choices.** Individuals and firms often have to make decisions that will affect future utility or profits, such as what type of investment to make, whether or not to take out a mortgage, or what type of bonds to sell. To simplify the issues, assume that individuals can borrow and lend at the same rate of interest. Thus, one dollar invested today at an interest rate of i is worth $(1 + i)^t$ dollars t periods into the future. Alternatively, the **present value** of receiving $(1 + i)^t$ dollars t periods from now is simply one dollar. Firms sell **bonds** to the public to borrow money. Bonds are sold at some price, with promises to pay the purchaser a fixed sum of money in each of a fixed number of periods. A bond that has no maturity date is known as a **consol**.

Key Words

Bond
Compensating
 variation
Consol
Consumer capital
Consumer surplus
Equivalent variation
Income index
Intertemporal choice
Laspeyres index
Lump-sum versus
 excise taxes

Paasche index
Present value
Price indices
Quantity indices
Reservation price
Supply of labor
Tragedy of the com-
 mons
Two-part tariffs

Case Study: The Energy Crisis in the United States

The oil embargo in 1973 resulted in an energy crisis in the United States. In the mid-1970s, the United States was importing nearly half its oil from the Organization of Petroleum Exporting Countries (OPEC). Although Americans eventually began to reduce their oil consumption in response to rising prices (by driving smaller cars and by switching from oil to natural-gas heating), the short-run or immediate response was not large. The oil shortage became a national crisis.

A For several years after the embargo, gasoline was rationed. Effectively, only so much gasoline was available at the pumps. Long lines formed, many people were turned away without full tanks, and on several occasions, violence broke

out in the lines. Analyze this rationing scheme. Let G^0 and G' be the preembargo and postembargo (fixed) supplies of gasoline. Assume that every gallon of gasoline requires q minutes of queuing time.

B Consider an alternative rationing scheme in which the government places a per-unit tax t on every unit of gasoline, but then gives the consumer a *lump-sum* rebate equal to tg_{-1}, where g_{-1} equals the pretax consumption level of gasoline. Under this scheme, consumers pay higher prices by t cents in the *current* year, then receive t cents back on every gallon of gasoline purchased in the *previous* year. Would this scheme be effective in decreasing the consumption of gasoline? Explain. Does the effectiveness of this program depend on its being a one-shot, unanticipated policy? Why or why not?

Exercises

Multiple-Choice

Choose the correct answer to each question. There is only one correct answer to each question.

1 Suppose that a certain bundle of goods costs $200 in year 0 and $250 in year 1. Then, if an individual actually spends $250 in year 1, and his preferences have not changed, which of the following is correct?
  a He is no worse off in year 1.
  b He must be better off in year 0.
  c He cannot be better off in year 1.
  d He is equally well off in the two years.
  e None of the above.

2 In Figure 5.1, the consumer chooses bundle A when the budget line is CC and bundle B when the budget line is DD. If the consumer's preferences have not changed, then which of the following is correct?
  a Points in area F are preferred to bundle A.
  b Points in area COC are inferior to bundle A.
  c Points in the shaded region are inferior to bundle B.
  d All of the above are true.
  e Only **b** and **c** are true.

FIGURE 5.1

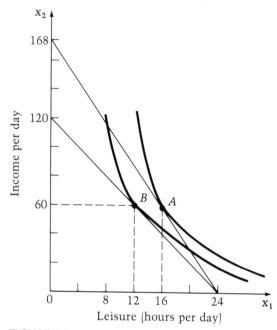

FIGURE 5.2

3 The supply curve of labor will be backward-bending in which of the following cases?

a If leisure is an inferior good

b If the substitution and income effects from an increase in the wage rate reinforce each other

c If an increase in the wage rate results in an increase in the amount of labor supplied on the market

d If the reduction in leisure due to an increase in the opportunity cost of leisure is less than the increase in leisure due to the corresponding increase in real income

e If none of the above is true

Use Figure 5.2 to answer questions **4** and **5**.

4 A utility-maximizing individual

a Is indifferent between the two income–leisure bundles A and B because they contain the same amount of income.

b Will choose to earn $120 income if the wage rate drops to $5 per hour.

c Is facing a wage rate of $7 when choosing bundle A.

d Only **b** and **c** are true.

e None of the above is true.

5 If the individual's wage falls from $7 to $5, which of the following is correct?

a The person will tend to consume less leisure owing to the substitution effect.

b The person will tend to take more leisure because of the income effect.

c The person is on the backward-bending portion of the labor supply curve.

d Leisure is an inferior good.

e None of the above is true.

6 Suppose that a tax of $1 on every unit of a good 1 is replaced by a lump-sum tax of $5. Under the per-unit tax, the individual consumed 5 units of good 1. Then, which of the following statements is true?

a The individual would not reduce his consumption of good 1.

b The individual would be worse off under this tax than under the first tax.

c The individual would consume less good 1 under the lump-sum tax.

d The individual would not be able to afford the same bundle of good 1 and everything else chosen under the per-unit tax.

e None of the above is true.

Refer to Figure 5.3 of an individual's utility-maximizing bundle of good 1, and to the composite good before and after a tax is imposed on that good, to answer questions **7** and **8**.

7 After a per-unit tax is placed on good 1,

a The consumer purchases less of the composite good.

FIGURE 5.3

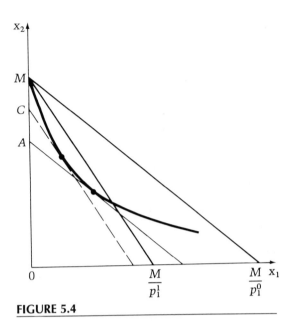

FIGURE 5.4

b The consumer chooses bundle A to maximize utility.

c The government collects AD tax revenues from this individual.

d The government collects BE tax revenues from this individual.

e None of the above is true.

8 If the government replaces the per-unit tax on good 1 with a lump-sum tax that leaves the individual at the same utility level as under the per-unit tax, then

a The government would collect fewer taxes than under the per-unit tax.

b The individual would consume less good 1 than under the per-unit tax.

c The individual would consume more good 1 than under the per-unit tax.

d Only **a** and **b** are true.

e Only **a** and **c** are true.

9 Figure 5.4 illustrates William Whiz's indifference curves for floppy disks for his personal computer, good 1, and all other goods, good 2. William's income is M. The same firm produces personal computers and floppy disks.

a If the price of the floppy disks is p_1^0, then the maximum price that William is willing to pay for the computer is distance MA.

b If the price of the floppy disks is p_1^1, then the maximum price that William is willing to pay for the computer is MC.

c The maximum price that William is willing to pay for the computer increases with a decrease in the price of the floppy disks.

d All of the above are true.

e Only **a** and **c** are true.

10 For a reduction in the price of a normal good,

a Consumer surplus overestimates consumers' true willingness to pay for the price reduction.

b Consumer surplus underestimates consumers' true willingness to pay for the price reduction.

c The quantity demanded of the good at the lower price along the compensated demand curve is larger than that quantity along the ordinary demand curve.

d The quantity demanded of the good will fall.

e None of the above is true.

True-False

11 If your current consumption bundle could have been bought 10 years ago for one-half of its current costs but your income 10 years ago was one-half of your current income and your tastes have not changed, then you must be equally well off compared with 10 years ago.

12 If the Laspeyres price index indicates your cost of living has increased but there has been no change in your disposable income, then you must be worse off than prior to the cost-of-living increase.

13 If the Paasche price index indicates your cost of living has increased but there has been no change in your disposable income, then you must be worse off than before the cost-of-living increase.

14 If the government wants to increase its revenue through a tax on some good, then it can collect more revenue through a lump-sum tax than through a per-unit tax that would leave the individual at the same level of utility.

15 Suppose that a consumer is willing to purchase f^* units of film at price p^*. Then, the maximum price that the consumer is willing to pay for the camera is the consumer surplus received from the f^* units of film if the income effect is zero.

16 Assume that an individual works 5 hours per day and earns $50 per day. If the government increases the income tax rate from 0% to 20%, then the individual will certainly increase his work hours to $6\frac{1}{4}$ to keep his income at the same level.

17 The supply curve for labor will be backward-bending if the substitution effect from an increase in the wage rate is smaller than the income effect when leisure is a normal good.

18 At low wages, the income effect for an increase in the wage is likely to dominate the substitution effect because the individual will want to increase her income by working more to offset the low wages.

19 Since you enjoy driving to the country so much every week, the "price" of your country trips is only the transportation expenses you incur per trip.

20 The higher the interest rate, the higher will be the price of the consol on the bond market.

Short Problems

21 Figure 5.5 shows the budget constraints faced by an individual in 1985 and 1986. Points A and B are the respective bundles of goods chosen in the two years. Can you say if the individual is

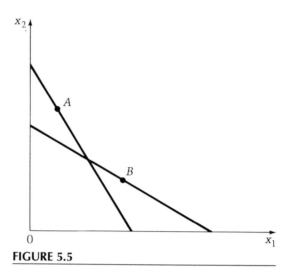

FIGURE 5.5

better or worse off in 1986 compared with 1985? Explain.

22 An individual consumes only two goods, good 1 and good 2. He spends all his income on these two goods. His consumption of good 1 and good 2 and the prices he faced in 1985 and 1986 are as follows:

	P_1	P_2	x_1	x_2
1985	10	15	20	10
1986	8	20	30	9

a In which period is he better off? Why?
b If you knew the indifference curves, show how you could calculate exactly how much income he needs in 1985 to reach the 1986 level of utility.

23 An individual can purchase housing either in the private housing market, in which she can buy any amount of housing she pleases at the market price, or in the public housing market, in which she is offered a particular amount of housing at a price lower than the private market price. Will she necessarily choose the public housing? If she does, will she consume more housing than she would have purchased on the private market? Explain.

24 At the University of Toronto, squash courts are allocated on a first-come, first-served basis.

Starting at 7:30 A.M., avid squash players can begin their attempts at reserving a squash court for the following day. A new squash plan has been recently introduced. For $100, a squash membership can be purchased, allowing the holder to book a court 1 week in advance. Only 300 of these memberships are available. Analyze this pricing scheme. Why was this membership offered? Why were only a limited number of memberships available?

25 The market for personal-computer (PC) software is very competitive. Active development of software is encouraged by IBM's liberal policy on providing information on its computer systems. Why might IBM be indifferent between facing competition in the software market rather than simply producing the software itself?

26 On an indifference curve diagram, illustrate the compensating variation and consumer surplus from a reduction in the price of a good with a zero income effect.

27 If Susan is offered a bond that will pay her $1000 in 3 year's time, and the current interest rate is 10%, then what price will she be willing to pay for the bond?

Long Problems

28 An individual has to choose between two jobs. The first job pays an hourly wage rate w_1 and requires him to work exactly 6 hours per day. The second job pays a lower hourly wage rate w_2, but he can work as many hours at this job as he likes. The two jobs are identical in all other characteristics, such as responsibility and boredom. In three separate diagrams, show the following:

a An individual who prefers the job paying w_1

b An individual who prefers the job paying w_2

c An individual who is indifferent between the two jobs

29 A worker is currently earning $6 per hour and is working 40 hours per week.

a Use indifference curves and budget constraints for the labor–leisure trade-off to illustrate this worker's optimizing decision.

b If the worker is offered an overtime wage of $9 per hour for all hours worked over 40, will

she increase her hours worked? Explain, using a diagram.

30 Consider a society with no income taxes. The government decides to impose an income tax equal to 20% of all earnings.

a Use an income–leisure graph to illustrate the effect of this tax on the budget constraint of a representative individual. Assume that the individual has no nonlabor income.

b Suppose that leisure is a normal good. Will the tax necessarily result in a decline in work time? Explain, using your diagram. Show the substitution and income effects for this change in the tax rate.

31 Reingard recently hit it lucky in a New York lottery. Her winnings are paid in $1000 *annual* increments for as long as she lives. She also earns $250 per month teaching at a New York university. Assume Reingard spends all of her annual earnings, and she cannot borrow against her future earnings.

a Draw a diagram of her utility-maximizing choice between leisure and all other goods. Given that Reingard lives a long and happy life, what is the present value of her stream of income earnings from the lottery ticket winnings?

b Suppose that her wage increases to $350 per month. Show the new optimum.

c Suppose that her lottery earnings increase by $600 per year. Show the new optimum.

d If Reingard is indifferent between a wage or lottery earnings increase, in which case, **b** or **c**, will Reingard work more? Explain.

32 A recent Berkeley graduate buys only three commodities — good 1, good 2, and good 3 — with his income. In his initial job location in Atlanta, he purchased the following quantities each month at the prices indicated.

| | Atlanta | |
	Quantity	Price ($)
Good 1	100	5
Good 2	200	8
Good 3	50	4

He is offered a new job in New York City at a substantially higher salary, $3200 per month.

The prices of goods 1, 2, and 3 in the new city are as follows.

New York City	
Good	Price ($)
Good 1	6
Good 2	10
Good 3	8

Is he worse off if he takes the job because of the higher prices, or do you need more information to tell? Explain.

33 A consumer spends his income on compact discs (CDs) and all other goods, good 2. CDs cost $20 per unit and the consumer's income is $300.

a Draw the consumer's budget constraint and show the optimum for a consumer who buys a positive amount of good 2 and CDs. Let the quantities of CDs and good 2 be x_1 and x_2, respectively.

b Now assume that a CD company offers him the following deal. For a membership fee of $100, he can buy all the CDs he wants for $10 each. Draw the new budget constraint under this offer.

c Under the offer, show that anyone buying more than 10 CDs before the plan is introduced will join the plan, but anyone buying less than 10 CDs may or may not join the plan.

d Draw an indifference curve diagram showing that if an individual is indifferent between joining and not joining the plan, then she would spend more money on CDs and purchase more CDs under the plan.

34 The Smiths, a family of four, spend $1000 out of their $6000 annual income on food. After conducting a thorough study, a government agency decides that $3000 is the minimum money required to provide proper nutrition for a family of four. Deciding that the Smiths cannot afford to pay more than $1000 for food out of their current income, the agency decides to make a gift to them each year of $2000 worth of food stamps, which may be used *only* on food.

a On a diagram, draw the Smiths' budget constraints before and after the gift of food stamps. Assuming convex indifference curves,

show the optimum before and after the gift. *Hint:* Measure food and all other goods in dollars. According to your diagram, has the government succeeded in its objective of ensuring that the Smiths get proper nutrition, that is, $3000 worth of food? Explain.

b Suppose that, instead of the food stamp program, the government gives the Smith family a cash subsidy of $2000 that can be spent on anything they wish. On the diagram you drew for **34a**, show the new budget constraint and the optimum. Is the government any closer to achieving its objective? Explain.

35 Laura earns $10,000 per year. She spends her income on education and composite commodity good 2. A unit of education costs $500 (think of a unit of education as one class). A unit of good 2 costs $1.

a Suppose that Laura maximizes utility subject to her budget constraint by consuming 8 units of education and spending $6000 on everything else. Indicate Laura's optimum on an indifference curve–budget constraint diagram. Now suppose that the government wants to subsidize Laura's education. It has three policies to choose among:
(1) Pay some portion of the price of each unit of education purchased.
(2) Give an equivalent cash subsidy.
(3) Give an equivalent subsidy-in-kind (that is, give Laura a voucher, or units of education).

b Suppose that the government decides to follow policy (1) by paying $250 per unit of education purchased by Laura. Redraw your diagram for **35a**, and show the new bundle of education and the composite commodity that Laura will choose under this government program. Indicate on the diagram the amount of money that the government is spending under this program. Will this program result in a shift in or a movement along the demand curve? Explain.

c Now suppose that instead of the per-unit subsidy, the government follows policy (2) and gives Laura a cash subsidy equal to the money spent under the program in **35b**. Redraw the diagram from **35b** and show the effect of this new policy on Laura's choice of education and good 2. Will Laura be better or worse off under this program than under program (1) analyzed in **b**? Explain. Will this program result in a shift in or a movement along the demand curve? Explain.

d Finally, suppose that instead of the per-unit subsidy in **35b** or the cash subsidy in **35c**, the government gives an education voucher as in policy (3). That is, the government spends the same amount of money as it did in **b** and **c** but "pays" Laura in units of education. Show on a diagram Laura's choice of education and good 2, and compare it to her choice under the cash-subsidy program in **c**. Is Laura better or worse off under this voucher program than under the cash subsidy program discussed in **c**? Explain. Will this program result in a shift in or a movement along the demand curve? Explain.

e What have you learned from this exercise?

36 Figure 5.6 is the ordinary demand curve of a representative consumer for bread. Assume that bread is a normal good and that the individual is currently consuming at a rate of 3 loaves per week at a per-unit price of $1. Because of a new computer-operated dough kneader, the cost of producing bread falls, and the equilibrium price drops to $0.50 per loaf. The government wants to determine the impact of the machine on consumer welfare and concludes that each individual has experienced an increase in welfare of *ABCD*.

a Would you agree that *ABCD* is the accurate measure of welfare? Why or why not?

b Draw the compensated-demand curve and indicate the change in the compensating variation due to the change in the price of bread.

Answers to Chapter 5

Case Study

A Suppose that there are N identical consumers. Let the initial budget constraint facing the individual be given by Ma in Figure A5.1; G^0/N is demanded. Now suppose that the oil embargo reduces supply to G'. The resulting queuing raises the total price of gas (price plus waiting costs), such that the consumer purchases bundle C.

The new total price of 1 gallon of gasoline is equal to the price paid at the pump plus the cost of waiting q minutes, hence, the cost of waiting q minutes can be measured by the change in the slope of the budget constraint. The value of the total queuing time is equal to the distance CD in the diagram.

Alternatively, a tax equal to the value of the queuing time could be placed on each gallon of gasoline. Suppose that each gallon requires q units of time, and w is the opportunity cost per unit of time. Then the tax $t = wq$ will cause each individual to choose point C in Figure A5.1. Although the individual is not better or worse off, the time spent working instead of queuing gener-

FIGURE 5.6

FIGURE A5.1

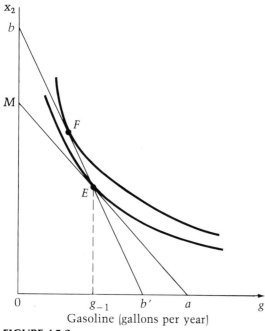

FIGURE A5.2

1 a	2 d	3 d	4 c	5 c
6 a	7 d	8 c	9 d	10 a

True-False

11 F	12 F	13 T	14 T	15 T
16 F	17 T	18 F	19 F	20 F

Short Problems

21 We cannot say because bundle A is not affordable in 1986 and bundle B is not affordable in 1985. Two possible sets of preferences are illustrated in Figure A5.3. In Figure A5.3a, the individual is better off in 1985; in Figure A5.3b, the individual is better off in 1986.

22 a To determine the period in which the individual is better off, calculate the Laspeyres and Paasche price indices and the expenditure index.

$$L = \frac{8 \times 20 + 20 \times 10}{10 \times 20 + 15 \times 10} = \frac{160 + 200}{200 + 150}$$

$$= \frac{360}{350} = 1.03$$

$$P = \frac{8 \times 30 + 20 \times 9}{10 \times 30 + 15 \times 9} = \frac{240 + 180}{300 + 135} = \frac{420}{435}$$

$$= 0.966$$

$$E = \frac{8 \times 30 + 20 \times 9}{10 \times 20 + 15 \times 10} = \frac{240 + 180}{200 + 150} = \frac{420}{350}$$

$$= 1.2$$

Since $E > L > P$, the cost of living has increased less than the increase in income; the individual is better off in 1986.

b The budget line for 1985 is $350 = 10x_1 + 15x_2$. The budget line for 1986 is $420 = 8x_1 + 20x_2$. The two budget lines are illustrated in Figure A5.4. The income needed in 1985 to reach the utility level in 1986 is found by shifting the 1985 budget line until it is tangent to the indifference curve reached in 1986. Thus, CD represents the income necessary in 1985 to reach the same utility level in 1986.

23 Assume that if the individual buys housing in the private market, her budget line is AB shown in Figure A5.5. If she buys public housing, *only* point D on budget line AC is attainable. Figure

ates income, which is collected by the government as taxes.

B Yes, the consumers would cut back consumption. To see this, suppose that last year's budget constraint is given by Ma, or

$$x_2 + p_g g = M$$

and last year's utility-maximizing bundle is E in Figure A5.2. The tax-rebate plan would change the budget line to

$$x_2 + (p_g + t)g = M + tg_{-1}$$

where g_{-1} is last year's consumption of gasoline. Note that the budget line under the tax-rebate plan passes through last year's bundle E with a steeper slope (that is, last year's bundle E is attainable). As shown in the Figure, the consumer would choose bundle F and purchase less gasoline.

The preceding answer assumes that the consumer is not aware that her actions could affect the lump-sum subsidy received. On the contrary, if the consumer realizes that any tax paid this year will be refunded next year, she may not adjust her actions in response to the tax.

(a)

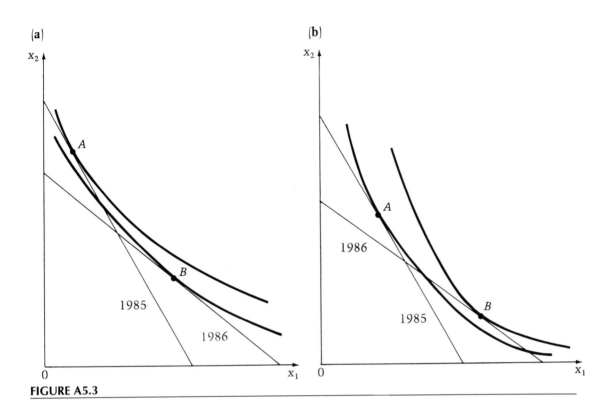

(b)

FIGURE A5.3

A5.5*a* shows the case in which public housing is not preferred. The utility-maximizing bundle in the private market is *E*, which is on a higher indifference curve than the one through *D*. If pub-

lic housing is chosen, the individual will not nec‐ essarily consume more housing. Figure A5.5*b* shows a case in which public housing is preferred but less housing is consumed than if housing were purchased in the private market.

FIGURE A5.4

24 Without the membership policy, the demand for squash courts would exceed the capacity. The rationing mechanism of first-come, first-served was inefficient because valuable time was wasted. The membership was a way for the university to recover some of the cost savings of individuals' time. Only a limited number were offered for distributional reasons. Realizing that many students may not be able to afford the membership, the university allowed a limited number of memberships (probably purchased by the wealthier faculty members) so individuals with a lower opportunity cost of time (probably students) could still make squash reservations with their time.

25 Software is a complementary component of computers. If the market for software is competitive, the software will be sold at the marginal cost of production. This enables IBM to sell the

(a)

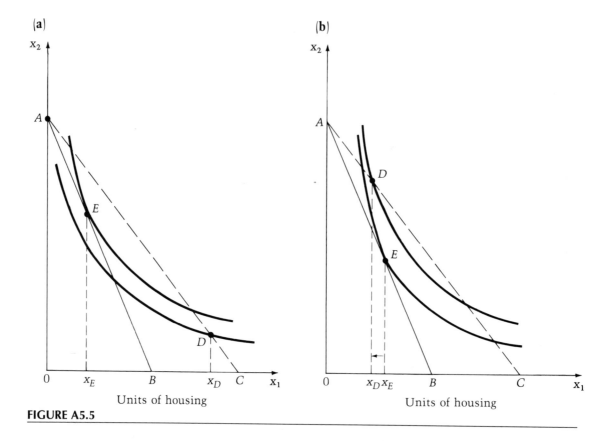

FIGURE A5.5

computers at a price equal to the consumer surplus from the use of the low-cost software. This pricing policy is the profit-maximizing pricing policy that IBM would want to follow if it sold *both* the computers and the software.

26 Let the price of good 1 fall from p_1^0 to p_1^1 as shown in Figure A5.6. The substitution effect is x_1^0 to x_1^1. The income effect is zero; hence, the substitution effect equals the total effect. In this case, the consumer surplus equals the compensating variation. Both measures give the maximum amount of money the individual is willing to give up to experience the price reduction. This amount of money, when it is given up, will leave the individual on the original indifference curve I_1. The compensating variation and consumer surplus in this case, are given by $M - M'$.

27 $$PV = \frac{\$1000}{(1+i)^t} = \frac{\$1000}{(1+0.1)^3} = 751.3$$

FIGURE A5.6

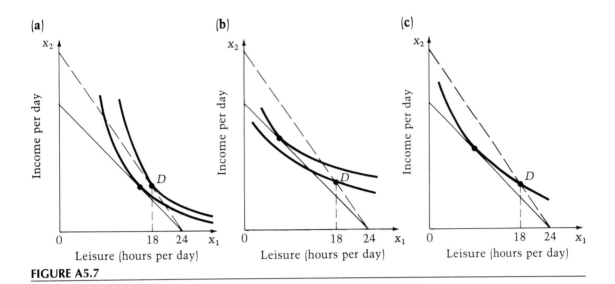

FIGURE A5.7

Long Problems

28 In each of the cases shown in Figure A5.7, the flatter income line represents the combination of income earned and leisure attainable when the wage rate is w_2. Point D on the dotted line indicates the *only* income–leisure combination that is attainable when the wage rate is w_1 and the individual can work only 6 hours.

29 a The maximum amount of money that the individual can earn in one week if she takes 0

hours of leisure is $24 \times 7 \times \$6 = \$1008$. The income line is AB in Figure A5.8.

b If the individual is offered $9 per hour for all hours over 40 hours, then her income line will get steeper for less than 128 hours of leisure. At maximum, the individual can earn: $40 \times \$6 + 128 \times \$9 = \$1392$. The new and the old income lines are in Figure A5.9. The individual will increase her hours of work.

30 a Let w be the daily wage rate for an individual. The income line without the tax is given by DE in Figure A5.10. The effect of the 20% tax is

FIGURE A5.8

FIGURE A5.9

FIGURE A5.10

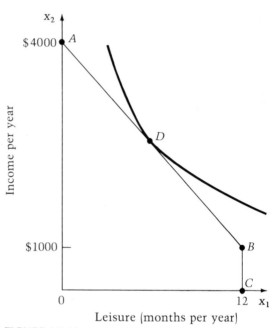

FIGURE A5.11

to pivot the income line inward. The maximum income that can be earned is $0.8 \times 365w = 292w$.

b If leisure is a normal good, the tax will not necessarily result in a decline in work time, as shown in Figure A5.10. The tax lowers the effective wage, resulting in an increase in leisure because of the substitution effect from x_1^A to x_1^C. The decline in real income decreases leisure from x_1^C to x_1^B. If the income effect outweighs the substitution effect, less leisure will be taken.

31 a Since Reingard earns $250 per month, her *maximum* annual income is $3000. She also receives $1000 per year from her lottery earnings, so her yearly budget line is *ABC*. Point *D* in Figure A5.11 indicates her utility-maximizing bundle. The present value of her stream of income from the lottery is $1000/0.08 = $12,500.

b If her wage rises to $350 per month, the slope of the budget line increases to $350 (from $250). Maximum income from teaching is now $350 \times 12 = $4200. The new utility-maximizing point is given by *E* in Figure A5.12*a*.

c If her lottery winnings increase by $600, the income line shifts upward, but the slope of the income line stays the same. The new utility-maximizing point is given by *F* in Figure A5.12*b*.

d If Reingard is indifferent between the two income increases, as shown in Figure A5.12*c*, she will choose to work more when the opportunity

cost of leisure is higher: that is, when the wage is higher.

32 The Laspeyres price index can be used to determine if he is better off in New York than in Atlanta. If the Laspeyres price index (based on the Atlanta bundle of goods) is less than the expenditure index (New York income divided by Atlanta income), then he is definitely better off in New York:

$$L = \frac{6 \times 100 + 10 \times 200 + 8 \times 50}{5 \times 100 + 8 \times 200 + 4 \times 50}$$

$$= \frac{600 + 2000 + 400}{500 + 1600 + 200} = \frac{3000}{2300} = 1.3$$

$$E = \frac{3200}{2300} = 1.39$$

Since $E > L$, he is better off in New York.

33 a The utility-maximizing bundle is given by *A* in Figure A5.13*a*.

b The new plan is shown in Figure A5.13*b*. The maximum number of CDs that can be purchased is 20; the maximum income that can be spent on everything else is $200.

c The two budget lines intersect at $x_1 = 10$. To see this, write the two budget lines:

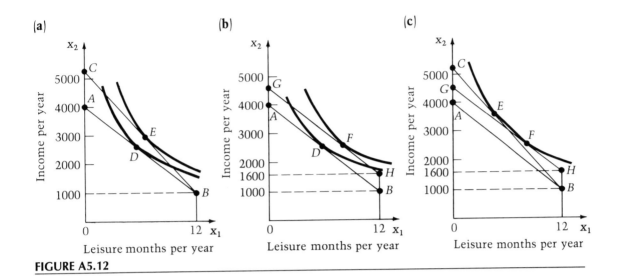

FIGURE A5.12

$$300 = x_2 + 20x_1 \quad \text{and} \quad 200 = x_2 + 10x_1$$

Substitute the second budget line into the first one:

$$300 = 200 - 10x_1 + 20x_1$$
$$x_1 = 10$$

As shown in Figure A5.14a, an individual buying more than 10 CDs will join the plan because a higher level of utility can be achieved. Individuals buying less than 10 CDs may or may not benefit from the plan. An individual who benefits from the plan is shown in Figure A5.14b.

d Figure A5.15 shows the individual to be indifferent between joining and not joining the plan. Comparison of point B, the utility-maximizing bundle under the plan, with point A indi-

FIGURE A5.13

(a)

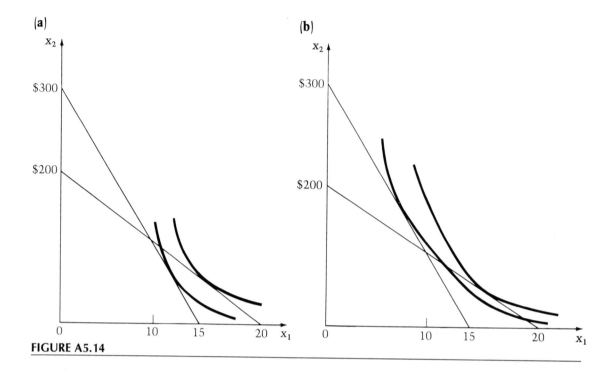

(b)

FIGURE A5.14

cates that the individual would purchase more CDs under the plan and have less money to spend on everything else.

34 a The original budget line is *AB* in Figure A5.16. The budget line with the $2000 food voucher is *BCD*. Before the voucher, they con-

sume the bundle given by point *E*; after the voucher, they consume the bundle given by point *C*. The way the indifference curves are drawn (they don't have to look that way), the Smiths spend only $2000 on food under the voucher.

b If the government gives a cash subsidy of $2000, the Smiths may choose to spend some of

FIGURE A5.15

FIGURE A5.16

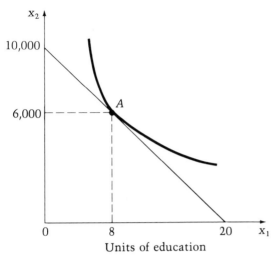

FIGURE A5.17

it on other goods. As shown in the figure, the budget line under the cash subsidy is *FD*. The Smiths choose point *G* on the budget line. In this case, the government is not closer to achieving its objectives; however, the Smiths are certainly better off.

35 a Laura's utility-maximizing bundle is given by point *A* in Figure A5.17.

b Under the per-unit subsidy, the budget line pivots outward as shown in Figure A5.18*a*. The government spends *BN*, the difference between the two budget lines at the utility-maximizing bundle *B*. This program will shift the demand

FIGURE A5.19

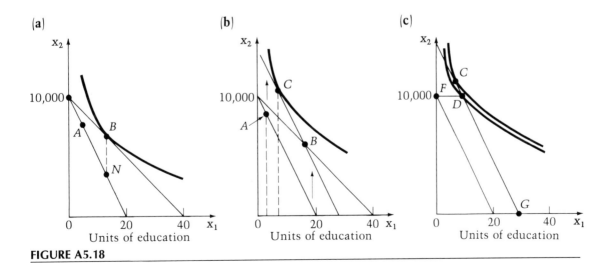

FIGURE A5.18

curve for education to the right; at every price, more units of education will be demanded.

c If the government gives a lump-sum subsidy equal to the amount spent on the program in **35b**, then the budget line will be a parallel increase in the original budget line with slope $p_1/p_2 = 500$ through point B. Laura chooses bundle C on a higher indifference curve, as shown in Figure A5.18b. The program will shift the demand curve for education to the right.

d Under the voucher scheme, the budget line will be the same as in **35c** except that bundles with more than 10,000 units of good 2 are not attainable. The new budget line is FDG. If Laura's bundle C in **35c** is as shown in Figure A5.18c then Laura will be worse off under the voucher scheme than under the cash subsidy. The best she can do is to consume bundle D under the voucher program. This program will shift the demand curve for education to the right.

e A lump-sum payment (cash subsidy) is more efficient than either a per-unit subsidy or a voucher. That is, given that the government spends the same amount of money on the individual in all cases, the recipient can be made no worse off and is usually better off with a cash subsidy than under the other two schemes.

36 a No. *ABCD* overestimates the true willingness to pay because bread is a normal good. That is, if the consumer surplus were actually taken away from the consumer, the individual would purchase less bread as a result of this income effect.

b The compensated demand curve is derived in Figure A5.19 for a decrease in the price of bread from $1 to $0.50. Bundles C and D are points on the ordinary demand curve; bundles C and E are points on the compensated demand curve. After the income effect is removed, the individual purchases x_1^E units of bread rather than x_1^D units at a price of $0.50. The compensating variation is given by the vertical distance AB in the figure.

6

CHOICE MAKING UNDER IMPERFECT INFORMATION

Chapter Summary

Risky Choices

In this chapter, we allow the consumer to enter the interesting and unpredictable world of **risk** and **uncertainty**. A **risky choice** has several possible outcomes, each of which might occur with some **probability.**

An example of a risky choice is a lottery. An individual, Martha, is a sweepstakes winner. Her prize is a choice between *A* dollars for certain and a gamble that pays $1 million with probability of 1/1,000,000 and 0 otherwise. Martha will choose the gamble if her reservation price for the gamble is at least as large as *A*. If Martha is risk-neutral, then her reservation price will equal the **expected value** of the gamble—the sum of the possible payoffs weighted by the probabilities of those payoffs being realized. In this case, Martha will take the gamble if *A* is not larger than $1.

Martha's reservation price may not equal the expected value of the lottery. Suppose that Martha has the opportunity to pocket $500,000 for certain or take a gamble that will make her a millionaire with a probability of $\frac{1}{2}$. For Martha *not* to take the gamble would seem perfectly reasonable. In this case, Martha's reservation price is less than $500,000, the expected value of the lottery.

Expected-Utility Hypothesis

This example suggests that the decision to undertake risk depends on something more than simply a comparison between the certain outcome (the opportunity cost of the gamble) and the expected payoff. Bernoulli argued that the reservation price of a risky choice is equal to the **expected utility** of that choice rather than to the expected monetary payoffs, where the expected utility is a weighted average of the utilities associated with the payoffs. The weights are probabilities of outcomes, where the probabilities are either objectively known or **subjective.**

In recent years, the expected-utility hypothesis has been theoretically justified, proving that an expected-utility function exists for a set of reasonable assumptions on preferences over risky prospects. The completeness, two-term consistency and three-term consistency assumptions discussed in Chapter 3 must all hold for these risky prospects. Nonsatiation implies that larger assured outcomes are always preferred to smaller ones. Three additional assumptions are also necessary. First, **continuity** guarantees that individuals are willing to make some trade-offs between risky and riskless prospects. Second, the **substitution assumption** says that for any given prospect, an equivalent compound prospect can be created. Finally, the **ordering assumption** states that if two prospects involve the same outcomes, then the most preferred prospect is the one with the highest probability of winning the better outcome. Together, these assumptions imply the **expected utility theorem:** If an individual prefers one prospect to another, then the preferred prospect has greater expected utility; if an individual is indifferent between prospects, then their expected utilities must be the same. Although the expected utility hypothesis can be used to analyze a variety of economic problems with risky prospects, it is not appropriate when preferences depend on the **state of the world.**

Attitudes Toward Risk

Under the expected-utility hypothesis, a taxonomy can be defined over an individual's attitudes toward risk. Define a **riskless asset** as one that offers the expected payoff from some lottery, A, with probability 1. Then, an individual is said to be **risk-neutral** if his utility from that **riskless prospect** equals the expected utility from the risky prospect A. Such individuals have a **constant marginal utility of wealth.** If the utility of the riskless prospect exceeds the expected utility from the risky prospect A, then the individual is **risk-averse** and has a **diminishing marginal utility of wealth.** In this case, the additional utility that is possible from undertaking the risky prospect is not large enough to offset the loss in utility that is possible from that prospect. Finally, an individual who is **risk-inclined** will receive more utility from the risky prospect than from the riskless option. We generally expect most individuals to be risk-averse.

Risk Pooling and Insurance

Risk-averse individuals attempt to shed risk. When two individuals face independent risks, they may agree to enter into a **risk pooling** arrangement, in which they share in any losses that either or both individuals incur. This risk-pooling arrangement is a type of **insurance.** To find out when an individual would **fully insure** herself against some risk (that is, pay for insurance that would fully compensate her in the event of a di-

saster), we need to determine the **certainty equivalent** of the prospect (that is, the amount of money that would leave the individual with a utility level equal to the expected utility of the risky asset). An individual will fully insure herself against risk if the cost of the insurance is less than the difference between the initial wealth and the certainty equivalent. If risk-neutral insurance firms are willing to supply the insurance, an individual can be left with a level of wealth equal to the expected wealth in the absence of insurance but without risk! A second mechanism by which risk is shed is **risk spreading.** In this case, an indivisible and risky asset is owned by several individuals or firms. Risk-averse individuals may prefer to own part of a risky asset rather than the entire asset.

Adverse Selection and Signaling

Informational problems arise in markets for insurance. An insurance rate for a particular category of individuals is based on the expected cost of supplying insurance for all individuals in that category. Where there is **asymmetry of information** — an individual knows he is a good driver but the insurance company does not, for example — there can be a market failure of **adverse selection.** Because "low-risk" individuals cannot communicate convincingly that they are low-risk, the insurance company can offer only one average rate, which will be attractive to high-risk individuals. Low-risk individuals will choose not to take out the insurance, and insurance rates will climb; hence, the low-risk group may be driven out of the market and, therefore, be unable to shed any of its risk. Akerlof coined this problem of asymmetric information in the market for used cars as the **lemons principle.**

If an individual could acquire a **signal** that informs the insurance company of his low-risk characteristic, then he could be offered an acceptable insurance policy. The signal that enables the low-risk individuals to shed their risk is **productive** if the policy, in the absence of the signal, would be acquired only by high-risk individuals. Examples of signaling are pervasive, especially in hiring practices.

Key Words

Adverse selection
Assured outcome
Asymmetric informa-
    tion
Certainty equivalent
Continuity assump-
    tion
Expected utility
Expected value
Insurance
Lemons principle
Marginal utility of
    wealth
Ordering assumption
Outcomes
Probability
Productive versus
    unproductive
    signals

Prospects
Reservation price
Risk
Risk-averse
Risk-inclined
Riskless asset
Risk-neutral
Risk pooling
Risk spreading
State-dependent pref-
    erences
Subjective probabili-
    ties
Substitution assump-
    tion
Uncertainty

Case Study: Getting a Free Ride

One summer while living in Florence, Italy, I traveled frequently by bus, a very inexpensive and convenient mode of transportation in Italy. Tickets to ride the bus anywhere in the city can be purchased in any tobacco shop for a mere 400 lire, approximately $0.25 in U.S. dollars (1985). Passengers ascend the bus from the back door and, immediately upon entering the bus, are required to punch their tickets into a machine in the back of the bus. There is no transit official in the bus to check that all passengers validate their tickets. After riding the bus twice a day for two weeks without having my ticket checked, I began to wonder if my last-minute dashes to the tobacco shop to buy a ticket were worth the effort, especially since the buses were so crowded that I had to push through the crowds to reach the ticket machine.

So one day, after evaluating this problem in uncertainty, I boldly decided to break the law and did not punch my ticket. However, I was very nervous. Despite the seemingly relaxed attitude of the public transit authorities, the Italians seemed to make every effort to validate their tickets. What motivated the Italians to be such law-abiding citizens?

One day I found out. A public transit official entered the bus at one of the stops. At that point, everyone (including myself) got out their tickets to proudly indicate that, indeed, their tickets had been punched moments earlier, all except for one person. Her ticket apparently had been used twice, and after a long shouting match, she had to purchase a ticket from the official for 40,000 lire (100 times the regular price) or get off the bus.

A Does a model of legal institutions based on self-interest behavior by consumers seem to apply to this situation? Explain.

B Given the frequency of monitoring and the fine for disobeying the law (including the reprimand by an authority), do you think the Italian public transit authority has adopted a good scheme for enforcing the law? Explain.

C Is there a possibility that a culprit might successfully bribe the law enforcer? Why or why not?

Exercises

Multiple-Choice

Choose the correct answer to each question. There is only one correct answer to each question.

1 A person who places a smaller utility on gaining $1000 than on losing an equal amount
   a Has an increasing marginal utility of money associated with larger amounts of money
   b Would pay $1000 for a lottery ticket that paid either $2000 with probability 1/2 or $0 with probability 1/2
   c Has a declining marginal utility of money associated with larger amounts of money
   d Is correctly described by both **b** and **c**
   e None of the above

Questions **2** and **3** pertain to a consumer with a utility function given by

$$U = \left(\frac{w}{500}\right)^{1/2}$$

where U is utility and w is wealth. Ordinarily, the consumer expects his income to be $40,500. However, he faces the possibility that his house will burn down, reducing his income to $4,500. This unfortunate event occurs with probability 1/3.

2 The consumer's expected utility, if uninsured, is

   a 57

   b 14

   c 114,000

   d 7

   e None of the above

3 The most the consumer would be willing to pay for full insurance is

   a $32

   b $98,000

   c $24,500

   d $16,000

   e None of the above

4 A lottery with a $\frac{1}{2}$ chance of winning $100,000 and $\frac{1}{2}$ chance of losing $80,000

   a May well be accepted by a risk averter

   b Will never be accepted by a risk averter

   c Will never be accepted by a risk-neutral person

   d Will always be accepted by a risk-averse individual

   e None of the above

To answer questions **5** to **7**, refer to Figure 6.1, which illustrates the utility function of two risk-averse individuals. Both individuals have initial wealth w_0. Each individual faces the uncertain outcome that her house will be robbed, in which case she will incur a loss of L. The probability of this event is p_1 for individual 1 and p_2 for individual 2. The proportion of low-risk individuals is $\frac{1}{2}$.

5 If the market for insurance is competitive and if insurance companies cannot distinguish between high-risk and low-risk individuals, then

   a Only individual 1 will purchase insurance.

   b Only individual 2 will purchase insurance.

   c Both individuals 1 and 2 will purchase insurance.

   d Neither individual will purchase insurance.

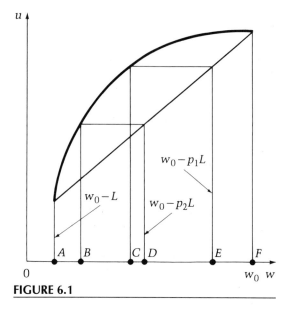

FIGURE 6.1

   e No firm will be willing to supply an insurance policy.

6 If the insurance company cannot distinguish between high-risk and low-risk individuals, then

   a The maximum premium that individual 1 is willing to pay for the insurance is CE.

   b The maximum premium that individual 2 is willing to pay for insurance is BF.

   c If both low- and high-risk individuals purchase insurance, the minimum price that the insurance company will be willing to accept for the insurance policy exceeds DF.

   d Since only low-risk individuals will purchase the insurance, the price of the insurance will be CF.

   e None of the above.

7 If low-risk and high-risk individuals can be identified and the market is competitive,

   a Insurance will be sold at two prices, BD for the high-risk individuals and CE for the low-risk individuals.

   b Insurance will be sold at two prices, DF for the high-risk individuals and EF for the low-risk individuals.

   c Only the high-risk individuals will buy insurance at a price of DF.

   d Insurance will be sold at one price, less than DF and greater than EF.

   e None of the above.

8 Suppose that the utility of wealth is given by $U(w) = w^{1/2}$. If there are two states of the world, each occurring with probability $1/2$, and a prospect pays $100 in state 1 and $36 in state 2, then the certainty equivalent of the prospect

    a Is $68

    b Is $8

    c Is $64

    d Cannot be calculated without more information

    e None of the above

9 For two prospects with the same expected value,

    a A risk-neutral individual will be indifferent between the two prospects.

    b A risk-averse individual will prefer the prospect with the larger spread in the outcomes.

    c A risk-inclined individual will prefer the prospect with the smaller spread in the outcomes.

    d A risk-averse individual will be indifferent between the two prospects.

    e None of the above.

10 An individual is risk-averse if

    a The certainty equivalent of a prospect is greater than the expected value of the prospect.

    b The expected utility of the prospect is larger than the utility of the expected value of the prospect.

    c The utility of the certainty equivalent is greater than the utility of the expected value of the prospect.

    d He is not willing to take a gamble at a price equal to the expected value of the gamble.

    e None of the above.

11 A signal that distinguishes between high- and low-productivity workers is productive if

    a The acquisition of the signal increases the individual's productivity.

    b Both high- and low-productivity individuals acquire the signal.

    c High-productivity individuals who would not accept a job at the wage offered without signaling are willing to work at the wage received after acquiring the signal.

    d The high-productivity individuals are able to recover some of the "subsidy" that their presence provides for the low-productivity individuals.

    e None of the above.

True-False

12 A risk-averse individual would never be willing to pay more than the expected loss from a risky project for full insurance.

13 Adverse selection is a market failure that occurs when individuals have information about themselves that they cannot communicate to the market.

14 A risk-averse individual prefers all certain prospects over a particular risky prospect.

15 Given two prospects with the same expected value, a risk-averse individual prefers the prospect with the smaller spread in the outcomes.

16 The certainty equivalent of a prospect for a risk-averse individual is less than the expected value of the prospect.

17 Given two prospects, (0.5, 0.5: 100, 0) and (0.7, 0.3: 30, 70), the risk-averse individual will definitely prefer the second prospect because the spread in the outcomes is smaller.

18 An expected utility maximizer with a utility function $U(w) = w^{1/2} + 0.1w$ would prefer to keep his initial wealth of $1000 rather than enter into a lottery (0.4, 0.6: $2500, 0). (The outcomes stated in the lottery include the initial wealth and the price of the lottery ticket.)

19 If high-risk and low-risk individuals cannot be distinguished by competitive insurance companies, then the price of insurance will be at least as large as an insurance company's expected costs of supplying insurance to a low-risk individual.

20 If the marginal utility of income is diminishing, then the expected utility of a prospect exceeds the utility of the expected value of the prospect.

*21 If a risk-averse individual with $500 income assigns a utility of 100 to $450 and a utility of 120 to $500, and if he is willing to pay $50 at maximum for a lottery ticket that pays $250 with probability $1/2$ and $0 with probability $1/2$, then the utility of $700 is 140.

Short Problems

22 Suppose that an individual is indifferent between $100 for certain and a 50/50 chance of

$200 and $50, and between $140 for certain and a 70/30 chance between $200 and $50. If the individual satisfies the axioms of expected utility theory, what can you say about the individual's preference between a 50/50 chance of $100 and $140 and a 50/50 chance between the following two gambles: a 50/50 chance between $200 and $50 and a 70/30 chance between $200 and $50? Explain. What assumption must be satisfied to answer the question?

23 Suppose that, in the absence of medical insurance, individuals who break an arm pay, on average, $500 for medical services. Assume the probability that an individual breaks her arm is 0.01 per year and the costs of providing insurance are zero. Will a competitive insurance industry provide insurance against the medical costs of broken arms at $5 for risk-neutral individuals, greater than $5 for risk-averse individuals, and less than $5 for risk-inclined individuals? Why or why not?

24 Explain, using a diagram, why a risk-averse individual, choosing between two prospects with the same expected value, prefers the prospect with the smaller spread in the outcomes.

25 Winfred Whiz is playing on a game show. He must choose between two offers. The first offer is a payment of $2000, which he can take for simply being on the show, or he can enter a gamble. In the gamble, he chooses one of two curtains that conceal two items. He makes a draw for curtain 1 or 2 from a hat; he receives the gift behind the curtain picked. He knows that behind one curtain is an automobile valued at $4000 and behind the other curtain is a set of encyclopedias valued at $500. If his initial wealth is $1000 and his utility function can be described by $U(w) = 1 - 1000/w$, then what must be the probability of drawing the car for Winfred to be indifferent between the two choices?

26 Explain the relationship between the certainty equivalent of some gamble and the maximum price of insurance that a risk-averse individual would be willing to pay.

27 A risk-neutral individual's preference ordering over prospects can be based entirely on the expected values of the prospects. Explain why this is true.

28 Let A, B, C, and D represent four gambles available to an individual, where

$$A = (0.8, 0.2: 4000, 0)$$
$$B = (1, 0: 3000, 0)$$
$$C = (0.2, 0.8: 4000, 0)$$
$$D = (0.25, 0.75: 3000, 0)$$

If the individual chooses B over A and C over D, is his behavior consistent with the axioms of expected utility theory? Explain.

29 Ms. Gamble currently has an income of $25,000. Assign the utility number 100 to this income level and the utility number 85 to the income level $20,000. It is known that Ms. Gamble would be willing to pay a maximum of $5000 for a lottery ticket that yields $10,000 with a probability of 3/5 (and yields zero otherwise). What is the utility number appropriate to the income level $30,000? Explain.

Long Problems

30 a Consider the following model provided by Spence in his 1973 paper.[1] Suppose that there are two types of people: high- and low-productivity workers. If a worker is known to be highly productive, then she would receive a wage of 2; if she is known to have low productivity, then she would receive a wage of 1. Assume that education does not increase an individual's productivity but simply awards the individual with a certificate. Assume that high-productivity individuals incur education costs $C^H = x/2$, where x = units of education, and that low-productivity individuals incur education costs $C^L = x$. Using this model of job market signaling, describe how education can have a value to certain individuals even if it does not increase their productivity.

b Are some signaling equilibria Pareto-improving over others? That is, would an increase or a decrease in the critical level of the signal, set by the employer to separate the good from the poor workers, make some employees better off without making others worse off? Explain.

---

[1] Spence, M. (1973) "Job Market Signalling," *Quarterly Journal of Economics.* **87**:355–374.

31 Many spokespersons of the women's movement have argued that women must be twice as good as men to be hired for many management positions. Explain how this argument could be valid, using the model of job market signaling in problem 30.

32 Betty Bat loves the New York Yankees. She has followed their exploits since she was 5 years old. This year they made it to the World Series. Betty has just thought up a clever plan. She has $1000 in savings that she has hidden under her bed. She could spend $600 of the $1000 in making Yankees championship paraphernalia: buttons, cups, pens, and so on. Then, if the Yankees win, she estimates that she would earn $1500. If the Yankees lose, she won't be able to sell any of her stock. Betty figures that the Yankees have a 0.6 chance of winning the World Series. Betty's utility function is given by $U(w) = w^{1/2}$.

    a If Betty is an expected utility maximizer, will she make the $600 investment into Yankees championship gadgets?

    b Calculate the certainty equivalent of Betty's clever prospect.

    c Suppose that a friend offers her insurance. He says to Betty, "If you pay me F dollars whether or not the Yankees win, then, in the event that the Yankees lose, I will pay you $1500, the amount that you would have earned had the Yankees won the World Series. If the Yankees win, I will pay you nothing." What is the maximum value of F that Betty is willing to pay for the insurance policy? If Betty's friend is risk-neutral, will he gain by this venture? Explain.

*33 An individual is about to place a bet on her favorite racehorse, Lightning Speed. She can make one of two bets. Each bet costs $100. In the first option, she bets that Lightning Speed will win the next race. If Lightning Speed wins, the individual will receive $1000 (not including the ticket price); otherwise, she receives $0. There is a 1/5 chance that the favorite horse will win. For the second option, she places a bet on Lightning Speed in the second and third races. If Lightning Speed wins in the second race, she receives a chance to play in the third race. There is a 1/4 chance that the favorite horse will win in the second race. If Lightning Speed wins in the third race, the individual receives $1000; if Lightning Speed loses in either the second or third race, she receives $0.

    a Assuming that the individual satisfies the assumptions of expected-utility theory, what must be the probability of Lightning Speed winning the third race for the individual to be indifferent between the two bets?

    b Which assumption of expected-utility theory has to be satisfied to answer a?

*34 Suppose $w_1 > w_2 > w_3 > w_4$, and $U(w_1) + U(w_4) = U(w_2) + U(w_3)$, where w is wealth. Show that any individual (regardless of preferences toward risk) would prefer $(p, 1 - p: w_1, w_4)$ over $(p, 1 - p: w_2, w_3)$ if $p > 1 - p$. Give intuition for this answer.

Answers to Chapter 6

Case Study

A The legal institution in question here is the method by which the Italian transit authorities have chosen to collect bus fares. Although the self-interested behavior of consumers suggests that they would like to save themselves the amount of the bus fare by cheating, they do not want to have to pay a fine if caught cheating. Thus, a model of legal institutions based on self-interested behavior does apply because the high fine compensates for the low probability of getting caught.

B If people are risk-averse and self-interested, they will obey the law if the expected utility from cheating is less than the utility from being honest. Given the costs of having frequent inspections, it seems likely that the Italian public transit authority has found an effective way to reduce cheating. The fine plus the humiliation of a public reprimand should lower the expected return from cheating to a point at which most passengers would obey the law.

C For many "crimes" with large fines, a culprit might attempt to bribe a law enforcer. However, in this case, the risk of receiving a more severe punishment for attempting to bribe a law enforcer, especially on a public vehicle, would deter such behavior.

Multiple-Choice

1 c	2 d	3 d	4 a	5 c	6 b
7 b	8 c	9 a	10 d	11 c	

True-False

12 F	13 T	14 F	15 T	16 T
17 F	18 T	19 T	20 F	*21 T

Short Problems

22 The individual is indifferent between a 50/50 chance of $100 and $140 and a 50/50 chance of (0.5, 0.5: 200, 50) and (0.7, 0.3: 200, 50). The substitution assumption requires that these relationships be true, that is, an equivalent compound prospect is found by substituting the $100 and $140 outcomes in the first prospect with their respective equivalent lotteries.

23 No. If the insurance company is risk-neutral, it will provide insurance at a price equal to the expected cost from an accident. The expected costs are $500(0.01) = 5$ for all individuals, regardless of their preferences toward risk.

24 Figure A6.1 shows an individual's utility function and two prospects $A = (1/2, 1/2: w_1, w_2)$ and $B = (1/2, 1/2: w_3, w_4)$. The expected values of the two prospects are equal: $(w_1 + w_2)/2 = (w_3 + w_4)/2 = w_e$. The expected utility of A, the prospect with the larger spread, is less than

the expected utility of B. Since a risk-averse individual has diminishing marginal utility of income, the individual prefers a prospect that has a smaller down-side risk (that is, the one with the chance of *losing* a smaller amount of money) than the one that has a chance of *winning* more money.

25 For Winfred to be indifferent between the two choices, the probability of drawing the car must satisfy

$$U(2000 + 1000) = p[U(4000 + 1000)] \\ + (1 - p)[U(500 + 1000)] \\ = U(1500) \\ + p[U(5000) - U(1500)]$$

Substituting the utility values into this expression gives

$$1 - \frac{1000}{3000} = 1 - \frac{1000}{1500} + p\left(\frac{1000}{1500} - \frac{1000}{5000}\right)$$

or

$$p = \frac{5}{7}$$

26 The certainty equivalent is the amount of money that with certainty would yield the same utility as the expected utility from a risky prospect. Full insurance would leave the individual at a certain level of income in all states of the world. The maximum price an individual would pay for insurance is the amount of money that would leave him at a utility level no less than the utility from the certainty equivalent wealth. Let I_r be the maximum demand price for insurance. Then $w_o - I_r = w_{ce}$, where w_{ce} is the certainty equivalent wealth. I_r and w_{ce} are illustrated in Figure A6.2.

27 For a risk-neutral individual, $U(w_e) = p[U(w_1)] + (1 - p)[U(w_2)]$, where w_1 and w_2 are two possible outcomes from a risky prospect and w_e is the expected value. Hence, $w_e = w_{ce}$, where w_{ce} is the certainty equivalent. Since a preference ordering over prospects is the same as a preference ordering over certainty equivalent wealth values, it can be defined over expected values for risk-neutral individuals.

28 If $B \, P \, A$, then

$$U(3000) > 0.8[U(4000)] + 0.2[U(0)] \quad (1)$$

FIGURE A6.1

FIGURE A6.2

If $C \; P \; D$, then

$$0.2[U(4000)] + 0.8[U(0)] > 0.25[U(3000)]$$
$$+ 0.75[U(0)] \qquad (2)$$

Both sides of equation (2) are multiplied by 4 and the equation is then rearranged to give

$$U(3000) < 0.8[U(4000)] + 0.2[U(0)] \qquad (3)$$

Since inequalities (1) and (3) cannot occur simultaneously, the behavior is not consistent with expected-utility theory.

29 Ms. Gamble has the option of taking the assured prospect of \$25,000 if she chooses not to buy a lottery ticket. Alternatively, she can purchase a ticket and face the risky prospect: $(3/5, 2/5: w_1, w_2)$, where w_1 and w_2 are given by

$$w_1 = 25,000 + 10,000 - 5000 = 30,000$$
$$w_2 = 25,000 + 0 - 5000 = 20,000$$

Since \$5000 is Ms. Gamble's reservation price for the lottery ticket, then it must be the case that

$$U(25,000) = 3/5[U(30,000)] + 2/5[U(20,000)]$$

Substituting $U(25,000) = 100$ and $U(20,000) = 85$ implies that $U(30,000) = 110$.

Long Problems

30 a If the employer does not know the productivity of workers, she can separate the high- and low-productivity workers through an education requirement. For example, she can set an education level x^* to separate the high- from the low-productivity workers. If $x \geq x^*$, she will pay 2; if $x < x^*$, she will pay 1.

As indicated in Figure A6.3, high-productivity workers earn more from getting x^* units of education because $2 - x^*/2 > 1$. Low-productivity workers earn more from not getting educated because $1 > 2 - x^*$, hence, there is a signaling equilibrium.

b If the level of the signal is raised above x^*, the low-productivity workers will be no worse off because they will continue not to get educated; however, for larger x^*, high-productivity workers will have to expend wasteful resources to acquire the additional units of the signal.

31 Use problem **30** to answer this question. Suppose that men and women face the same costs $C = x/2$ for acquiring x units of education. However, because employers have less information on women's abilities, they require the cutoff education level between high- and low-productivity women to be higher than the cutoff for men. For example, if women have education $x \geq x_w^*$ education, then they will be paid 2; if men have education $x \geq x_m^*$, where $x_w^* > x_m^*$, they will be paid 2. Figure A6.4 shows the cost curves and the signaling cutoff level for men and women. Note that $2 - x_m^*/2 > 1$, so men will get x_m^* units of education. However, $2 - x_w^*/2 < 1$, so women do not get the required amount of the signal to get the higher wage (even though they are equally productive). For women to receive the same wage as men in this model, they must have lower costs of getting educated (that is, they must be more productive).

FIGURE A6.3

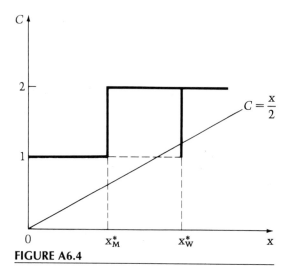

FIGURE A6.4

32 a If the Yankees win (state 1), Betty will earn $1500 in revenues less the $600 from the investment, or net revenues of $900. Given her initial income of $1000, $w_1 = \$1900$. If the Yankees lose, she will lose the $600 and have a total wealth of $w_2 = \$400$. Betty will undertake the investment if the expected utility from the prospect exceeds the utility from keeping the $1000 under her bed. That is,

$$U(1000) < 0.6[U(1900)] + 0.4[U(400)]$$

Substituting in the expression for the utility function gives

$$1000^{1/2} < 0.6(1900^{1/2}) + 0.4(400^{1/2})$$
$$31.6 < 26.15 + 8 = 34.15$$

Yes, Betty will invest the $600 in the risky prospect.

b The certainty equivalent is that level of wealth w_{ce} that yields the same utility as the prospect; that is,

$$w_{ce}^{1/2} = 34.15, \quad \text{so} \quad w_{ce} = \$1166.22$$

c Betty receives $1500 if the Yankees win or lose (or a net revenue of $900 in addition to the initial income) under the insurance plan. At maximum, she is willing to pay the amount of money from her total certain income of $1900 that will leave her at the same level of utility as with the certainty equivalent. That is,

$$(1900 - F)^{1/2} = 34.15$$

and so

$$F = \$733.78$$

Betty is willing to pay no more than $733.78 for the insurance policy. The friend will offer the insurance policy because the expected cost of the policy, $0.4(1500) = \$600$, is less than F.

*33 a The two prospects can be written as

$$A = (1/5, 4/5: w_o + 900, w_o - 100)$$
$$B = (1/4, 3/4:$$
$$[p, 1 - p; w_o + 900, w_0 - 100], w_o - 100)$$

The expected utility from each prospect is

$$V_A = (1/5)[U(w_o + 900)] + (4/5)[U(w_o - 100)]$$
$$V_B = (1/4)\{p[U(w_0 + 900)] + (1-p)[U(w_o - 100)]\}$$
$$\quad + 3/4 \,[U(w_o - 100)]$$
$$= (1/4)\,p[U(w_o + 900)]$$
$$\quad + (1 - 1/4p)[U(w_o - 100)]$$
$$= \hat{p}[U(w_o + 900)] + (1 - \hat{p})[U(w - 100)]$$

Then, $V_A = V_B$ if $\hat{p} = (1/4)p = 1/5$, which implies $p = 4/5$.

b To answer part **a**, the substitution assumption of compound prospects must be satisfied, that is, the simple prospect $(1/5, 4/5: w_o + 900, w_o - 100)$ must be equivalent to the compound prospect B.

*34 An individual prefers $A = (p, 1 - p: w_1, w_4)$ over $B = (p, 1 - p: w_2, w_3)$ if

$$p[U(w_1)] + (1 - p)[U(w_4)] > p[U(w_2)]$$
$$+ (1 - p)[U(w_3)]$$
$$p[(U(w_1) - U(w_2)] > (1 - p)$$
$$[U(w_3) - U(w_4)]$$

Then, since $U(w_1) + U(w_4) = U(w_2) + U(w_3)$, $U(w_1) - U(w_2) = U(w_3) - U(w_4)$, and substitution yields

$$p[U(w_1) - U(w_2)] > (1 - p)[U(w_1) - U(w_2)]$$
$$\text{or} \quad p > 1 - p$$

When $p = 1/2$, the lotteries are identical; hence, if $p \neq 1/2$, the lottery with the larger payoff in the more likely state of the world is preferred. For example, if $p > 1/2$, then because $w_1 > w_2$, lottery A is preferred. If $p < 1/2$, lottery B is preferred because the payoff in the more likely state of the world is higher for lottery B than for lottery A.

7

THE THEORY OF THE FIRM

Chapter Summary

What Is the Firm?

We begin our analysis of the firm. For the most part, the textbook view of the firm is that of a "black box," an entity that takes inputs and turns them into outputs for sale. Modern theory of the firm has given economists insights into the existence and internal organization of the firm. In this chapter we ask why firms are organized as they are, why they exist, and what determines their sizes.

Organization of the Firm

Firms vary in size and organizational structure. One important dimension of the organizational structure of the firm is the degree of separation between **ownership** and **control**. In an **owner-managed firm,** one person owns the firm and makes all the decisions. In a **partnership,** both the ownership and the decision-making responsibilities rest with two or more individuals. In the predominant organizational structure of the **publicly held corporation,** management and control are almost entirely separate. Whatever the organizational structure, there is a person or persons who have claim to the profits. They are called the **residual claimants.**

The first big puzzle at the heart of the theory of the firm is the following: A firm is a cooperative venture, requiring all individuals to work toward the objectives of the firm, whatever they may be. Why would individual workers who are motivated by self-interest behave in such a way to promote the interests of this cooperative venture? The simple answer is that the firm adopts an institutional structure that best achieves its objectives, given the self-interests of individuals. For example, if quality of output is pursued by the firm, individuals should not be paid according to their production volume alone.

Optimal Institutional Arrangement

If the self-interested behavior of individuals is intrinsically in conflict with the firm's interest, why are firms made up of more than one person? Corporations with hundreds or thousands of employees are the norm rather than the exception. To answer this question, we compare two simple organizations: a one-person firm and a two-person partnership. If there is no technological advantage in having two individuals work as a **team,** as in a partnership, then indeed, a one-person firm is the optimal institutional arrangement. In this case, the individual is the sole residual claimant and is rewarded the entire profits earned from his effort. Under an equal partnership, the individuals receive only one-half the earnings from their efforts and, hence, have less of an incentive to work hard. The result is less income and lower utility for each partner compared with the single-person firm. In this case, the **Pareto-optimal organizational form** is the single-person firm, because no other organizational form will leave all parties at least as well off and at least one party better off.

Team Effort and Partnerships

If we recognize that the team effort of two individuals can raise the output of the firm compared with the sum of the outputs from two individuals struggling on their own, then a partnership may be desirable. However, if costs of **monitoring** individuals are zero, then an alternative, owner-managed structure to the partnership is Pareto-preferred. Under this alternative, one teammate is contractually obligated to put forth the optimal effort; she receives zero for any level of **shirking.** The other teammate, who adopts the role of the owner and manager, is also motivated to put forth the optimal effort because she is the exclusive residual claimant; hence, this owner-managed arrangement is Pareto-preferred to a partnership and to a single-person firm.

When is a partnership Pareto-optimal? Note that the owner-managed firm has an advantage over the partnership in that a single individual captures all the profits from her efforts but has the disadvantage that the other partner is paid a fixed salary, independent of the profits that could be earned from additional effort. Therefore, the second individual must be monitored. Because the payment to both individual's in a partnership is tied partly to the profits produced by their efforts, then the incentive to shirk is limited; hence, if monitoring costs are very high, the partnership will be the preferred institutional arrangement. The Pareto-preferred organizational form selected depends on the possible productivity gains and monitoring costs associated with any given set of circumstances.

Specialization and Division of Labor

Adam Smith provided another reason for observing multiperson firms: **specialization and division of labor.** When tasks can be sequentially divided and workers can specialize in one or a few of them, output is expected to rise as a result of practice and repetition, reduction in setup time, and technical progress. Other reasons for observing multiperson firms are risk sharing and risk pooling.

Why are firms the sizes that they are? Why do they not transact in the market to obtain inputs rather than produce inputs within the firm, or vice versa? Coase suggests an answer to these questions: When the organizational costs of operating within a firm exceed the **transaction costs** of coordinating activities through the market, the firm will stop its expansion.

Firms may not have a choice between producing inputs or transacting in the market. If the inputs used are **specific** (as opposed to **generic**) and used solely by a particular firm, then that firm will have a difficult time convincing someone else to provide them. Both parties will require contractual protection, guaranteeing that the input will be produced and purchased at some specified price. Whether or not the market is used will depend on the trade-off between coordination difficulties within a firm and contracting costs in the market.

Key Words

Generic inputs	Residual claimant
Learning by doing	Shirking
Monitoring costs	Specialization and
Owner-managed firm	division of labor
Pareto-optimal	Specific inputs
organizational form	Team production
Partnership	Transactions costs
Private incentives	
Publicly held corporation	

Case Studies

I. Self-Imposed Punishments

An American was taking a boat ride up the Yangtze River when she observed a disturbing sight. A group of strong but exhausted men, rowing the boat, were being whipped and shouted at by an overseer. She complained of this brutality to the captain, demanding that he immediately stop this torture. He reluctantly informed her that there was nothing that she nor anyone else could do because the men were the ones who hired the overseer to punish them in this way.[1]

---

[1] Anecdote by S. Cheung in J. C. McManus (1975), "The Cost of Alternative Economic Organization," *Canadian Journal of Economics*, **8**(August):334–350.

A Explain why the rowers of the boat were willing to pay for such treatment.

B How might the overseer be encouraged to put forth the optimal level of effort?

II. Reneging on the Contract

In the 1960s, Standard Oil of Ohio contracted to purchase oil from Pure Oil, which operated out of the Oklahoma oil fields. It also contracted with Carter Oil to build a pipeline from the Oklahoma fields to Illinois that would connect onto the Illinois–Ohio pipeline. Soon after signing the contract, Standard Oil attempted to renege on the contract, arguing that the price and transport costs were unreasonable. The real trouble began when large oil discoveries were made in Illinois, lowering the price of Illinois crude significantly below that of transported Oklahoma crude. Standard Oil tried to break the terms of the contract. After expending large court fees, Standard Oil was forced to uphold the terms of the agreement.

A What was the source of the problem in this contractual agreement? Under what conditions would the parties agree to such an arrangement?

B Standard Oil incurred large contracting costs outside the firm. Is there a way that it could have avoided these costs by coordinating its activities within the firm rather than through the market? Explain.

Exercises

Multiple-Choice

Choose the correct answer to each question. There is only one correct answer to each question.

1 Multiperson firms can arise under which of the following conditions?
   a When the production from more than one individual working together exceeds the sum of output from individual efforts
   b When the risks from capital investments required for production are large
   c When the costs of monitoring are small
   d All the above
   e Only **a** and **c**

2 A piece rate paid to workers has which of the following effects?
   a Induces workers to produce a high-quality product
   b Always results in a divergence between the interests of the individual worker and the interests of the firm
   c Induces the workers to produce a large volume of product
   d Does not reward the worker for any of the added product from his effort
   e None of the above

To answer questions **3** and **4**, refer to Figure 7.1, which shows the income–effort line for individual 1 under a single-person firm $0B$, given by $y_1 = Ae_1$ and the indifference curves for the individual. Lines CD and EF are income–effort lines under a partnership.

3 Suppose that an individual enters into a partnership in which all profits are split equally between the two individuals, and both individuals have identical preferences and technologies. Then, the effort that each individual will put forth in equilibrium
   a Is e_1^0
   b Is e_1^1
   c Is e_1^2

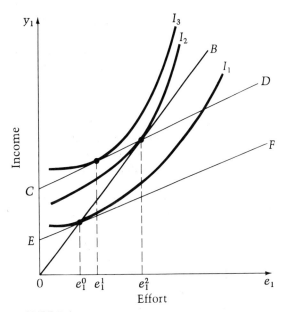

FIGURE 7.1

d Cannot be shown because the diagram illustrates only *one* individual's indifference curves and income–effort line

e None of the above

4 Suppose that the partnership results in a higher level of output than the sum of outputs from individual efforts; that is, $y = B(e_1 + e_2)$, where $B > A$. Then, which of the following is true?

a The partnership can never be a Pareto improvement over the single-person firm.

b The partnership may be a Pareto improvement over the single-person firm if B is sufficiently large.

c The partnership will always be a Pareto improvement over the single-person firm if monitoring costs are sufficiently low.

d The partnership will always be a Pareto improvement over the single-person firm if the individuals are risk-neutral.

e None of the above.

5 Suppose that the output of a team exceeds the sum of the outputs from individual production; then, which of the following is true?

a A partnership is always a Pareto improvement over a single-person firm.

b An owner-managed organization always dominates a partnership.

c An owner-managed organization dominates a partnership if monitoring costs are sufficiently low.

d A partnership always dominates an owner-managed organization because it does not require monitoring.

e None of the above.

6 In which of the following ways is team production different from specialization?

a Individuals' effort levels can be assessed under team production but not under specialization.

b Team effort is more productive than isolated production, whereas specialization is less productive than isolated production.

c Specialization occurs in stages; team production does not.

d There are setup costs for every job in specialized production, but there are no setup costs for jobs produced by a team.

e None of the above.

7 A residual claimant of a firm

a Is paid a fixed wage

b Receives the profits of the firm after all wages and costs are paid

c Has the incentive to put forth less effort than under a fixed-wage contract

d Is always the manager of the firm

e None of the above

8 Production activities are likely to be organized within a firm rather than through the market when

a Market transaction costs are small.

b Benefits from increased output from team production are less than the costs of monitoring the team.

c Specialization and division of labor increase production.

d The production process requires generic assets.

e All the above.

9 Specific capital required by a firm's production process

a Has no (or very few) alternative uses

b Will be produced in the firm requiring it if contracting costs are large

c Can result in bargaining problems when it is produced by a firm other than the one requiring it

d All the above

e Only **b** and **c**

True-False

10 When monitoring costs are high, a partnership may be a Pareto improvement over the owner-managed team.

11 If there are no benefits from team production, then the one-person firm dominates the partnership organization of the firm.

12 When team production is more productive than individual production, a partnership is always more efficient than an owner-managed organization because in the owner-managed case only one person is a residual claimant.

13 When team production is more productive than individual production, an owner-managed organization is preferred to a single-person firm if monitoring costs are zero.

14 Fixed-wage contracts encourage more shirking than contracts that tie the wage to output, holding everything else constant.

15 Team production and specialization in production are identical in that the effort of each worker is impossible to assess.

16 In the absence of a contract or good will, a firm requiring a specific input is more likely to produce the input within the firm rather than purchase the input in the marketplace.

17 Firms are more likely to emerge when transaction costs of writing and enforcing contracts are large.

18 Specialized production and team production are the same in that both are sequences of separate, specialized activities.

19 Because competitive markets pay workers the value of their marginal product, thus inducing the efficient level of effort, there is no need for firms ever to integrate into input production (that is, pay workers to produce some good within the firm).

Problems

20 Explain why firms integrate into input production (that is, pay workers to produce some goods within the firm) rather than use the market for these transactions.

21 List some factors that determine the size of a firm.

22 Using the theory developed in this chapter, explain the poor teaching performance by some professors at your university.

23 To purchase eight tickets for the subway, an individual must pay $5 and then deposit one of the tickets in the ticket box. Why doesn't the subway clerk simply give seven tickets for the $5 and allow the customer entry into the station?

24 In small towns, McDonald's hamburger franchisees pay a fixed initial fee for the franchise and receive a large percentage of profits earned. Why are both the franchisee and the owners residual claimants?

25 After World War I, British coal miners were paid a piece rate—that is, a payment per ton of coal—to encourage them to work at an efficient level of effort. Nevertheless, many of the coal mines in Britain were shut down before all the economically extractable coal was mined. A suboptimal *amount* of effort by the coal miners cannot be blamed for the inefficient production of coal. Can you suggest a reason why the economically extractable coal was not mined? (*Hint:* Because the coal miners' wages were tied to the output, monitoring was, perhaps wrongly, presumed to be unnecessary.)

26 Two individuals are deciding whether to form a partnership or to continue operating as single-person firms. For the case of team production (two workers), the output–effort relationship is $y = B(e_1 + e_2)$, where y is total income and e_i is the effort of the ith worker, $i = 1, 2$; for a single-person firm, $y_i = Ae_i$, where y_i is the ith individual's income, and $A < B$. All workers have identical preferences over effort and income: Utility increases in y_i and decreases in e_i. Workers choose the utility-maximizing level of effort, given the income–effort relationship.

a If monitoring costs are zero, which institutional arrangement—a single-person firm, an equal partnership, or an owner-managed firm—will be Pareto-dominant? Explain, using a diagram.

b Suppose that monitoring costs are equal to M and are equally split between the two individuals. On a diagram, show a situation in which the individuals are indifferent among all three forms of organization.

***27** Small raspberry farms in the Frazer Valley in British Columbia hire pickers every summer to harvest the crop. There are two aspects to the performance of a berry-picker: A good picker picks a lot of berries each day and picks the rows *clean* (that is, does not leave the small berries or the hard-to-get-at berries on the bushes). The contract established between the farm owners and the pickers specifies that the pickers be paid a rate per pound or volume for the amount picked (usually about one-third of the wholesale value). In addition, the rows that a picker has finished are checked randomly for cleanliness. If the rows are not clean, then the picker does not receive the payment.

a Identify the potential moral hazard problems in berry picking under a piece-rate contract (that is, the incentives to shirk). Analyze the efficiency of the particular organizational arrangement described in solving these problems.

b Describe some alternative contracts that could be established for berry picking and compare them with the observed contract.

*28 Sarah and Sean are furniture movers. They are interested in adopting the efficient organizational form for a moving business. Working alone, each as a production function of $y_i = 3e_i$, where y_i is income in dollars and e_i is effort in hours. Working together as a team, because of the advantages of team production in moving, they are able to achieve the production function $y = 4(e_1 + e_2)$, where y is now total income. Both have utility functions given by

$$U_i = \frac{y_i}{(e_i + 2)^2}$$

so that

$$\mathrm{MRS}_i = \frac{2y_i}{(e_i + 2)}$$

a If both individuals set up *independently* as owner-managers, find the level of effort expended by each, the income received, and the utility level attained. (*Hint:* Draw a diagram and decide what you need to calculate before doing anything else.)

b If Sarah and Sean form a *partnership*, sharing their total income equally, what will the effort levels, income, and utilities be?

c Explain the two factors at work that lead your answer to **b** to be different from that to **a**.

d What are the Pareto-optimal levels of effort, income, and utility for team production by Sean and Sarah?

e What organizational form might Sean and Sarah adopt to achieve **d**? What condition is required for this to be possible?

Answers to Chapter 7

Case Studies

I A The rowers realized that every member of the team has an incentive to shirk. In the absence of shirking, output from the team exceeds the sum of output from individual efforts. Hence, the rowers hired a monitor to prevent the team members from shirking.

B Make him a residual claimant.

II A Specificity of capital that led to small numbers bargaining. The parties would agree to a binding contract only with large penalties for reneging on the contract.

B Standard Oil could have expanded its firm to include production of oil from Oklahoma oil fields. Then, when Illinois oil prices fell, it could have purchased Illinois crude and sold the Oklahoma crude locally.

Multiple-Choice

1 d	2 c	3 a	4 b	5 c
6 c	7 b	8 c	9 d	

True-False

10 T	11 T	12 F	13 T	14 T
15 F	16 T	17 T	18 F	19 F

Problems

20 When transaction costs of writing separate contracts for every market transaction are large, input supplies are uncertain, the benefits from team production exceed the costs of monitoring the team, or specialization and division of labor increase production, firms will integrate into input production.

21 When the cost of carrying out a transaction within the firm exceeds the cost of that transaction in the marketplace, a firm will stop growing. Increasing monitoring costs and diseconomies of scale will affect the size of the firm.

22 The output of a university — knowledge acquired by the students — is a product of team effort by all professors. However, there is little monitoring of professors' efforts (except for end-of-year evaluations), and because wages are not tied to effort (except through merit increases), the professor has an incentive to shirk.

23 This is a monitoring device to ensure that the clerk does not attempt to pocket any of the revenues from ticket sales.

24 When monitoring costs are high, franchisees are made residual claimants to ensure that they maintain the quality and reputation of McDonald's. Since the owners of McDonald's are also residual claimants, they have the incentive to continue to develop new products and to advertise.

25 Because the coal miners' wages were tied to their effort, the miners attempted to produce large volumes of coal. This meant mining the coal in the large seams that was easiest to extract. Since the miners were not monitored, they passed over coal in the narrow seams, which was more difficult to reach. The large setup costs of returning the capital equipment to the unmined coal exceeded the return from this coal, which would have been economical to extract in the first shift.

26 a The owner-managed arrangement dominates the other two relationships. The income–effort lines for individual 1 under the owner-managed, partnership, and single-person firms are given by $0C$, DB, and $0A$, respectively, in Figure A7.1. In a single-person firm, the individual maximizes utility at E; under a partnership, the individual moves to point F; and in the owner-managed arrangement, the individual chooses point G.

b Monitoring costs will shift line $0C$ down by $M/2$ to $0'C'$. In Figure A7.2, the individual is

FIGURE A7.2

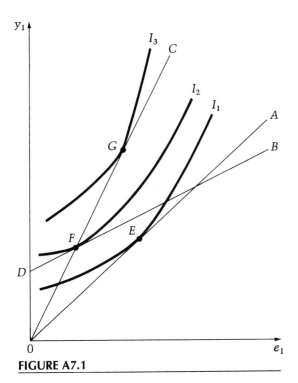

FIGURE A7.1

shown to be indifferent between the owner-managed situation at point G and the partnership (where monitoring is not necessary) at point F. Furthermore, the optimal levels of effort and income under a single-person firm at point E yield the same utility as the alternative arrangements.

*27 a The moral hazard (shirking) problem in berry picking under a piece-rate contract is in the cleanliness of the picking. Under this contract, and at a given effort level, the picker is interested in maximizing the quantity of berries picked per hour. In balancing the "intensive margin" of more berries picked in a section against the "extensive margin" of moving faster down the sections, the picker will tend to move very quickly, reaching for the large berries on the outside branches and leaving both the small berries and the berries in the middle of the bushes that are hard to reach. The farmer, however, wants to maximize the *stock* of output from a field, where the stock equals the intensity (pounds of berries per section) times the number of sections. Under various contracts, a conflict could arise between the intensity desired by the farmer and that supplied by the pickers. The actual contract, which includes a piece rate and a random check for cleanliness, eliminates this potential conflict.

b The observed contract is a sharing contract. Two other contracts could be offered: a wage contract and rental contract. Under a wage contract, the worker receives a fixed amount and, therefore, must be monitored. If his effort were monitored directly but could not be monitored perfectly, then the potential shirking problem would be reversed compared with the piece-rate contract; the worker would have no incentive to choose the wrong intensity but would be inclined to shirk on effort to the extent that he could get away with it. As in the first contract, the worker must be monitored.

A rental contract has the picker buying the rights to a given plot of land for the season, then selling the berries herself after picking them. All incentive problems in picking are *internalized*. However, this arrangement leads to buyers spending money to determine the quality of the plots that they are considering purchasing. This expenditure on information may be costly.

*28 a Set MRS equal to marginal product of effort:

$$\frac{2y_i}{e_i + 2} = 3$$

Substitution of the production function $y_i = 3e_i$ yields $6e_i/(e_i + 2) = 3$, which implies that $e^* = 2$, $y^* = 6$, and $U^* = \frac{3}{8}$. The solution is illustrated in Figure A7.3 for $i = 1$.

b Now MRS equals marginal product of effort, where the marginal product is one-half of the *total* marginal product; that is,

$$\frac{2y_i}{e_i + 2} = 2$$

implies that $y_i = e_i + 2$. Substitution of the individual's production function $y_i = 2(e_i + e_j)$ into this equation gives $2(e_i + e_j) = e_i + 2$. By symmetry, $e_i = e_j = e'$ in equilibrium, $e' = \frac{2}{3}$, $y' = 2 \times \frac{4}{3} = \frac{8}{3}$; $U' = \frac{3}{8}$. The solution is illustrated in Figure A7.4 for $i = 1$.

c The partnership is more productive because of team production, but the partnership involves an efficiency loss because each worker receives only one-half of the marginal product of

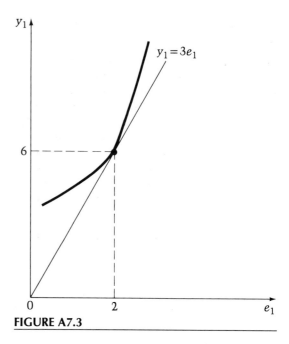

FIGURE A7.3

increased effort; hence, effort is reduced in equilibrium. In this example, these two effects cancel, leaving utility unchanged.

d Set MRS equal to total marginal product:

$$\frac{2y_i}{(e_i + 2)} = 4$$

Substitute production function $y_i = 4e_i$ to yield $e'' = 2$; $y'' = 4 \times 2 = 8$; $U'' = \frac{1}{2}$.

FIGURE A7.4

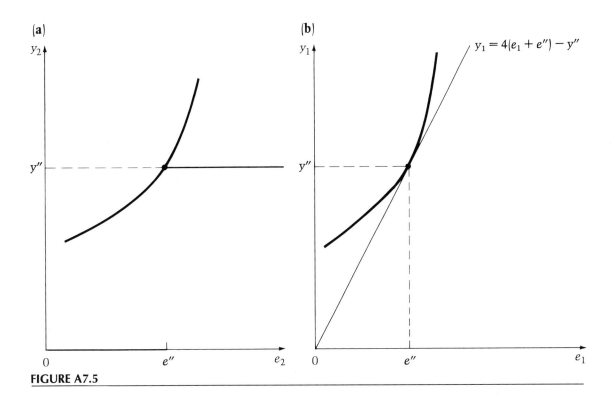

(a)

(b)

$$y_1 = 4(e_1 + e'') - y''$$

FIGURE A7.5

e Either worker—say, Sarah—could set up as owner-manager and hire the other worker on the following contract: Put forth e'' effort and earn y'' income or get zero for any effort level less than e''. Given this contract, e'' will be the optimal level of effort for Sean, as shown in Figure A7.5a. Given that Sarah is now the residual claimant, she gets the full marginal product of any increase in her own effort; hence, she will put forth the Pareto-efficient amount e'' and get y''. Sarah's solution is shown in Figure A7.5b. (Sarah's effort and income are subscripted by 1, Sean's by 2.) The condition required for this solution is costless monitoring of Sean's effort.

8

PRODUCTION AND COST: ONE VARIABLE INPUT

Chapter Summary

In this chapter, we abstract from the complexities of the firm's internal organization and concentrate on the production decisions. The firm is treated simply as an organization that buys inputs and transforms them into goods and services for the market.

The Production Function

Basic to all the firm's production decisions is the **production function** of the firm, $y = F(z_1, \ldots, z_n)$, which is the relationship between quantities of inputs (the z_1) and the maximum output that can be produced (y). The production function describes the output that can be produced when inputs are used in a **technically efficient** manner. The production technology can be one of several types — inputs can be used in **fixed proportions** or in **variable proportions** in production.

To put the production function in perspective, we must emphasize that the firm wants to profit maximize; that is, it wants to maximize its revenues from sales of output while minimizing its costs of production. Thus, **profit-maximization** implies **cost-minimization**. The **long-run planning horizon** is such that the firm can vary all of its inputs, whereas in the **short run**, the firm can vary some but not all of its inputs. In both the short run and the long run, the cost-minimizing firm finds the least expensive bundle of inputs, given their **rental prices,** that will produce some given amount of output.

As is intuitively clear (and rigorously discussed in later chapters), the decision about which inputs to employ by a firm depends on how "productive" an input is, relative to its cost. For this reason, we isolate increases in the **total product** or **output** attributable to a particular input, holding the other input(s) fixed. As first recognized by Malthus, the total product curve is characterized by **diminishing marginal productivity** of a variable input, holding all other inputs fixed in quantity. That is, as *additional* amounts of an input are applied to fixed factors, the *additional* output produced eventually begins to decline. Similarly, the **average product,** the total product divided by the quantity of a variable input employed, will also begin to decline after some level of a variable input. The relationship between the average and marginal products is the following: When the marginal product exceeds (is less than) the average product, the average rises (falls); when marginal product equals average product, average product is at a maximum.

One Variable Input

Consider the case in which all inputs but one are fixed in quantity. In this case, the short-run production function is defined by the total product

(TP) function, $TP(z_1) = F(z_1, \bar{z}_2, \ldots, \bar{z}_n)$. From the short-run production function, we can derive the **short-run cost function** and the seven short-run cost concepts: the **short-run total cost STC(y)**, **short-run variable costs VC(Y)**, **short-run fixed costs FC**, **short-run average costs SAC(y)**, **short-run average variable costs AVC(y)**, **short-run average fixed costs AFC(y)**, and **short-run marginal costs, SMC(y)**. STC(y) equals the sum of VC(y) and FC. The variable-cost function is found simply by turning the total product function on its side; more precisely, transform the variable input axis to variable costs by multiplying the input quantities by the input price and then interchange the axes. The AVC(y), variable costs divided by output, has an inverse relationship with the average product: As average product rises, average variable costs fall, and vice versa. An analogous relationship holds between the SMC(y), the additional costs of producing additional output, and marginal product. Adding the fixed costs to the variable costs gives the short-run total costs; adding AFC(y), total fixed costs divided by output, to the average variable costs gives SAC(y). Hence, we have the seven short-run cost curves and related production relationships that are necessary for analyzing the firm's production decisions in the short run.

An Application: Traffic Congestion

Many of the issues associated with cost and production functions can be illustrated in a simple model of traffic congestion. Suppose that a commuter can choose between two alternative routes to get him to work. The costs to the commuter are measured in terms of the money value of time spent commuting, which in turn depends on the number of cars on each of the alternative routes. In this case, the output is the total number of commuter trips made on each road.

From this simple model, we find that if there is unrestricted access to both roads — that is, if both roads are common property — then commuters equate their average commuting costs on each route. This equilibrium is suboptimal from a cost-benefit perspective because it does not minimize the total commuting costs to society. To attain the socially optimal number of cars on each road, commuters should instead equate their marginal commuting costs on each of the

routes. One possible solution to this problem is to levy a toll — that is, to restrict access — on one of the routes in order to shift the private equilibrium to the optimum. Note that we could reinterpret this example to reflect the issues of multiplant production. To minimize total variable costs of production, given that output is produced in two or more plants, set the short-run marginal costs of production equal in all plants.

Key Words

Average product
Common-property resources
Cost-benefit criterion
Diminishing marginal productivity
Fixed-proportions production
Free disposal
Long-run costs
Marginal product
Production function

Rental price
Short run
Short-run total costs, variable costs, fixed costs, average costs, average variable costs, average fixed costs, marginal costs
Technical efficiency
Total product
Variable-proportions production

Case Study: Paying the Toll

Commuters traveling from Oakland to San Francisco, California, must cross the Bay Bridge to get to work every morning. Even though a toll of $1.50 must be paid to cross the bridge, this route is congested; the traffic moves so slowly during rush hour that the average time to travel the 8 miles from Oakland to San Francisco is 1 hour.

Commuters have an alternative mode of transportation, the public transportation system called BART. BART is effectively congestion-free. A round-trip ticket from Oakland to San Francisco on BART costs approximately $3. Using BART, commuting time to San Francisco from Oakland, including the time to walk from the BART station to one's workplace, is approximately 50 minutes.

A Describe the optimization rule that a commuter uses in deciding which mode of transportation to use.

B Suppose that the only relevant costs are the toll costs, public transit tickets, and time costs. (Ignore other costs such as costs of gasoline, depreciation of the car, and parking costs.) Given the optimization rule you suggested in **A**, what would be the implicit value of a commuter's time?

C Suppose that the time it takes to travel from Oakland to San Francisco is a function of the flow of traffic across the bridge in 1 hour, X. Assume that for a flow of traffic less than 1000 cars per hour, it takes 15 minutes to drive the desired distance, but for a flow of traffic greater than 1000 cars per hour, the average time for a commuter to travel that distance becomes $t = 0.00025X$, where t is measured in hours. It can be shown that the flow of traffic that minimizes commuters' travel costs is $X = 2000$. Given the implicit wage you found in part **A**, does a toll of $1.50 and public transportation costs of $3 achieve this optimal flow of traffic? What is the economic problem here?

D If the current equilibrium is suboptimal, suggest two ways in which the optimal allocation of commuters to the two transportation modes might be achieved.

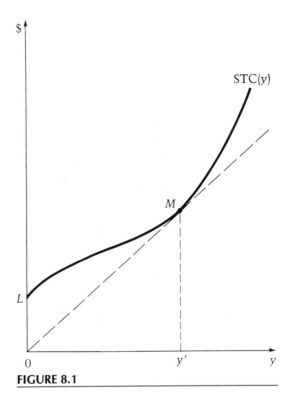

FIGURE 8.1

Exercises

Multiple-Choice

Choose the correct answer to each question. There is only one correct answer to each question.

Refer to Figure 8.1 to answer questions **1** and **2**.

1 A firm producing y' units of output
 a Is minimizing average variable costs of production
 b Is minimizing average total costs of production
 c Faces fixed costs equal to My'
 d Faces a marginal cost smaller than the average total cost of production
 e None of the above

2 In Figure 8.1, which of the following is shown?
 a Total fixed costs decline for increases in output.

 b Average total costs at y' equals My' divided by Oy'.
 c Marginal costs are increasing for all values of output.
 d Average variable costs at y' equal the difference between My' and $0L$ divided by $0y'$.
 e Both **b** and **d**.

3 The law of diminishing returns to a variable input
 a Assumes that at least one input is held fixed
 b Refers to the behavior of the marginal product of the variable input
 c Implies that an increase in the fixed factor would increase total product
 d All the above
 e Only **a** and **b**

4 Suppose that 2 dozen bagels can be produced with 2 workers, and 4 dozen bagels can be produced with 6 workers. Then, which of the following is correct?
 a Average product is $\frac{1}{2}$.
 b Average variable costs are rising.

c The marginal product is higher than the average product.

d The marginal product of labor is 2 (dozen bagels).

e None of the above.

5 The production function $y = \min(az_1, bz_2)$ implies which of the following?

a Good Y can be produced with variable proportions of input 1 and input 2.

b The production of 1 unit of good Y requires more of input 1 than input 2 if $a > b$.

c If input 1 and input 2 are being used in the proportion b/a, then an increase in the quantity of only one of the inputs will not increase output.

d If input 1 and input 2 are being used in the proportion b/a, then an increase in the quantity of only one of the inputs will increase output.

e None of the above.

6 Which of the following defines the average variable cost?

a The price of the variable input divided by the marginal product of that input

b Total variable costs divided by the quantity of the variable input hired

c The additional cost of hiring another unit of the variable input

d The price of the variable input divided by the average product of that input

e None of the above.

To answer questions **7** and **8**, refer to Figure 8.2. Assume that input 1 is the variable input in the production of good Y.

7 In Figure 8.2,

a The average product of input 1 is maximized at point A.

b Average fixed costs are constant.

c The slope of AVC equals the slope of ATC at every output.

d None of the above.

e Both **a** and **c**.

8 At point B,

a The average product of input 1 is at a maximum.

b The slope of the total cost curve is less than the slope of the total variable cost curve at the same output.

c The average product is rising.

d The marginal product is less than average product.

e None of the above.

9 Four servings of spaghetti *alle vongole* require 16 ounces of spaghetti, 8 ounces of tomato sauce, 12 ounces of clams, and 4 ounces of garlic. Suppose that a cook has 98 ounces of spaghetti, 60 ounces of tomato sauce, 54 ounces of clams, and 30 ounces of garlic. Then the maximum number of individuals that he can feed is

a 28

b 24

c 20

d 18

e None of the above

True-False

10 If marginal product is decreasing, then average product must also be decreasing.

11 For a fixed-proportions technology, inputs cannot be substituted for each other in production.

12 The marginal product of input 1 derived from the production function $y = \min(az_1, bz_2)$, diminishes for increases in input 1.

13 If the average product is declining, then average *total* costs must be increasing.

14 The short run is that period of time during which some inputs cannot be varied.

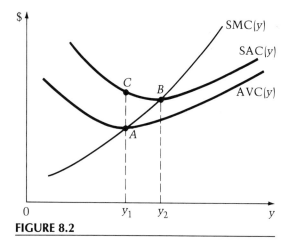

FIGURE 8.2

15 The slope of the short-run total cost curve equals the slope of the short-run variable cost curve at every output.

16 Average fixed costs are constant for all output levels.

17 A profit-maximizing firm never operates on the declining portion of the total product curve.

Short Problems

18 Give an intuitive argument in support of the law of diminishing returns.

19 Suppose that a firm produces with one variable factor of production and that marginal product decreases for all levels of the input used. Draw the total product curve of the firm and show how the average and marginal product curves are derived from the total product curve.

20 The production function relating two inputs and output y is given by

$$y = z_1^{1/2} z_2^{1/2}$$

and the marginal product of z_1 equals $MP_1 = z_2^{1/2}/(2z_1^{1/2})$.

  a Determine the expression for the average product curve for input 1, holding $z_2 = 4$. Illustrate the marginal and average product curves.

  b Derive the short-run total cost curve for the production relationship described in **a**.

21 Explain why the difference between the average total cost and average variable costs is large for low-output levels and small for high-output levels.

22 An alfalfa farmer in Montana produces bushels of alfalfa y using land (input 2) and labor (input 1) according to the production function, where the marginal product of labor is $(2z_2^{1/2})/z_1^{1/2} - 1$. The farmer has 16 acres of land for alfalfa production. In addition, she has unlimited amounts of her own labor services for producing alfalfa (that is, her opportunity cost of time is zero). How many units of her labor will she use, given that she employs all 16 acres of land? Explain.

Long Problems

23 Suppose that a firm's short-run total cost function is given by

$$STC(y) = a + by$$

where a and b are positive constants and y is output. Only one variable and one fixed factor are used in production.

  a Find the total variable costs, total fixed costs, average total costs, average variable costs, average fixed costs, and marginal costs.

  b Assume that the price of the variable input is w. Find expressions for the total product, average product, and marginal product.

  c Do you think that these cost and production relationships are realistic? Why or why not?

24 Suppose that a farmer in North Dakota has a fixed amount of labor and two plots of land, A and B.

  a If the marginal productivity diminishes on both plots, what distribution of labor on the two plots of land will maximize output? Use economic intuition as to why your solution is correct.

  b Now suppose that the marginal product of labor increases on plot A and diminishes on plot B. Would only plot A be cultivated? Explain, using a diagram.

25 Milkshakes are produced at the local soda fountain with two inputs: Theodore's time, input 1, and the set of fixed ingredients (1 cup of milk, 1 tablespoon of malt, 1 scoop of ice cream), input 2. The number of milkshakes produced can be no greater than Theodore's time multiplied by the speed s (measured in number of milkshakes per hour) at which Theodore works. Theodore also knows that when he makes milkshakes very quickly, he spills a large amount of the ingredients. Hence, his production is constrained by the technological relationship that says that the number of milkshakes he can make *per set of ingredients* can be no greater than $10/s$. In other words, if Theodore makes 10 milkshakes per hour, he can produce 1 milkshake for every set of ingredients, but if he makes 20 milkshakes per hour, he needs twice the ingredients because one-half of them land on the floor. This production relationship has an upper bound of 1; he cannot make more than 1 milkshake per set of ingredients. Given these relationships, determine the speed at which Theodore will work as a function of z_1 and z_2 (quantities of inputs 1 and 2) and the production function for milkshakes.

Answers to Chapter 8

Case Study

A Commuters will equate the average commuting costs of using the two modes.

B Let w be the implicit value of time per hour. Then the average cost of using public transportation is $\$3 + (\frac{5}{6})w$; the average cost of driving is $\$1.50 + (1)w$. Equating these costs implies $w^* = \$9$.

C No. Since it takes 1 hour to cross the bridge, the flow of traffic must solve $0.00025X = 1$; that is, $X = 4000$. Note that $X = 4000$ is also found by equating average commuting costs of driving and public transportation. The average commuting costs of public transportation are

$$\$3 + \frac{5}{6}w = \$3 + \frac{5}{6}(\$9) = \$10.50$$

The average commuting costs of driving are

$$\$1.50 + (\$9)(0.00025X) = \$1.50 + 0.00225X$$

Equating these costs gives $X = 4000$.
    The economic problem is one of common property in which commuters do not internalize adequately the costs that they impose on others by their decisions. That is, to determine which mode to take, commuters equate average commuting costs, rather than the marginal commuting costs of driving and public transportation.

D The flow of traffic can be reduced by increasing the toll to cross the bridge or reducing the cost of public transportation.

Multiple Choice

1 b	2 e	3 d	4 b	5 c
6 d	7 a	8 d	9 d	

True-False

10 F	11 T	12 F	13 F
14 T	15 T	16 F	17 T

Short Problems

18 Consider the case of land. If the law of diminishing returns did not hold, only cultivated land would be used to produce food; new land would never be brought into production. Alternatively, one can think of a small rice paddy in Asia. Initially, as labor is added to the plot, output and productivity increase. However, if too many laborers come to work on the plot, they begin to get in each other's way, and there is not enough work to keep them all busy. This is when diminishing returns to labor set in.

19 When the marginal product decreases as the input increases, it implies that the slope of the total product curve declines throughout, as shown in Figure A8.1. The average product at a point is given by the slope of a ray from the origin to that point on the total product curve. Note

FIGURE A8.1

that the slope of a ray from the origin falls as z_1 increases. Furthermore, $AP(z_1) > MP(z_1)$ at every z_1.

20 a If $z_2 = 4$, $y = z_1^{1/2}(4^{1/2}) = 2z_1^{1/2}$. Average product and marginal products are given by $AP_1 = 2z_1^{1/2}/z_1 = 2/z_1^{1/2}$ and $MP_1 = 1/z_1^{1/2}$. To plot AP_1 and MP_1, let $z_1 = (4, 9, 16)$. At these values, $MP_1 = (\frac{1}{2}, \frac{1}{3}, \frac{1}{4})$ and $AP_1 = (1, \frac{2}{3}, \frac{1}{2})$, as shown in Figure A8.2.

b The short-run total cost is the sum of the variable costs and the fixed costs. Variable costs are found by inverting the production function and multiplying z_1 by the wage rate. That is,

$$y = 2z_1^{1/2} \quad \text{so} \quad z_1 = \frac{y^2}{4}$$

Multiply z_1 by w_1 and define the short-run variable cost $VC(y) = w_1 z_1$. Then,

$$VC(y) = w_1 z_1 = \frac{w_1 y^2}{4}$$

The fixed input is z_2, so fixed costs are found by multiplying $4 (= z_2)$ by its price w_2; thus, $FC = 4w_2$. Total costs are

$$STC(y) = VC(y) + FC = \frac{w_1 y^2}{4} + 4w_2$$

21 The difference between the short-run average cost and the average variable cost is the average fixed cost. That is,

FIGURE A8.2

$SAC(y) = AVC(y) + AFC(y) \qquad$ so
$$SAC(y) - AVC(y) = AFC(y)$$

As output increases, $AFC(y)$ declines, and $SAC(y) - AVC(y)$ goes to zero.

22 The farmer will use an amount of labor such that $MP_1 = 0$. For $z_2 = 16$, $MP_1 = (2)(4)/z_1^{1/2} - 1 = 0$, which implies $z_1 = 64$. If she were to use more than 64 units of labor, the MP_1 of labor would be negative and output would decline. If she used fewer than 64 units, the MP_1 would be positive; more output could be produced at zero opportunity cost.

Long Problems

23 a Total variable costs $= by$, total fixed costs $= a$, average total costs $= (a + by)/y$, average variable costs $= b$, average fixed costs $= a/y$, and marginal costs $= b$.

b Let z_1 be the quantity of the variable factor. To find the product curves, we must invert the variable cost curve, where $VC(y) = wz_1$. Then, since $VC(y) = by$, $wz_1 = by$ and, therefore,

$$y = \frac{wz_1}{b}$$

Then, $AP(z_1) = y/z_1 = w/b$ and $MP(z_1) = \Delta y/\Delta z_1 = w/b$.

c These production relationships are not realistic in that they do not exhibit diminishing marginal productivity. In this case, the marginal product w/b is a constant and, therefore, is independent of output.

24 a If marginal product of labor (input 1) diminishes on both plots, the farmer will want to allocate labor to the two plots until the marginal products are equal. To see this, suppose that $MP_1^A > MP_1^B$. Then by transferring labor from plot B to plot A, total output can be increased. As this transfer continues, MP_1^A falls and MP_1^B increases; output is maximized at $MP_1^A = MP_1^B$. The argument is similar for $MP_1^A < MP_1^B$.

b If the marginal product increases on plot A and diminishes on plot B, then (1) only A will be used, (2) only B will be used, or (3) both plots will be cultivated. The three possibilities are plotted in Figure A8.3, in which the marginal product of labor on plot A is measured from left to right, and the marginal product of labor on plot B is measured from right to left.

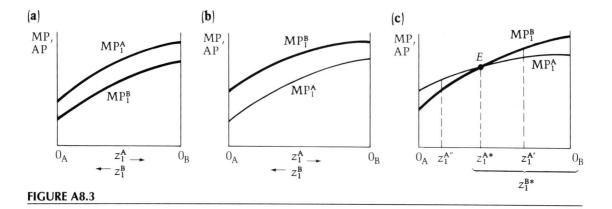

FIGURE A8.3

(1) Only plot A is cultivated. In Figure A8.3*a*, the MP_1^A increases in z_1 and MP_1^B declines in z_1. Because $MP_1^A > MP_1^B$ for every unit of labor, all labor is used on plot A.

(2) Only plot B is cultivated. As shown in Figure A8.3*b*, the marginal product of labor on plot B, though declining in z_1, is greater than the marginal product of labor on plot A.

(3) Both plots are cultivated. In Figure A8.3*c*, the two marginal product curves cross; z_1^{A*} units of labor are used on plot A, and z_1^{B*} units are used on plot B. To see that this allocation maximizes output, consider an increase in labor on plot A—say, to $z_1^{A'}$. Since $MP_1^B > MP_1^A$, this will result in a decline in output. If labor is reduced—say, to $z_1^{A''}$—$MP_1^A > MP_1^B$ and again there is a reduction in total output. Hence, output is maximized at point E.

25 There are two constraints to this production relationship. Let m be the total number of milkshakes produced and s be the speed (milkshakes per hour) at which Theodore works. Then $m \leq$ sz_1 implies that the number of milkshakes produced can be no greater than Theodore's time multiplied by his speed. The second constraint, $m/z_2 \leq 10/s$, is a "technological relationship" which says that the number of milkshakes made per set of ingredients can be no greater than 10 divided by the speed. The speed s at which the maximum number of milkshakes can be produced, given these two constraints, is found by equating $m = sz_1$ and $m = 10z_2/s$. That is,

$$sz_1 = \frac{10z_2}{s}$$

and so

$$s^* = \left(\frac{10z_2}{z_1}\right)^{1/2}$$

Substituting s^* into either of the constraints yields the production function

$$m = \left(\frac{10z_2}{z_1}\right)^{1/2} z_1 = (10z_1z_2)^{1/2}$$

9

PRODUCTION AND COST: MANY VARIABLE INPUTS

Chapter Summary

Many Variable Inputs

We now explore a firm's input and output decisions when it has sufficient time to vary *several* production inputs to achieve the lowest possible production costs for every output. The production function of the firm in the long run can be described by **isoquants**, which are curves of all combinations of input that yield the same output level. Isoquants are negatively sloped, and they are usually characterized by a diminishing **marginal rate of technical substitution**, which implies that increasing amounts of one input must compensate for decreasing amounts of other inputs to keep output constant. Two special cases — perfect substitutes and perfect complements in production — are represented by straight-line and right-angled isoquants, respectively.

Derivation of the Long-Run Cost Function

In the **long run**, the firm can vary *all* inputs in production. To derive the long-run cost function, an important ingredient in model development in later chapters, we need to determine the combination of inputs that minimizes the costs of producing every output level. The *algebraic* solution to this problem is a set of **conditional input demand functions** that give the cost-mini-

mizing level of input as a function of input prices and the output level. Substitution of these input demands into the cost identity (sum of inputs weighted by their respective prices) yields the **long-run cost function**.

This algebraic solution can be illustrated on an **isoquant–isocost** diagram. An isocost curve gives the combinations of inputs that can be purchased at a particular outlay or cost, given input prices. When isoquants are smooth and convex and the solution to the cost-minimization problem is interior, then the cost-minimizing combination of inputs that produce a given level of output is described by two conditions: (1) The optimal input bundle must lie *on* the relative isoquant, and (2) the marginal rate of technical substitution, also defined as the ratio of the marginal products of input 1 to input 2, must equal the ratio of the prices of input 1 to input 2.

Comparative Statics

Comparative statics analysis reveals interesting information about the relationships among output, inputs, and input prices. While holding output constant, one can show that if the price of an input that is used in positive amounts rises, then the minimum cost of producing that output will also rise. In addition, the amount of the input in question that is used either stays constant or decreases, but it never increases. If the prices of all inputs increase by the same factor, then the cost-minimizing bundle of inputs will remain unchanged, and the minimum cost of producing an output will rise by the same factor.

Suppose, instead, that we hold input prices constant but allow output to change. As output increases, holding input prices constant, the cost-minimizing combinations of inputs map out the **output expansion path**, from which the long-run total cost function is derived. As output rises, if the quantity demanded of an input rises (falls), the input is said to be **normal (inferior)**. If the production function is **homothetic,** the output-expansion path is a ray through the origin.

Returns to Scale

Production functions can exhibit constant, increasing, or decreasing returns to scale. If **constant returns to scale** (CRTS) prevail, an increase in the scale of production by s — that is, s times the quantities of *all* inputs used in production — results in s times the original level of output; output increases more than s times for **increasing returns to scale** (IRTS) and less than s times for **decreasing returns to scale** (DRTS). This responsiveness of output to a change in the scale of production is measured by the **scale elasticity of output,** or the percentage change in output y for a percentage change in the scale of production s.

When the production function is homothetic, the cost-minimizing problem can be expressed in terms of one variable: the scale factor, s. In this case, the same method used in Chapter 8 for deriving the short-run total cost from the production function can be employed here. Thus, **long-run marginal costs** LMC(y) and **long-run average costs** LAC(y) have the same relationship as their short-run counterparts. Another important relationship is between the returns to scale and the LAC(y) curve. If there are IRTS, the LAC(y) curve declines; for DRTS, the LAC(y) curve increases.

Relationship Between the Short-Run and Long-Run Curves

For every output level, there is a cost-minimizing combination of inputs and, hence, an optimal plant size or a level of the fixed input that is optimal for that output during production in the short run. For example, at some output — call it y' — there is a short-run cost curve that is tangent to the long-run cost curve. For output levels

larger or smaller than y', short-run costs exceed long-run costs because there is a larger or smaller use of the fixed factor that would produce the output at lower costs in the long run. Where the long- and short-run costs are tangent, so are the SAC(y) and LAC(y) curves at y'. Again, at higher and lower levels than y', SAC(y) exceeds LAC(y). At y', the long- and short-run marginal costs are equal. For larger output levels, the cost increases from additional output are smaller in the long run than in the short run [LMC(y) < SMC(y)], but for smaller output levels, the *cost savings* are larger in the long run than in the short run [LMC(y) > SMC(y)].

Costs and the Market Structure

A review of these various long-run relationships gives us some insight into the conditions under which we would expect to find firms. If the production technology exhibits DRTS throughout, we would expect the good to be produced at the smallest possible scale; that is, by the household. For CRTS, there is neither an advantage nor a disadvantage to producing at a larger scale and, hence, no compelling reason to observe firms. However, for IRTS, there is a definite disadvantage from small-scale production, and we would expect to see a few large firms. Finally, if the LAC(y) curve is U-shaped and the output corresponding to the minimum value is relatively small, we might expect to see many small firms in the market. Alternatively, if the minimum value of the LAC(y) curve is relatively large, we might expect to see a monopoly or oligopoly.

Key Words

Complements and substitutes in production
Conditional input demand functions
Homothetic production functions
Input substitution
Isocost curves
Isoquants
Long run
Long-run average costs (LAC)
Long-run marginal costs (LMC)
Marginal rate of technical substitution (MRTS)
Normal and inferior inputs
Output expansion path
Returns to scale
Scale elasticity of output

Case Study: Is the End of the World in Sight?

In the early 1960s, the Club of Rome published a report, *The Limits to Growth*,[1] that created great anxiety among politicians, academicians, and the general population for the following decade. Using computer models of the world economy, the Club of Rome prophesied that doomsday was near at hand. Developing nations of the world were rapidly depleting the earth's natural resources, and without resources, production of consumption goods was impossible. The Club made a strong warning to conserve our natural resources or accept the consequences of our extravagant behavior.

Panic struck many countries around the world. In Japan, land speculation and inflation increased, and policies of rapid industrial growth met resistance from environmental groups and the general public. Many people, however, were skeptical of the report, arguing that it promoted unnecessary panic. J. Stiglitz wrote a paper[2] showing that if assumptions different from those adopted by the Club of Rome were made, the world could go on indefinitely with everyone enjoying some constant level of consumption, even with a finite stock of resources! Although Stiglitz did not deny that human activity may indeed result in the demise of the world, his paper suggested that it would not necessarily result from exhaustion of our natural resources.

A Given the Club of Rome's conclusions, what do you think the long-run production function assumed in their report looked like? Explain.

B Describe a production function relationship alternative to the one in question **A**, which Stiglitz may have had in mind. If this represented the true "production function" for the world economy, why would resource exhaustion be less of a problem? Do prices of inputs have anything to do with the argument? Explain.

C It would seem that a judicious conclusion to make from this debate is something in between the argument of the Club of Rome and that of Stiglitz. Indeed, conventional supplies are nonrenewable, but this does not necessarily imply that future economic growth must be limited. You gave one argument for this in question **B**. Suggest other reasons that a declining resource base may not stifle future growth. What other changes might take place in the economy?

Exercises

Multiple-Choice

Choose the correct answer to each question. There is only one correct answer to each question.

1 For a given output, long-run average cost—$LAC(y)$—equals short-run average cost—$SAC(y)$—and $LAC(y)$ is greater than long-run marginal cost, $LMC(y)$. Then,
  a The $LAC(y)$ curve is rising.
  b The $LAC(y)$ curve is falling.
  c The $SAC(y)$ curve is at its minimum.
  d $SAC(y)$ equals $LMC(y)$.
  e Only **c** and **d** are true.

2 The production function $y = z_1 + 2z_2 + 5$ exhibits which of the following?
  a IRTS
  b CRTS
  c DRTS
  d Diminishing marginal product of labor
  e None of the above

3 If the marginal rate of technical substitution of input 2 for input 1, $MRTS(z_1, z_2)$, is $\frac{1}{3}$ in firm A but $\frac{2}{3}$ in firm B, then
  a Only firm A is minimizing its production costs.
  b Only firm B is minimizing its production costs.
  c Firm A's amount of input 2 is twice that of firm B.
  d Output in firm A could be increased if firm A traded 3 of input 1 for 2 of firm B's input 2.
  e None of the above is true.

[1] D. H. Meadows, D. L. Meadows, J. Randers, W. W. Behrens III (1972), *The Limits to Growth*, New York: Universe Books.
[2] J. Stiglitz (1974), "Growth with Exhaustible Natural Resources: Efficient and Optimal Growth Paths," *The Review of Economic Studies*, Symposium on the Economics of Exhaustible Resources, pp. 139–152.

For questions **4** and **5**, refer to Figure 9.1.

FIGURE 9.1

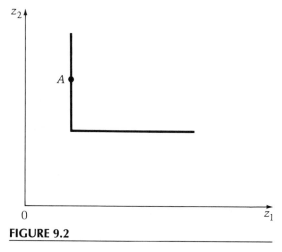

FIGURE 9.2

4 If the price of input 1 is $10 per unit, then

a Five units of input 2 will minimize the cost of producing 10 units of output.

b The price of input 2 is $400.

c There must be IRTS.

d The total outlay (cost) of 10 units of output is $1000.

e None of the above.

5 If the firm is currently operating at a plant size of 5 units of input 2 while producing 10 units of output in the short run, then

a It would be minimizing the costs of producing 10 units of output in the long run.

b It could reduce the production costs of producing 10 units of output in the long run by building a smaller plant.

c It could reduce the production costs of producing 10 units of output in the long run by building a larger plant.

d 100 units of input 1 minimize the short-run variable costs of producing 10 units of ouput.

e Both **b** and **d** are true.

6 At point A on the isoquant in Figure 9.2, which statement is true?

a The marginal products of both input 2 and input 1 are negative.

b The marginal products of both input 2 and input 1 are zero.

c The marginal product of input 2 is zero, and the marginal product of input 1 is positive.

d The marginal product of input 2 is positive, and the marginal product of input 1 is zero.

e None of the above is true.

7 Suppose that a producer minimizes the cost of producing a certain output level with 200 units of labor and 100 units of capital. Then

a The per-unit price of capital per unit must be twice as expensive as labor per unit.

b Labor per unit must be twice as expensive as capital per unit.

c The marginal rate of technical substitution of capital for labor must equal $\frac{2}{1}$.

d The marginal rate of technical substitution of capital for labor must equal $\frac{1}{2}$.

e None of the above is true.

8 Suppose that the production function is $y = az_1 + bz_2$, so the marginal rate of technical substitution of input 2 for input 1 is a/b. If w_1 is the price of input 1, w_2 is the price of input 2, and $w_1/w_2 > a/b$, then

a Input 1 and input 2 are complements in production.

b Only input 2 will be used to minimize the cost of producing any output level.

c Only input 1 will be used to minimize the cost of producing any output level.

d The marginal cost of production is rising.

e None of the above is true.

9 Suppose that the production function for good Y is given by

$$y = \min(2z_1, 3z_2)$$

Then,

a LMC(y) is constant for all output y.

b The ratio of input 1 to input 2 required by the production process is $\frac{2}{3}$.

c The ratio of input 1 to input 2 required by the production process is $\frac{3}{2}$.

d Both **a** and **b** are true.

e Both **a** and **c** are true.

10 The marginal rate of technical substitution of input 2 for input 1

a Equals the absolute value of the slope of the isoquant at every point

b Is the amount of input 2 that can be replaced by a unit of input 1 to keep output at the same level

c Is declining for convex isoquants

d All the above

e Only **a** and **c**

11 Conditional input demand functions give which of the following?

a The maximum quantities of inputs that can be purchased at various input prices

b The cost-minimizing quantities of inputs, conditional on an output level and input prices

c The combinations of inputs that can be purchased at various total costs

d The combinations of inputs that can produce a particular output level

e None of the above

12 The conditional input demands for input 1 and input 2, given the production function $y = \min(az_1, bz_2)$, are

a $z_1 = ay$, $z_2 = by$

b $z_1 = by$, $z_2 = ay$

c $z_1 = y/a$, $z_2 = y/b$

d $z_1 = y/b$, $z_2 = y/a$

e None of the above

13 At point A in Figure 9.3, which statement is true?

a The marginal productivity per dollar of input 1 exceeds the marginal productivity per dollar of input 2.

b The marginal productivity per dollar of input 2 exceeds the marginal productivity per dollar of input 1.

c Total costs of producing y^* units of output are minimized.

d The ratio of the marginal product of input

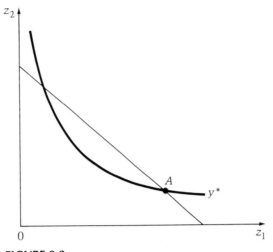

FIGURE 9.3

1 to input 2 exceeds the ratio of the input prices of input 1 to input 2.

e None of the above.

14 If the production function in Figure 9.4 is homothetic, then

a The marginal rate of substitution is constant along the ray $0A$.

b If the minimal cost of producing 1 unit of output is C^*, then the minimal cost of producing $\frac{1}{2}$ unit of output must be $\frac{1}{2}C^*$.

c All cost-minimizing bundles for the input price ratio w_1^*/w_2^* lie on the ray $0A$.

d All the above.

e Only **a** and **c**.

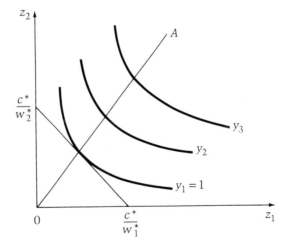

FIGURE 9.4

True-False

15 An LAC(y) curve is U-shaped because input prices are decreasing for low output levels and increasing for high output levels.

16 If a production technology exhibits IRTS, then a 10% increase in output will result in less than a 10% increase in the long-run total costs of production.

17 If an equal percentage increase in the use of all inputs results in a smaller percentage increase in the quantity produced, a firm's production function is said to exhibit decreasing returns to scale.

18 The scale elasticity of output equals the slope of the production function, $Y(s)$.

19 Since short-run and long-run marginal costs are equal at the point at which the short- and long-run cost curves are tangent, the LMC(y) curve has the same slope as the SMC(y) curve.

20 To minimize the costs of producing a given amount of output, the marginal products of all inputs must be equal.

21 If a production process uses the two inputs of labor and capital, then an increase in the wage rate will cause a firm to increase its use of capital, with output held constant.

22 An increase in the wage rate always results in an increase in the use of capital, for constant total costs.

23 The isoquants for a production technology characterized by fixed proportions are straight lines.

24 DRTS implies that the LAC(y) curve is decreasing.

25 Any input bundle on an isocost curve yields a higher output than any point below the isocost curve.

26 Isocost curves are homogeneous of degree one in input prices.

27 The costs of producing a given level of output falls when the price of an inferior factor of production increases.

28 The LAC(y) curve intersects the LMC(y) curve where the average factor productivity $[Y(s)]/s$ is at a minimum.

Short Problems

29 You observe that a firm has increased its output during a particular month in response to an increase in demand and that it has experienced an increase in the average cost of production. Assuming that neither technology nor input prices have changed, can you tell whether the firm is producing in a region of increasing, constant, or decreasing returns to scale? Explain.

30 A firm minimizes its production costs subject to a quantity constraint $y = y^*$ (or, alternatively, maximizes output subject to costs equal to C^*), as illustrated in Figure 9.5 by point A. The firm produces its product with input 1 and input 2, which cost w_1 and w_2 per unit, respectively. What two conditions characterize this solution?

31 If a firm's production technology is characterized by CRTS for all output levels, then can the firm's SAC(y) curve be U-shaped? Explain, using diagrams.

32 Homothetic production functions have the property that the slopes of the isoquants are equal along a ray from the origin. Why does this imply that the cost-minimizing bundles of inputs lie along a ray from the origin for a particular ratio of input prices?

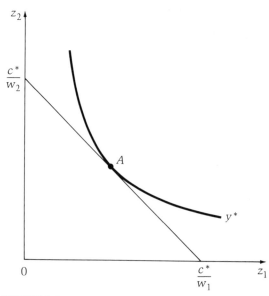

FIGURE 9.5

33 Explain how particular characteristics of the production technology for a good can influence the existence of firms and the market structure in that industry.

34 Calculate the arc scale elasticity of output between input combinations (z_1, z_2), $(4, 4)$, and $(16, 16)$ for the production function $y = z_1^{1/2} z_2$.

Long Problems

35 Suppose that a firm produces a product with two inputs, labor (input 1) and capital (input 2). Labor costs $3 per unit and capital costs $5 per unit. The firm maximizes output subject to the constraint that it does not spend more than $1000.

   a Draw the firm's cost constraint. Give the firm a set of convex isoquants and show an optimum for the output-maximizing firm on the graph. Label the optimal quantities of capital and labor z_2^* and z_1^* and the isoquant $y = 100$.

   b Using the same isoquants you used in **a**, show the firm's optimum, which minimizes the costs subject to the constraint that $y = 100$. What is the level of cost at the new optimum? How do the optimal values of labor and capital compare with those you found in **a**?

   c Suppose that the wage rises to $5 per unit. Show the effect of this increase on the quantity demanded of labor when (1) the firm maximizes output subject to the constraint that costs are $1000, and (2) the firm minimizes costs subject to the constraint that $y = 100$.

36 Suppose that the long-run total cost of producing 100 units of output is $1000. Labor (input 1) costs $10 per unit, capital (input 2) costs $10 per unit, and these are the only two inputs used in production. The firm is currently producing 100 units of output and is using the cost-minimizing combination of 50 labor and 50 capital.

   a On an isoquant diagram, show that an increase in output from 100 units to 150 units will result in higher short-run total costs, average costs, and marginal costs than in the long-run counterparts.

   b Show that a decrease in output from 100 units to 50 units will result in higher short-run total costs and average costs than in the long-run counterparts, but will result in marginal costs that are lower in the short run than in the long run.

   c Give an intuitive explanation for these relationships between the short- and long-run cost curves.

37 The table shows a relationship between output y and long-run total cost $TC(y)$ for a firm.

y	$TC(y)$	y	$TC(y)$
100	100	400	300
200	150	500	425
300	200	600	600

   a Draw a set of appropriate isoquants and isocosts, assuming two inputs 1 and 2.

   b In another diagram, draw the $LAC(y)$ and $LMC(y)$ curves of the firm.

   c In the diagram for question **b**, draw the $SAC(y)$ curve when input 2 is optimally chosen for 600 units of output.

38 Show how you would derive the firm's $TC(y)$ curve given constant factor prices of $100/unit of input 1 and $200/unit of input 2 and a set of convex isoquants for the firm. Also assume that the firm's production technology is homothetic and initially exhibits IRTS for low output levels and eventually exhibits CRTS for *all* higher output levels. What do the corresponding long-run marginal cost and average cost curves look like? Explain.

*39 Four production functions are

$$y = z_1^{1/2} z_2^{1/2} \qquad (1)$$

$$y = 2z_1 + \frac{z_2}{2} \qquad (2)$$

$$y = 2z_1^{1/4} + \frac{z_2}{2} \qquad (3)$$

$$y = \min(z_1, z_2) \qquad (4)$$

   a Determine whether the production functions exhibit increasing, decreasing, or constant returns to scale for all levels of output. Explain.

   b Express the production functions in terms of one variable, the scale factor s. Then derive an expression for the point scale elasticity of output for each newly defined production function.

   c Determine which of the production functions are homothetic.

40 Suppose that 10 units of a good can be made with one of only three fixed-proportion technologies: Process A uses 10 units of capital (input 1) and 2 units of labor (input 2); process B uses 5 units of capital and 8 units of labor; process C uses 2 units of capital and 15 units of labor.

a Draw the "kinked isoquant" curve for 10 units of output.

b Can 10 units of output be made with $3\frac{1}{2}$ units of capital and $11\frac{1}{2}$ units of labor? If so, how can this be achieved? Can 10 units of output be made with $9\frac{1}{6}$ units of capital and 3 units of labor? If so, how can this be achieved?

c What do your answers in **b** imply about the restrictiveness (or unrestrictiveness) of the assumption of smooth isoquants?

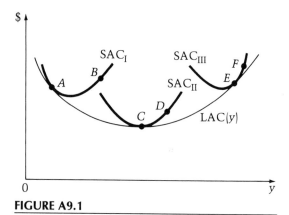

FIGURE A9.1

Answers to Chapter 9

Case Study

A The long-run production function exhibited fixed proportions, where no or little substitution between exhaustible resources and other inputs is possible.

B Stiglitz allowed for greater substitutability between resources and other inputs, a characteristic of the Cobb–Douglas production function, for example. In this case, diminishing resources could be replaced by other inputs; for example, capital. As a resource is exploited, its price rises, encouraging firms to replace it with other inputs.

C The long-run production function is based on existing technology. New types of technology (for example, replacing oil with solar power) could enable the world to circumvent the problem of a shrinking resource base.

Multiple-Choice

1 b	2 c	3 d	4 b	5 b
6 c	7 e	8 b	9 e	10 d
11 b	12 c	13 b	14 e	

True-False

15 F	16 T	17 T	18 F	19 F
20 F	21 T	22 F	23 F	24 F
25 F	26 T	27 F	28 F	

Short Problems

29 No, it is not possible to tell. Recall that returns to scale deal with the long run because such returns ask how output changes when *all* factors

of production are variable. A month may not be long enough for all inputs to vary. If the firm was operating at point *A* in Figure A9.1 and moved along SAC$_I$ to point *B*, then it is on the IRTS section of the LAC(y) curve. If it started at point *C* on SAC$_{II}$ and moved to *D*, then it is on the CRTS section of the LAC(y) curve. SAC$_{III}$ indicates a situation in which the firm is on the DRTS portion of the LAC(y) curve.

30 Costs are minimized when the input bundle z_1^*, z_2^* satisfies

$$\text{MRTS}(z_1^*, z_2^*) = w_1/w_2 \quad \text{and} \quad y^* = f(z_1^*, z_2^*)$$

31 Yes. Figure A9.2 illustrates a production technology that exhibits CRTS and the short-run average cost curves are U-shaped.

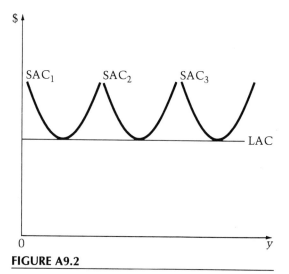

FIGURE A9.2

32 Cost-minimizing input bundles satisfy the condition $\text{MRTS}(z_1, z_2) = w_1/w_2$. That is, $\text{MRTS}(z_1, z_2)$ is equal to the constant input price ratio for all output levels. Since the $\text{MRTS}(z_1, z_2)$ is constant along a ray from the origin for homothetic production functions, those input bundles along the ray are cost-minimizing bundles for the input price ratio equal to the constant $\text{MRTS}(z_1, z_2)$.

33 If the production technology exhibits IRTS for all levels of output, then only one firm can be sustained in the industry. Since average costs of production fall as output increases, the firm has an incentive to capture all the demand in the market at any given price to have the largest output possible. For CRTS, there is no obvious incentive for firms to enter because a good can be produced at the same average cost regardless of the scale of production. If the production technology exhibits DRTS, then the good is best produced at the smallest possible scale; for example, by the household. For an initial range of IRTS that is not too large, firms will arise. Where the efficient scale is small, a competitive market will develop; where the scale is large, oligopoly is likely to be the market structure.

34 The arc scale elasticity is defined by

$$e = \frac{\Delta y/y}{\Delta s/s}$$

where y is output, and s is scale of production.
For the particular problem,

$$\frac{\Delta s}{s} = \frac{(16 - 4)}{(16 + 4)/2} = \frac{12}{10} = \frac{6}{5}$$

At $(4, 4)$, $y = 2 \times 4 = 8$; at $(16, 16)$, $y' = 4 \times 16 = 64$. Then,

$$\frac{\Delta y}{y} = \frac{(64 - 8)}{(64 + 8)/2} = \frac{56}{36}$$

The arc elasticity is $e = (56/36)(5/6) = 35/27$. Note that the production function exhibits IRTS.

Long Problems

35 a The output-maximizing input bundle, subject to a total outlay of $1000, is given by point A in Figure A9.3.

b The cost-minimizing bundle subject to $y = 100$ is the same point A in the figure. Costs are $1000 at this point.

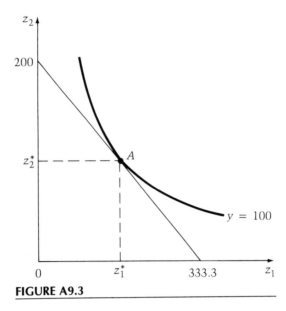

FIGURE A9.3

c (1) If labor costs rise to $5 per unit, the isocost line will pivot inward, as shown in Figure A9.4a, when costs are constrained to equal $1000. This has the effect of reducing the quantity demanded of labor from z_1^A to z_1^B as shown.
(2) If the firm minimizes costs subject to $y = 100$, the isocost in Figure A9.4a shifts out parallelly until it is tangent to the isoquant at point C, as shown in Figure A9.4b. The change in the quantity of labor is measured by the substitution effect: The quantity of labor demanded falls with an increase in the wage rate, holding output constant.

36 a The isoquants $y = 100$ and $y = 150$ are shown in Figure A9.5. In the long run, the costs of producing 150 units of output are given by the isocost curve AB. In the short run, capital is fixed at 50, and costs of production are given by isocost CD, which are larger than the long-run costs. Since average costs = total costs/output, $\text{LAC}(y) < \text{SAC}(y)$ for $y = 150$. The marginal costs of producing the additional 50 units of output in the long run are

$$\frac{\text{costs given by } AB - 1000}{50}$$

In the short run, the marginal costs are

$$\frac{\text{costs given by } CD - 1000}{50}$$

(a)

(b)

FIGURE A9.4

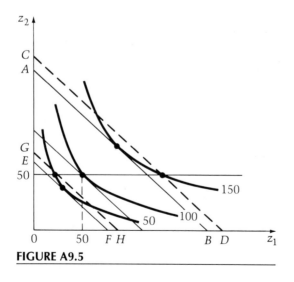

FIGURE A9.5

Hence, $SMC(y) > LMC(y)$.

b The long-run cost of producing 50 is given by isocost curve EF; the short-run cost of producing 50 is given by GH. As before, $STC(y) > LTC(y)$. Note that the $LMC(y)$ is

$$\frac{1000 - \text{costs given by } EF}{50}$$

and the $SMC(y)$ is

$$\frac{1000 - \text{costs given by } GH}{50}$$

Since costs for EF are less than costs given by GH, $LMC(y) > SMC(y)$.

c In the short run, the relationships described hold because capital is not flexible. In the long run, inputs can be adjusted to lower costs. For increases in output, $SMC(y) > LMC(y)$ because the *increase* in costs is greater in the short run;

for decreases in output, $SMC(y) < LMC(y)$ because the *cost-savings* from decreasing output are less in the short run than in the long run.

37 a Let $w_1 = w_2 = \$1$. Then the isocost–isoquant map can be drawn as in Figure A9.6.

b The $LAC(y) = LTC/y$ and $LMC(y) = \Delta LTC/\Delta y$ schedules are shown in the table.

Q	LAC(y)	LMC(y)
100	1	1
200	0.75	0.50
300	0.66	0.50
400	0.75	1
500	0.85	1.25
600	1	1.75

The $LAC(y)$ and $LMC(y)$ curves are plotted in Figure A9.7. $LMC(y)$ is plotted in between quantity values; for example, the $LMC(y)$ between 100 and 200 units of output is plotted at $y = 150$.

c When z_2 is optimally chosen for $y = 600$, the cost-minimizing level is given by z_2^* in Figure A9.6. For any output greater or less than $y = 600$, $SAC(y)$ will exceed $LAC(y)$. For $y > 600$, $SMC(y)$ will exceed long-run marginal costs, and for $y < 600$, $SMC(y) < LMC(y)$. These relationships are shown in Figure A9.7 by $SAC(y)$ and $SMC(y)$.

38 An example of a production function that satisfies the technological requirements is shown in Figure A9.8. At an output of 10, 5 units of

FIGURE A9.7

FIGURE A9.6

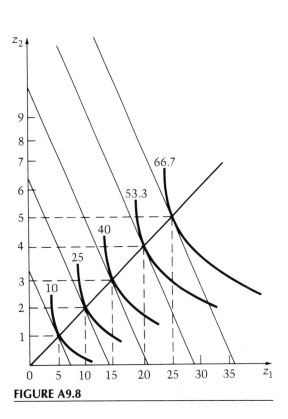

FIGURE A9.8

labor (input 1) and 1 unit of capital (input 2) are required. The scale is doubled and output increased by $2\frac{1}{2}$ times. The scale increases by 50% from 10 labor and 2 capital, and output increases to 40 (75%). Beyond this point, an increase in the scale by some proportion increases output by the same proportion. For simplicity, the production function is assumed to be homothetic, so the expansion path is a straight line from the origin.

Because the production function is homothetic, we know that the costs of production increase proportionately with the scale of production. The costs are

$$TC(10) = 700$$
$$TC(25) = 1400$$
$$TC(40) = 2100$$
$$TC(53.3) = 2800$$
$$TC(66.7) = 3500$$

The cost function is graphed in Figure A9.9a. Average costs initially decline up to 40 units of output and are constant afterward. Marginal costs fall initially and then increase up to 40 units of output and are constant thereafter. The LMC(y) and LAC (y) schedules are shown in the table.

Q	LMC(y)	LAC(y)
10	70	70
25	46.6	56
40	46.6	52.5
53.3	52.5	52.5
66.7	52.5	52.5

The long-run marginal and average cost curves are graphed in Figure A9.9b.

*39 a (1) CRTS. Let $y^0 = (z_1^0 z_2^0)^{1/2}$. Multiply z_1^0 and z_2^0 by λ. Then the new output is

$$y' = (\lambda z_1^0 \lambda z_2^0)^{1/2} = \lambda (z_1^0 z_2^0)^{1/2} = \lambda y^0$$

(2) CRTS. Let $y^0 = 2z_1^0 + z_2^0/2$. Multiply z_1^0 and z_2^0 by λ. Then the new output is

$$y' = 2\lambda z_1^0 + \frac{\lambda z_2^0}{2} = \lambda \left(2z_1^0 + \frac{z_2^0}{2}\right) = \lambda y^0$$

(3) DRTS. Let $y^0 = 2(z_1^0)^{1/4} + z_2^0/2$. Multiply z_1^0 and z_2^0 by λ. Then the new output is

$$y' = 2(\lambda z_1^0)^{1/4} + \frac{\lambda z_2^0}{2}$$

so

$$y' = \lambda^{1/4} 2(z_1^0)^{1/4} + \frac{\lambda z_2^0}{2} < \lambda \left(2(z_1^0)^{1/4} + \frac{z_2^0}{2}\right) = \lambda y^0$$

(a)

(b)

FIGURE A9.9

Hence, since y' is less than λy^0, the production function exhibits DRTS.

(4) CRTS. Let $y^0 = \min(z_1^0, z_2^0)$. Multiply z_1^0 and z_2^0 by λ. Then,

$$y' = \min(\lambda z_1^0, \lambda z_2^0) = \lambda \min(z_1^0, z_2^0) = \lambda y^0.$$

b (1) Let $z_1^0 = 1$, $z_2^0 = 1$. Then $Y(1) = 1$ and $Y(s) = s^{1/2} s^{1/2} = s$.

(2) Let $z_1^0 = 1$, $z_2^0 = 1$. Then $Y(1) = 2 + \frac{1}{2} = 2\frac{1}{2}$ and $Y(s) = 2s + s/2 = 2\frac{1}{2} s$.

(3) Let $z_1^0 = 1$, $z_2^0 = 1$. Then $Y(1) = 2^{1/4} + \frac{1}{2} = 1.69$ and $Y(s) = 2s^{1/4} + s/2$.

(4) Let $z_1^0 = 1$, $z_2^0 = 1$. Then $Y(1) = 1$ and $Y(s) = s$.

Calculus is needed to calculate output elasticities, where output elasticity $= (dy/ds)(s/y)$. Since production functions (1), (2), and (4) exhibit CRTS, the output elasticity equals 1. For production function (3).

$$e = \frac{(\frac{1}{2} s^{-3/4} + \frac{1}{2}) s}{2s^{1/4} + s/2} = \frac{(s^{1/4} + s)}{2(2s^{1/4} + s/2)}$$

c (Need calculus). If a production function is homothetic, then along a ray from the origin, the MRTS of input 2 for input 1 is constant. Since the input ratio is constant along a ray, the MRTS for a homothetic production function must depend only on the input ratio. Since production functions (1), (2), and (4) exhibit CRTS, they are homothetic. To see this, consider (1).

$$\text{MRTS} = \frac{\text{MP}_1}{\text{MP}_2} = \frac{z_2}{z_1}$$

To check whether production function (3) is homothetic, the MRTS is derived:

$$\text{MRTS} = \frac{\text{MP}_1}{\text{MP}_2} = \frac{0.5 \, z_1^{-3/4}}{0.5} = \frac{1}{z_1^{3/4}}$$

Since MRTS depends on absolute rather than relative amounts of the input, it is not constant along a ray from the origin; therefore, the production function is not homothetic.

*40 a The isoquant is given by ABC in Figure A9.10.

b If $3\frac{1}{2}$ units of capital and $11\frac{1}{2}$ units of labor are used, then a combination of processes B and C is used. Let λ be the proportion of the 10 units of output that is produced using process B, and $1 - \lambda$ the proportion of output produced with process C. (See point D.) Then, since process B

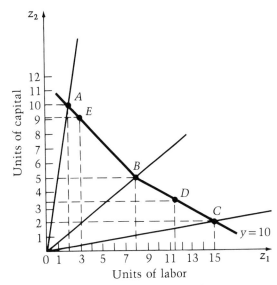

FIGURE A9.10

uses 5 units of input 2 and 8 units of input 1 and process C uses 2 units of input 2 and 15 units of input 1, the actual amounts of labor and capital that will be used to produce 10 units of output are

$$z_1 = \lambda 8 + (1 - \lambda)15 = 15 - 7\lambda$$

and

$$z_2 = \lambda 5 + (1 - \lambda)2 = 2 + 3\lambda$$

Substitute $z_2 = 3\frac{1}{2}$ and $z_1 = 11\frac{1}{2}$ into these expressions to get $\lambda = \frac{1}{2}$. That is, $3\frac{1}{2}$ units of input 2 and $11\frac{1}{2}$ units of input 1 will yield 10 units if 5 units of output are produced using process B and 5 units of output are produced with process C.

To use 3 units of labor and $9\frac{1}{6}$ units of capital, processes A and B are needed. Now let λ be the proportion of output produced with process A. Then,

$$3 = \lambda 2 + (1 - \lambda)8 \Longrightarrow 3 = 8 - 6\lambda \Longrightarrow \lambda = \frac{5}{6}$$

and

$$9\tfrac{1}{6} = \lambda 10 + (1 - \lambda)5 \Longrightarrow 9\tfrac{1}{6} = 5 + 5\lambda \Longrightarrow \lambda = \frac{5}{6}$$

Hence, $\frac{5}{6}$ of the 10 units of output are produced with process A and $\frac{1}{6}$ with process B. See point E in Figure A9.10.

c The answers in **b** give a justification for the assumption that isoquants are smooth.

10

THE THEORY OF PERFECT COMPETITION

Chapter Summary

Assumptions of Perfect Competition

Perfect competition is a compelling model for understanding our price system. The formal theory is built on the assumption of the existence of a **large number** of **price-taking** buyers and sellers, **perfect information**, a **homogeneous product**, and **perfect mobility**. One is hard-pressed to come up with real-world examples that have these characteristics of the ideal, perfectly competitive market. Some agricultural markets appear to come closest; but in the case of wheat, for example, the existence of a small number of large, price-setting grain companies makes that example questionable. Then why bother with perfect competition?

Many of the reasons for studying perfect competition can be seen in the context of a simple exchange economy — an economy in which goods are traded but not produced. Consider two individuals, Diane and Curtis, on an island, each with an initial allocation of two island goods, fish and bananas. Curtis has all the fish; Diane has all the bananas. A shipwrecked sailor — the **Walrasian auctioneer** — suddenly appears and begins to announce prices at which Diane and Curtis can trade their goods. Given these prices, Diane and Curtis determine their demands and supplies of bananas and fish that maximize their utilities, subject to their budget constraint de-fined by their initial allocations and the announced prices. An **equilibrium** occurs when total demands equal total supplies at the announced prices.

The Competitive Equilibrium

The competitive equilibrium of this simple exchange economy highlights some fundamental characteristics of perfect competition. First, given the initial allocation of goods in the economy, the gains from trade are realized. If the initial allocation had been different, the final equilibrium would also have been different. Note that the competitive equilibrium does not rectify initial inequalities. (This issue will be discussed in more detail in Chapter 16.) Most important, however, is the fact that perfect competition provides a **Pareto-efficient** allocation of resources in the absence of externalities. This means that no reallocation can make some people better off without making others worse off.

Just how applicable is this model of perfect competition? We already understand that models do not have to capture all the complexities of the real world to be useful. In providing an abstraction of the salient features of markets that look like perfect competition, the forces at work in this model appear very much like the ones that direct the allocation of resources in a capitalistic price system. **Experimental economics** has provided strong support for the robustness of the competitive model. In simple environments of economic trading, the outcomes predicted by the competitive model are often attained, even when the assumptions of many traders and perfect information are relaxed.

The Short Run

The perfectly competitive firm is assumed to maximize profits. The firm will achieve this objective in the short run by producing an output level at which marginal revenue equals the short-run marginal cost of production. Since the firm is a price-taker, this rule is restated as **price equals marginal cost**. There are two additional requirements for profit maximization. First, the output level for which $p = SMC(y)$ must be on the upward-sloping portion of the marginal cost curve. Second, the firm must be able to cover at least its variable costs of production; otherwise, it will simply shut down and avoid these costs. These requirements imply that the short-run supply curve for the firm is the upward-sloping part of the short-run marginal cost curve above the average variable cost curve. The industry short-run supply curve is the horizontal summation of the firms' short-run supply curves. **Competitive equilibrium** in the short run is described by the intersection of the aggregate demand and the short-run supply curves. This equilibrium is efficient because there are no gains from further trading. The total surplus of consumers and producers is maximized under this allocation.

The Long Run

As in the short run, the long-run equilibrium is characterized by demand equals supply; however, the **industry long-run supply curve** is more complicated to derive. As in the short run, each firm makes its long-run plan by equating its **long-run marginal cost** and the price. The difference is that the industry long-run supply is not simply the horizontal summation of the firms' long-run marginal cost curves. In the long run, firms can enter the industry if economic profits are being made by established firms. Similarly, established firms can exit the industry if they are making losses. Hence, the **long-run equilibrium** for the industry is not achieved until profits equal zero. In the former case, profits are reduced to zero by

the entry of new firms and the expansion of output; in the latter case, the exit of firms and the consequent reduction of output raise profits to zero. In long-run equilibrium, then, price equals **efficient average cost** [the minimum of the $LAC(y)$ curve], which in turn equals $LMC(y)$ $SAC(y)$, and $SMC(y)$. That is, all firms must operate at the minimum of their $LAC(y)$ curves in the long-run equilibrium.

What does this equilibrium condition tell us about the long-run supply curve of the industry? It depends on whether the prices of inputs as industry output expands stay constant, increase, or decrease; that is, if the industry is a **constant-cost, increasing-cost**, or **decreasing-cost industry**, respectively. Consider a constant-cost industry. Starting at some long-run equilibrium, suppose there is a shift in the demand curve to the right. Established firms will equate their $SMC(y)$ to the increased price and contemplate a further increase in output in the long run. However, entrants will also see that there are profits to be had by following this same rule and will enter the industry. By the very nature of a constant-cost industry, the expansion of output by both the established firms and entrants *will not increase the costs of production*. Entry will continue until price is once again equal to efficient average cost, yielding a long-run industry supply that is horizontal at the minimum of the $LAC(y)$ curve. Similar analysis indicates that the long-run industry supply curve for an increasing-cost industry is positively sloped, whereas a decreasing-cost industry is characterized by a negatively sloped industry supply curve.

The effect on the competitive equilibrium of changes in exogenous variables — such as prices of substitute or complement goods, income, or technological change — can be analyzed by **comparative statics** exercises. Impediments to the competitive market mechanism (for example, rent control) will prevent the market-clearing price and quantity from being achieved, resulting in a loss of surplus. In particular, rent controls result in a noncompetitive equilibrium because they interfere with the allocative function of the price mechanism in perfect competition. Usually, such controls are aimed at some normative goal. Positive economic analysis can be used to determine whether these normative objectives are being achieved.

Key Words

Constant-, increasing-, decreasing-cost industries
Cost-benefit measures
Efficient average cost
Efficient scale of production
Exchange economy
Experimental economics
Externalities
Long-run competitive equilibrium
Market impediment

Pareto efficiency
Perfect competition
Perfect information
Price ceiling/price floor
Price-taking behavior (large numbers)
Producer and consumer surplus
Profit maximization
Short-run competitive equilibrium
Walrasian auctioneer

Case Study: The Market for Agricultural Commodities

The market for agricultural products in North America is characterized by many price-taking farmers and consumers. This competitive market captures the attention and concern of policy-makers because of the volatility in prices, and hence in incomes, that farmers face owing to random and often uncontrollable effects on their crops, especially weather. Even when farmers are fortunate enough to harvest a bumper crop, farm income suffers because the demands for most agricultural products are price-inelastic. An increase in the supply of a particular crop decreases the price and the farmers' incomes from that product.

In response to these problems, the government has proposed various schemes. We examine some of them in this case study. In considering the effects of these programs, let the initial competitive price of the agricultural commodity be $4 per bushel. For each of the three proposed schemes, analyze the short-run implications for the industry before entry or exit can occur.

Scheme 1—The government imposes a price floor of $8 per bushel on the agricultural commodity. Any quantity not sold to the public at that price is purchased by the government and destroyed.

Scheme 2—The government ensures that farmers will receive $8 per bushel by offering a per-unit subsidy on every unit of the commodity sold.

Scheme 3—Quotas are imposed on farmers' output of corn to raise the equilibrium price to $8 per bushel.

A Which program has the largest impact on the output of corn compared with the initial competitive equilibrium? Compare the change in quantity supplied by the farmers under each system.

B The original goal of these programs was to stabilize farm income. Which program has the largest impact on the revenues received by farmers? Which program offers the highest producer surplus for farmers?

C Which program is the most expensive for the government (and hence, the taxpayers) to implement? Discuss the merits of each program from the government's point of view.

Exercises

Multiple-Choice

Choose the correct answer to each question. There is only one correct answer to each question.

For questions **1** and **2**, refer to Figure 10.1. In

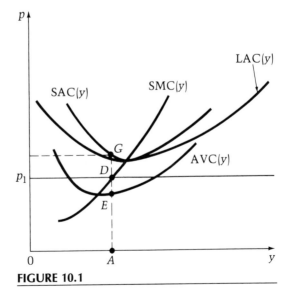

FIGURE 10.1

the short run, a representative profit-maximizing firm operates at a plant size with short-run average cost curve SAC(y).

1 If a firm faces a price p_1 in the short run, it will do which of the following?

    a Make positive profits

    b Incur a loss equal to DE times $0A$

    c Exit from the industry and make no loss at all

    d Incur a loss equal to GD times $0A$

    e None of the above

2 If all firms in the competitive industry have cost curves as shown in the figure, then in long-run equilibrium

    a There will be more firms in the industry than in short-run equilibrium.

    b Firms will make positive profits.

    c Prices will rise to the minimum of the LAC(y) curve.

    d Firms will make a loss equal to GD times $0A$.

    e None of the above.

3 If a perfectly competitive firm earns a profit of $1000 per year and faces CRTS in production, which of the following is true?

    a In the long run, it can double its profits by doubling all its inputs.

    b It can raise price as its profits begin to erode.

    c It can make the same profit in the long run.

    d It will make no profits at all as firms enter the industry.

    e None of the above.

4 An allocation of goods among individuals and resources among firms is said to be Pareto-optimal if

    a Consumers' surplus is maximized.

    b It is not possible to make someone better off without making anyone else worse off.

    c It is possible to make someone better off without making anyone else worse off.

    d The utilities of all individuals are equal.

    e Only **a** and **b**.

5 In the short run, an excise tax imposed on perfectly competitive firms is passed entirely onto the buyers in the form of a higher price if

    a Demand is perfectly price-inelastic.

    b Supply is perfectly price-elastic.

    c Demand is perfectly price-elastic.

    d Both **a** and **b**.

    e None of the above.

6 Figure 10.2 is an ordinary demand curve for good Y. If the income elasticity of demand for Y equals 0, then the area ABp^*

    a Underestimates the consumers' willingness to pay for the opportunity to purchase good Y at price p^*.

    b Overestimates the consumers' willingness to pay for the opportunity to purchase good Y at price p^*.

    c Is an exact measure of consumers' willingness to pay for the opportunity to purchase Y at price p^*.

    d Is one-half the consumers' true willingness to pay for the opportunity to purchase good Y at price p^*.

    e There is not enough information to answer this question.

7 Which of the following is *not* an assumption of perfect competition?

    a The number of suppliers is large enough that no one produces a significant proportion of the output, and all demanders and suppliers are price-takers.

    b All individuals have perfect knowledge.

    c The products sold by all firms in the market are homogeneous.

    d Each firm faces a downward-sloping demand curve.

    e All the above are assumptions of perfect competition.

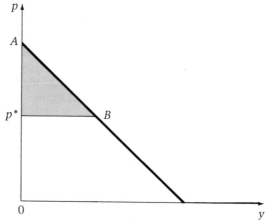

FIGURE 10.2

8 If an industry is an increasing-cost industry, then

   a The long-run industry supply curve is positively sloped.

   b The long-run industry supply curve is negatively sloped.

   c The supply curve for inputs used in the production is horizontal.

   d The short-run average cost curve cannot be U-shaped.

   e None of the above.

True-False

9 If all individuals have identical linear demand curves, then the price elasticity of the market demand in absolute value is higher at every price level than the absolute value of the price elasticity of the individual demands.

10 Since long-run profits for a competitive firm are always zero, it will never pay a competitive firm to adopt a cost-reducing innovation.

11 If a lump-sum tax is placed on firms in a competitive industry, the entire tax will be passed onto the consumers in the form of a higher price in the short run, but none of the tax will be passed onto the consumer in the long run.

12 The greater the increase in demand, the higher is the long-run price of a good produced in a competitive increasing-cost industry.

13 If each firm is initially earning positive profits in a perfectly competitive industry, then there will be entry of new firms, price will fall, and the output of each firm will be smaller in the final long-run equilibrium.

14 Since every firm in a competitive industry earns zero economic profit in long-run equilibrium, then a fall in the market price would mean that no firms could survive in the long run.

15 If all firms minimize costs and face the same input prices but different production functions, then all firms will use inputs in the same proportion.

16 The horizontal summation of the LMC(y) curves of individual firms is not the long-run supply curve for the industry.

17 If two individuals have identical preferences, there are no benefits from trade.

18 The competitive equilibrium price depends on the initial distribution of resources.

*19 A lump-sum subsidy to bread producers will shift the market demand for flour further to the right in the long run than will a per-unit subsidy on bread, if the total payments given to bread producers are equivalent under the two subsidy programs.

*20 The long-run price of wheat under a lump-sum subsidy paid to wheat farmers will result in a higher price of wheat in the long run than would a per-unit subsidy paid to wheat farmers, if the total subsidies paid to each farmer are equivalent under the two subsidy arrangements.

Short Problems

21 Consider a competitive industry with a long-run demand curve

$$y_d = 40 - 2p$$

and long-run supply curve

$$y_s = 4p - 20$$

   a Find the equilibrium price and quantity.

   b Suppose that consumers must buy the product from a third person who charges $6 per unit for his services. Find the new equilibrium quantity and price.

22 Discuss why "scalping" at sports events (individuals buy several tickets in advance and sell them for very high prices just before a game) may be desirable from an efficiency point of view. Usually this activity is frowned on by the promoters of such events. Why?

23 Compare the effect of a $1 per gallon tax on gasoline with a sales (ad valorem) tax of $t\%$ of total gasoline expenditures on equilibrium price and quantity, assuming that the gasoline market is competitive. Using a diagram, show when the two types of taxes will result in the identical equilibrium price and quantity.

24 The demand and supply curves for wheat in a bad and good year are shown in Figure 10.3. The demand curves are the same in the 2 years. What would happen to total expenditures on wheat if supply were to increase slightly to the right in Figure 10.3a? What would happen to

(a)   **(b)**

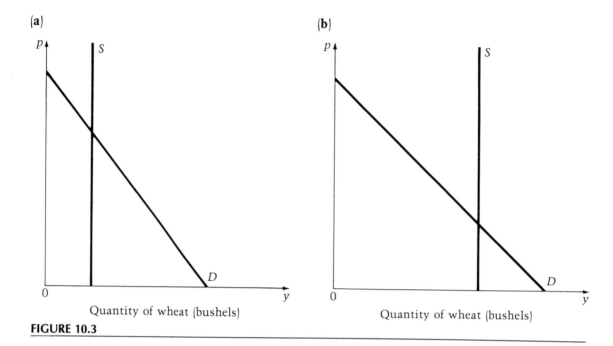

Quantity of wheat (bushels)   Quantity of wheat (bushels)

FIGURE 10.3

total expenditures if supply were to increase slightly to the right in Figure 10.3*b*? Explain.

25 Discuss this statement: Price controls are useful to provide adequate housing for those in the lower income levels who would not otherwise be able to afford it.

26 Suppose that a per-unit tax of $1 is placed on producers in a competitive market. Using diagrams, indicate whether none, some, or all of the tax is passed onto the consumer in the form of a higher price in the short run for each case.
    a Demand is perfectly price-elastic.
    b Demand is perfectly price-inelastic.
    c Supply is perfectly price-elastic.

Long Problems

27 A common agricultural policy is to assign quotas on egg production such that each producer is allowed to sell eggs only up to the amount allotted under his or her quota. Assume that eggs are produced in a perfectly competitive, constant-cost industry; individual quotas are set at a level less than the former output levels; and the government does not purchase any eggs from the producers.
    a Using diagrams, determine the short-run

effects of this quota scheme on the egg market and on an egg farmer. Would a farmer have the incentive to cheat by producing more than his or her quota? Explain.
    b If quotas are placed on the output of individual farmers but not on the industry output, then what will be the long-run effects? Explain, using diagrams.
    c Briefly discuss the advantages and disadvantages of such a quota system.

28 The table gives a relationship between the quantity of feed fed to a hen and the dozens of eggs obtained.

Feed fed (pounds)	0	4	8	12	16	20
Eggs obtained (dozens)	2	12	20	26	30	32

Assume that all other inputs are held constant and that their total cost is $5. Suppose that the cost of feed is $2 per pound and the price of eggs is $2 per dozen. Assume that eggs and feed are sold in a competitive market.
    a Calculate the following:
    (1) The profit-maximizing number of eggs to produce
    (2) The profit-maximizing amount of feed to give a hen

b Derive the marginal and average product curves for feed and the marginal and average cost curves. Plot the marginal cost, average total cost, and marginal revenue functions. Indicate your answer in **a**(1) by a point C.

29 Industry Y is a perfectly competitive, constant-cost industry. It is currently in a position of long-run equilibrium. Market demand in the industry is given by

$$y = 1500 - 25p$$

The short-run market supply curve is given by:

$$y = 15p - 100 \quad \text{for} \quad p \geq 10$$
$$= 0 \quad \text{for} \quad p < 10$$

There are 25 firms in the industry.

a Calculate the equilibrium market price and quantity and the equilibrium quantity produced by each firm.

b Each firm is currently operating at the optimal plant size. What must be the minimum short-run average variable costs for this plant and the efficient average cost? Explain.

c Now suppose that the government imposes a tax of $10 on producers for each unit of the commodity produced.

(1) Illustrate on a diagram the loss in consumer surplus plus producer surplus as a result of this tax. If the consumer surplus is to be an accurate measure of willingness to pay to purchase the good at lower prices, what must be true?

(2) What will happen to the price paid by consumers in the long run? Explain.

30 In the 1960s, the governments of the United States and Canada imposed price controls on natural gas. The price of natural gas was set below the world price.

a Using a diagram, show the short-run effects of the price ceiling on natural gas in the domestic market for natural gas and on one of the domestic firms.

b During this time, the prices of goods using natural gas—for example, electricity—were not controlled. Would you expect the price ceiling on natural gas to cause electricity to be cheaper than it otherwise would be in the short run? Use diagrams to answer. Assume that natural gas is used as a variable input in the production of electricity.

31 The federal government finds it necessary to increase its tax revenues. It decides that part of this increase will come from the imposition of a tax on a competitive industry that formerly has not been taxed. Two proposals are under consideration regarding the form of the tax:

(1) A licensing arrangement by which every firm in the industry must pay a flat fee of $F per year

(2) A tax on sales by which each firm would be required to pay a tax of $t on each unit produced and sold

Analyze the long-run effects of these alternative taxing schemes on
a Market price
b Output per firm
c Output of the industry
d The number of firms in the industry

32 Grand Ola, Inc. produces a breakfast cereal in a constant-cost, perfectly competitive industry. Its average cost curve is U-shaped. The firm is currently operating at $y = 10$. The minimum of the long-run average cost curve is at $y = 10$ with average costs equal to $30.

a What is the long-run equilibrium price of cereal? Explain.

b The price falls to $22. Should the firm shut down in the long run? Why or why not? Should it shut down in the short run? Why or why not?

c Suppose that the rent of the land on which the factory stands falls in the next period. If the price of cereal is $30, how does this rent decrease change the quantity that the firm produces in the short run? Explain and illustrate the effect of this rent decrease on the short-run cost curves.

d What effect will an increase in the price of wheat (an input) have on the long-run output of each firm? On the number of firms in the long run? On the long-run industry output? Explain.

e The producers of Nutty Bread, who use the Grand Ola breakfast cereal as an ingredient, receive a per-unit subsidy from the Department of Agriculture. The subsidies come from general tax funds. How will this affect the equilibrium price and industry output for breakfast cereal in the long run? Explain, using diagrams.

*33 Suppose that an advance in microchip technology reduces the average cost of producing computers by $100 at every output level. Assume that the long-run average cost curve is U-shaped and the computer industry is a constant-cost industry. Also assume that the minimum of the long-run average cost is at 400 units of output per year.

   a If the inventor of the new chip offered her invention to firms at a per-unit cost of $50, what would be the long-run effects on price and quantity produced by the firm and the industry as a result of the invention? Describe the effects, using diagrams.

   b Suppose that the inventor were to charge a fixed total royalty of $20,000 per year to each firm using the invention instead of the $50 royalty. Show the effect that this fee will have on the average and marginal cost curves of each firm. Under which royalty payment scheme would the long-run price of computers be lower? Explain.

Answers to Chapter 10

Case Study

A The results of the three schemes are illustrated in Figure A10.1. Under scheme (1), shown in Figure A10.1a, the price floor of $8 per bushel implies that although y_2 units are supplied, only y_1 units are demanded. The government must enter the commodity market and purchase the excess supply $(y_2 - y_1)$. Thus, although output has increased, the quantity actually consumed has fallen dramatically. Under scheme (2) in Figure A10.1b the supply curve shifts to S'. In these conditions, both the quantity supplied and the quan-

tity demanded increase to y_2 as the consumer price is allowed to fall to p_1. Under scheme 3 in Figure A10.1c, the government must ensure that output never rises above y_1 to guarantee a price of $8 per bushel. Thus, it is only when quotas are imposed that output actually falls relative to the competitive equilibrium commodity; scheme 3 reduces the output.

B When either a price floor or a per-unit subsidy is introduced, farmers receive $8 per bushel on the quantity that they supply to the market, y_2. Thus, each of the first two schemes raises farmers' incomes compared with the competitive equilibrium of $4 per bushel and output y_0. Under a quota system, the price per bushel is still $8, but output is only y_1, so revenues are much lower than under the first two schemes. The quota system will, however, yield higher revenues than the competitive equilibrium if demand is inelastic with respect to price. Producer surplus is the difference between the price actually received per unit of output and the price that producers are willing to accept for any given quantity, as measured by the height of the supply curve. The producer surplus under each scheme is illustrated in Figure A.10.1 by diagonal lines. Producer surplus is much larger under the first two schemes compared with the third.

C The cost to the government of a price-floor scheme is determined by the amount of excess supply it must purchase — in this case, $y_2 - y_1$ — at the price of $8 per bushel. In the per-unit subsidy case, the government must make up the dif-

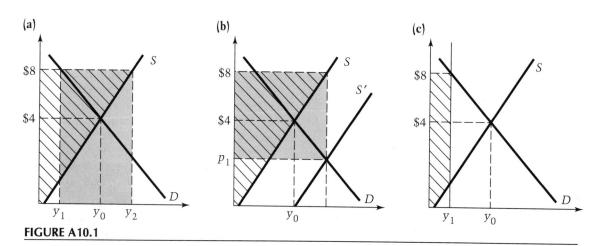

(a) **(b)** **(c)**

FIGURE A10.1

ference between the producer price ($8 per bushel) and the consumer price (p_1 per bushel) on the total number of units sold y_2. The total costs of each of these schemes, if we ignore administration costs, are represented in Figures A10.1*a* and A10.1*b*, respectively, by the shaded region. The actual total cost of each scheme depends on the elasticities of the demand and supply functions. So, it is impossible to say which scheme is more expensive without more information. By imposing quotas, the government avoids having to make direct payments to the farmers; however, administration costs and welfare costs are involved in the artificial restriction of output. When discussing the merits of these programs, it should be remembered that in choosing its policies, the government is concerned not only with expense but also with staying in power and keeping the electorate happy.

Multiple-Choice

1 d	**2** c	**3** d	**4** b
5 d	**6** c	**7** d	**8** a

True-False

9 F	**10** F	**11** F	**12** T	**13** T	**14** F
15 F	**16** T	**17** F	**18** T	***19** T	***20** F

Short Problems

21 a Quantity demanded equals quantity supplied, where

$$40 - 2p = 4p - 20$$

from which $p^* = 10$. Substitute $p = 10$ into either the demand or supply to get equilibrium quantity $y^* = 40 - 2 \times 10 = 20$.

b If consumers must pay $6 to a third person, then the price paid by consumers is $p = p_s + 6$, where p_s is the price received by suppliers; p_s is substituted for p in the supply function. Demand and supply curves become

$$y_d = 40 - 2(p_s + 6); \quad y_s = 4p_s - 20$$

Equating y_d and y_s gives

$$40 - 2(p_s + 6) = 4p_s - 20$$

$$p_s = 8$$

The price paid by consumers is $p^* = 8 + 6 = 14$,

and quantity demanded and supplied in the market is found by substituting $p = 14$ into the demand curve: $y^* = 40 - 2(8 + 6) = 12$. This solution is illustrated in Figure A10.2.

22 Suppose that, in the absence of scalping, the price of tickets is at $\bar{p}$, which is below the equilibrium price in Figure A10.3; that is, y_d individuals want tickets and y_s tickets are available. Under a first come, first served rationing scheme, the individuals with the lowest surplus may be the lucky ones to get the tickets. Alternatively, if a scalper gets the tickets and sells them to the individuals willing to pay the highest prices for the tickets, then total surplus from the sale of y_s tickets could be as large as the shaded area. The activity is frowned upon for equity reasons: Promoters feel that all individuals — not just those willing (and able) to pay high prices for the tickets — should have the opportunity to view the event.

23 Assume that the taxes are placed on the consumer. A tax of $1 per gallon has the effect of shifting the demand curve down by $1 at every quantity. This is shown by demand CD in Figure A10.4*a*. In this case, the new equilibrium quantity is y^*. The price paid by consumers is p^*. An ad valorem (sales) tax has the effect of pivoting the demand curve. The demand curve under the ad valorem tax is EB in Figure A10.4*b*. The two demand curves will yield identical solutions

FIGURE A10.2

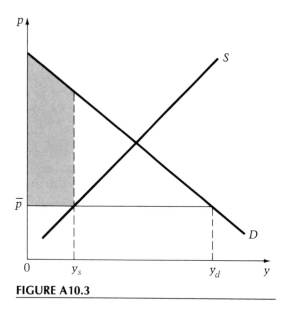

FIGURE A10.3

when they intersect the supply curve at the same point, as shown in Figure A10.4b.

24 a Since the intersection of demand and supply is on the elastic portion of the demand curve, total expenditures increase when supply curves increase and equilibrium price falls.

b The intersection of demand and supply is on the inelastic portion of the demand curve.

When equilibrium price falls, total expenditure falls.

25 Price controls in the housing market result in a shortage of available housing. Price controls help the low-income individuals who are fortunate enough to receive adequate housing, but there will be some (and perhaps many) who will be unable to purchase the housing.

26 a A tax of $1 will shift the supply curve upward by $1. If demand is perfectly elastic, the price will not change. None of the tax is passed on to consumers. This situation is illustrated in Figure A10.5a.

b Figure A10.5b shows the case in which demand is perfectly inelastic. The entire tax is passed on to consumers.

c As before, the tax shifts the supply curve upward by $1 at every quantity. The minimum price that firms will accept for the product, given the tax, is $p_0 + 1$. The consumer pays the entire tax, as shown in Figure A10.5c.

Long Problems

27 a In Figure A10.6, the firm is shown to be in long-run equilibrium, producing y_0 eggs at price p_0; industry output is ny_0. Individual quotas of $\bar{y}$ are then imposed. In the short run, the supply

(a)

(b)

FIGURE A10.4

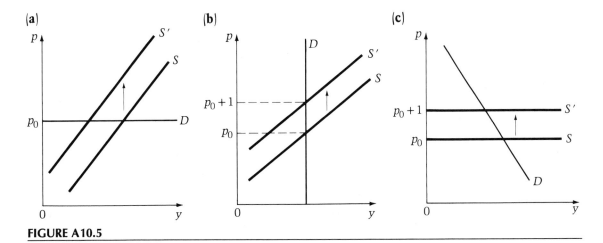

FIGURE A10.5

curve of the firm changes from SMC to *ABC*; industry supply changes from *SS* to *SBS'*. Market price and quantity are p_s and $n\bar{y}$, respectively, under the quota. At a price p_s, each farmer would like to increase profits by producing more than his quota; in particular, where $p_s = \text{SMC}(y)$.

b In the long run, firms are making profits. Some farmers will enter the industry. As this happens, the supply curve will shift to *S"S"*; that is, where firms are breaking even when producing $\bar{y}$ eggs at a market price of p_L.

c The quota system is inefficient in that the

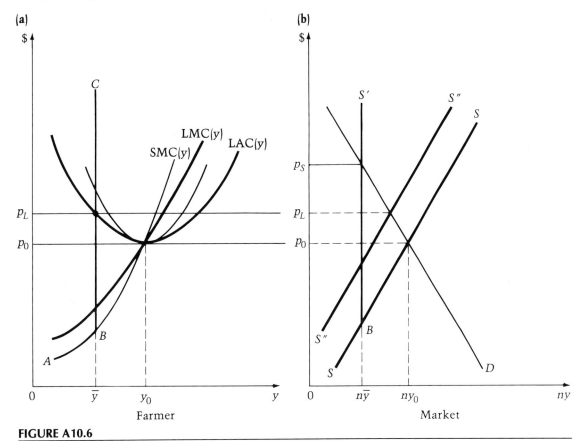

FIGURE A10.6

price is artificially high: At the quota, the price exceeds the marginal cost of producing eggs. Since demand is likely to be price-inelastic, total revenues to farmers will increase.

28 Multiply the quantities of feed by $2 and add $5 to get the total costs. Multiply the quantities of eggs by $2/dozen to get total revenue.

Total costs	5	13	21	29	37	45
Total revenues	4	24	40	52	60	64

a To find the profit-maximizing number of eggs to produce and amount of feed to use, derive the marginal cost and marginal revenue schedules. (*Caution:* Eggs are not increasing in *unit* increments; for example, the marginal cost between 2 and 12 dozen eggs is $(13 - 5)/(12 - 2) = \$0.80$).

Quantity	2	12	20	26	30	32
Marginal costs		0.80	1.00	1.33	2.00	4.00
Marginal revenue		2.00	2.00	2.00	2.00	2.00

(1) The profit-maximizing output level is where $p = MC(y)$ or between 26 and 30 units (or the average of 28).

(2) The profit-maximizing feed is the amount required to produce between 26 and 30 units; that is, between 12 and 16 pounds of feed (or the average of 14 pounds).

b The marginal and average product curves are plotted in Figure A10.7*a*. For example, the marginal product between 0 and 4 units of feed is $(12 - 2)/(4 - 0) = 2.5$; the average product of 4 units of feed is $12/4 = 3$. The cost curves are plotted in Figure A10.7*b*.

Feed	0	4	8	12	16	20
Marginal product	2.5		2	1.5	1	0.5
Average product	∞	3	2.5	2.2	1.9	1.6

Quantity	2	12	20	26	30	32
Marginal costs	0.80		1	1.33	2	4
Average costs	2.5	1.08	1.05	1.1	1.23	1.4

(a)

(b)

FIGURE A10.7

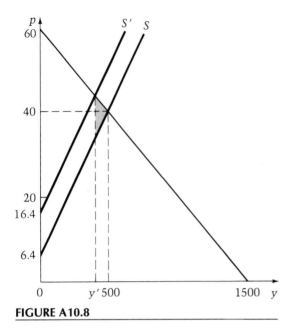

FIGURE A10.8

29 a Equilibrium market price and quantity are found by equating supply and demand.

$$1500 - 25p = 15p - 100$$
$$p = 40$$
$$y = 15 \times 40 - 100 = 500$$

The equilibrium quantity per firm is 20.

b The minimum short-run average variable cost is 10; at any price below 10, the firms refuse to supply the market and output is zero. The efficient average cost is 40.

c (1) The loss in surplus is given by the shaded area in Figure A10.8. For consumer surplus to be an accurate measure of willingness to pay, the income effect must be zero.

(2) Each firm's cost curves increase by $10 at every output, so the efficient average cost increases from $40 to $50. In the long run, firms will drop out of the market until the price increases to $50.

30 a The firm is shown in Figure A10.9a and the market in Figure A10.9b. In the absence of

FIGURE A10.9

Quantity of electricity

FIGURE A10.10

price controls, equilibrium price is p^*. Under the price control at $\bar{p}$, the firm equates $\bar{p}$ with $SMC(y)$ and produces $\bar{y}$ units of output. Market quantity supplied is $\bar{Y}_s$; quantity demanded is Y_d.

   b Since natural gas is an input into the pro-

duction of electricity, the supply curve for electricity will be affected by the price control. Suppose, for simplicity, that one unit of natural gas is used to produce one unit of output. Then the supply curve for electricity shown in Figure A10.10 is given by $S'AB$. As shown, there are two effects on the supply curve. First, a reduction in the price of electricity reduces costs of production, thereby shifting the supply curve to the right. Second, the quantity of electricity is restricted to $\bar{Y}_s$ units because of limited quantities of natural gas. Price of electricity rises from p_E^* to p_E'.

31 The initial equilibrium before either proposal is imposed on the firm is given by p_0, y_0, and $n_0 y_0$; and n_0 firms are in the market. The cost curves are LAC_0 and LMC_0, and supply and demand are S_0 and D in Figure A10.11.

   (1) Under the flat-free charge, F increases the $LAC(y)$ curve only. The $LAC(y)$ curve slides up the $LMC(y)$ curve to LAC'. Firms exit the industry in the long run; the supply curve shifts to S'; price rises to p'; firm quantity rises to y'; and market quantity drops to $n'y'$, $n' < n_0$. The equi-

(a)

(b)

FIGURE A10.11

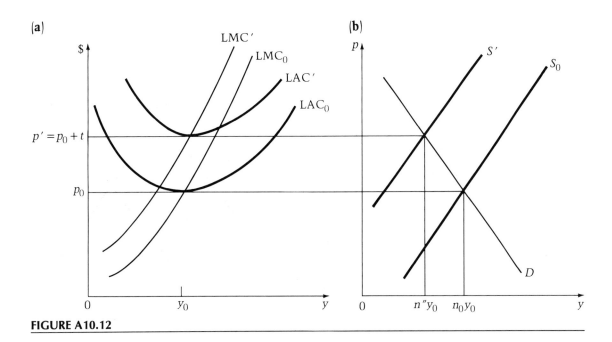

(a)

(b)

FIGURE A10.12

libria before and after the lump-sum tax are illustrated in the figure.

(2) Under the excise tax, the LAC(y) and LMC(y) curves shift up by t to LMC' and LAC', as in Figure A10.12. Again, firms exit the industry; supply shifts to S' and price rises to p' (where $p' = p_0 + t$); firm output remains unchanged; and industry output falls to $n''y_0$, $n'' < n_0$.

32 a It is $30. The long-run price equals the minimum of the LAC(y) curve because competitive firms cannot earn profits in the long run.

b The initial equilibrium is shown in Figure A10.13a. If the price falls to $22, the firm will want to exit from the industry in the long run because it is making negative profits. In the short run, the firm will not shut down if it is covering its variable costs.

c Rent on land is a fixed cost of production. The decrease in the rent will result in a movement of the SAC(y) curve from SAC_0 down the SMC(y) curve to SAC' in Figure A10.13b. This does not change the supply curve of the firm. Hence, the short-run market price and the quan-

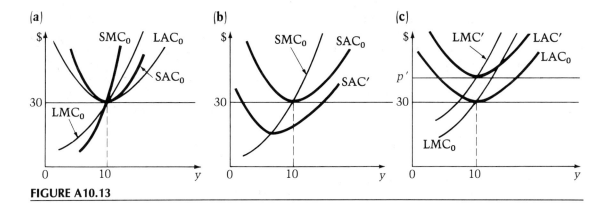

(a)

(b)

(c)

FIGURE A10.13

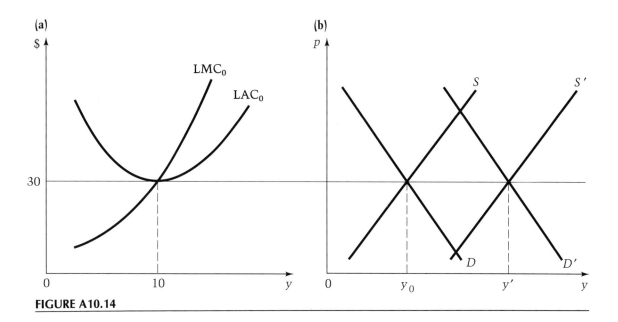

(a)

(b)

FIGURE A10.14

tity produced by the firm do not change, as shown in Figure A10.13b.

d An increase in the price of wheat will increase the LMC(y) and LAC(y) curves. This change is indicated in Figure A10.13c for the case in which the minimum of the LAC(y) curve does not change. (This may not always be the case.) Since firms are making negative long-run profits, firms will drop out of the industry; the industry supply curve will shift to the left; industry quantity will fall; and the market price will rise to p'. The firm quantity will stay the same (in this case). However, if the minimum of the LAC(y) curve had fallen to $y < 10$ or increased to $y > 10$, then the firm quantity would have fallen or increased, respectively.

e The subsidy will increase the production of Nutty Bread and thus the demand for Grand Ola cereal. The increase in demand will result in profits to the firms; more firms will enter the industry until price falls to its original level at a higher output because the industry is a constant-cost industry. This equilibrium solution is illustrated in Figure A10.14.

*33 The effect of a $100 per unit decrease in costs is shown in Figure A10.15. LMC_0 and LAC_0 fall by $100 at every output level (to LMC' and LAC', respectively). The minimum of the LAC(y) curve remains at 400.

a If the inventor offers her technology for $50 per unit, then LMC_0 and LAC_0 will fall at every output by only $50 to LMC_a and LAC_a rather than by the full $100, as shown in Figure A10.16. The equilibrium price falls to $p_0 - 50$; firm quantity stays at 400; market quantity rises from $400n_0$ to $400n_a$, $n_a > n_0$.

b If a fixed fee of $20,000/year is charged,

FIGURE A10.15

(a)

FIGURE A10.16

(a)

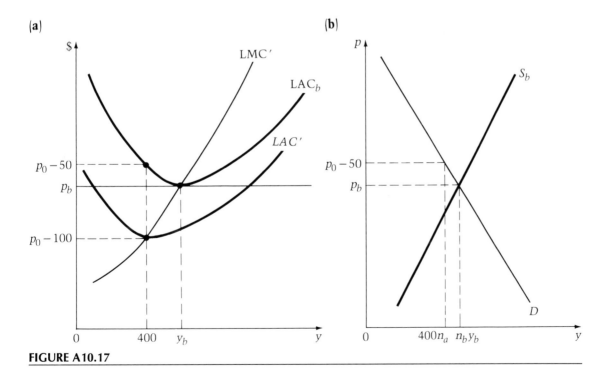

FIGURE A10.17

LMC′ — the LMC(y) curve under the new technology with no license fee — will not change. However, the LAC′ slides up LMC′ to LAC$_b$. At y = 400, the average cost increases by 50. The long-run average and marginal cost curves under the new technology with no license fee — LAC′ and LMC′ — and under the new technology with the $20,000 fee — LAC$_b$ and LMC′ — respectively, are shown in Figure A10.17. Note that the firm and market quantity (y$_b$ and n$_b$y$_b$, respectively, n$_b$ > n$_0$) are larger under the lump-sum royalty than under the per-unit royalty in Figure A10.17a (400 and 400n$_a$, respectively). Also, the market price under the lump-sum fee, p$_b$, is lower than the price under the per unit fee, p$_0$ − 50.

11

MONOPOLY

Chapter Summary

Examples of Monopoly

Monopoly is a market structure that is the opposite of competition. In theory, it refers to a single firm that is producing a good for which no close substitutes exist. In practice, a monopoly is not always easy to identify because close substitutes for a good are often difficult to define. For example, the producers of Coca-Cola, though appearing to virtually monopolize the soft-drink market, looks like a harmless competitive firm in the market for all beverages. A single firm providing electricity in a town is a straightforward example of a monopolistic market.

Pricing Behavior of Monopoly

After a monopoly has been identified, its pricing behavior is relatively easy to predict. As with a competitor, we assume that a monopolist is a profit maximizer and, hence, that it chooses the output level that equates marginal revenue and marginal cost. Unlike a competitor, the monopolist faces a **downward-sloping demand curve** and a **downward-sloping marginal revenue curve**. The punchline to the monopoly problem is that the monopolist sets a *price greater than its marginal cost* and, therefore, greater than the competitive price that would prevail under the same cost and demand conditions. This tendency of a monopolist to produce too little of its product is an example of a **market failure**: There are unrealized gains

from trade that no one — neither the consumer nor the monopolist — has been able to capture.

Development of Monopolies

How does a monopoly come about? Several ways are suggested: The government may create an exclusive franchise; a firm may discover a new product and obtain a patent that gives it monopoly rights for 17 years; a firm may have exclusive rights to a low-cost resource; a firm may be a **natural monopoly** by nature of the production technology; or the monopolist just may have been at the right place at the right time to be able to deter the entry of other firms into the market. The Sylos postulate suggests that potential market entrants take the output of existing firms as given. Thus, the decision of whether or not it is worthwhile to enter the market depends only on the residual demand, that portion of market demand not supplied by the monopolist.

Regulation of Monopolies

The social desirability of a monopoly and the type of government action used against it depend partly on the reason for the monopoly. For example, although recognizing that public utilities are natural monopolies, the government may want to limit their profits. A common mechanism used is **average cost pricing**, in which the price is set equal to the average cost of production. Since price equals average cost rather than marginal cost, an inefficient amount of output is produced. Moreover, the monopolist does not have the incentive to minimize production costs. If the regulation is on the **rate of return** on investment, and that allowable rate of return exceeds the price of capital, then the monopolist will use an inefficient mix of capital and other inputs. Too much capital will be used in production relative to the efficient mix of inputs. In a more efficient mechanism, which requires considerable information on the part of the government, the regulatory agency gives a subsidy equal to the consumer surplus less the total revenue generated by the sales earned at the current price. Alternatively, if an innovator secures a **patent** that gives monopoly rights over its invention, then no action will be taken against the monopoly unless it uses this legal monopoly to acquire monopoly power illegally elsewhere. The purpose of the patent system is to encourage technological change. In the case of a natural resource monopoly, the government may try to encourage more competition in the industry by forcing the monopolist to divest some of its holdings.

Price Discrimination

If the monopolist were a bit more clever, it could capture some of those unrealized gains through **price discrimination**; that is, the monopolist could charge different prices to different customers. However, mere savvy is not all it takes for successful price discrimination. The monopolist must be able to segment its market and to charge each segment a different price. The monopolist may engage in one of three types of price discrimination. The first is **perfect price discrimination**: A different price is charged for each unit sold. In this case, the monopolist manages to extract *all* the unrealized gains from trade and even redistributes some surplus from the consumers to itself. The second is **ordinary price discrimination**: The monopolist identifies groups of customers and charges them different prices. The third is **multipart pricing**: A different price is set for different blocks of the good or service.

Although it is the most common, ordinary price discrimination still requires the monopolist to segment the market in such a way that there can be **no arbitrage** (resale between groups) and in a way that will elicit **different elasticities of demand**. The monopolist can assign the

groups, such as adults and children, or can resort simply to **self-selection**; that is, to induce individuals to assign themselves to the appropriate market group. Advanced-booking discounts for airplane travel and after-holiday sales are examples of the self-selection market segmentation mechanism. Individuals with more inelastic demands will not take advantage of these reduced prices. However the groups are assigned, the monopolist's profit-maximizing strategy is to set the marginal revenues equal across all markets, which in turn are set equal to the marginal cost of production. This scheme results in higher prices for customers who have relatively more inelastic demands.

Patent Policy

In a static, nonchanging world such as we have studied so far, monopolies are associated with inefficiency; however, in a dynamic world, patent monopolies may actually help to reduce inefficiency. If patents are not allowed, then an inventor must compare the present value of future monopoly profits with the costs of developing a specific idea or invention. If others can quickly imitate the invention, future monopoly profits will be small, and there is little private incentive to engage in research. Alternatively, a patent, by making the benefits of an invention **appropriable** for the inventor, extends the period of time over which he or she is able to earn monopoly profits. From the government's point of view, the optimal patent policy should maximize the value of the invention to society by setting marginal social benefit equal to its marginal social cost.

Key Words

Arbitrage	Natural monopoly
Average cost pricing	Ordinary price
Efficiency criterion	discrimination
Entry deterrence	Patent monopoly
Franchise monopoly	Perfect price discrimination
Marginal revenue	nation
Market failure	Rate-of-return
Monopoly	regulation
Monopoly by management	Resource monopoly
	Self-selection
Multipart price discrimination	Sylos postulate

Case Study: Sorting Out the Differences Between Construction Workers and Dentists

Several years ago, a chemical company sold plastic molding powder (methyl methacrylate) to two types of customers: construction companies and dentists. The plastic powders sold to the construction companies and dentists were identical except for two things: It was rumored that an arsenic compound was put into the plastic powder sold to the construction companies, and the price of the plastic powder sold to the dentists was 25 times higher.

A What economic principle does this case involve?

B What was the chemical company trying to achieve by putting arsenic in the molding powder sold to the construction firms?

C Do dentists and construction firms have the same demand curve for molding powder? What might make their demand curves differ?

D Are the two necessary conditions for ordinary price discrimination satisfied in this case? Explain.

E This chemical company has some sort of market power that allows it to price discriminate. Suggest some possible sources of its market power.

Exercises

Multiple-Choice

Choose the correct answer to each question. There is only one correct answer to each question.

Use the following information to answer questions 1–3. Three monopolists want to maximize their profits in the long run. The demand curve facing each firm is linear and given by $p = 100 - y$, where p = price and y = quantity. The average cost curve is U-shaped. Sufficient information to make a recommendation has been provided (see table).

	Price ($)	Quantity	Total Cost ($)	LAC ($)	LMC ($)
Firm 1	70	—	—	50	40
Firm 2	—	40	600	At minimum	—
Firm 3	80	—	2,000	—	60

1 What should firm 1 do to maximize profits?
 a Stay at current position
 b Increase price and reduce quantity
 c Decrease price and increase quantity
 d Exit from the industry
 e None of the above

2 What should firm 2 do to maximize profits?
 a Stay at current position
 b Increase price and reduce quantity
 c Decrease price and increase quantity
 d Exit from the industry
 e None of the above

3 What should firm 3 do to maximize profits?
 a Stay at current position
 b Increase price and reduce quantity
 c Decrease price and increase quantity
 d Exit from the industry
 e None of the above

4 If regulators guarantee a natural monopolist a return on capital in excess of the cost of capital, what will the owners of the natural monopoly do?
 a Substitute from capital to other inputs
 b Not produce a given output at minimum cost
 c Reduce investment in the firm
 d All the above
 e None of the above

To answer questions **5** and **6**, refer to Figure 11.1.

5 Suppose that a monopolist producing in the market in Figure 11.1 is not allowed to practice any form of price discrimination. At y_1, the monopolist
 a Would be maximizing profit
 b Would set price equal to p_1
 c Would earn a profit of CD
 d Would do all the above
 e Would do only **a** and **b**

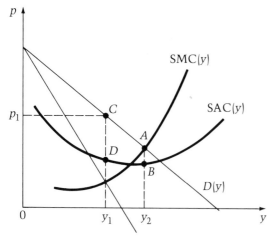

FIGURE 11.1

6 Now suppose that the monopolist in Figure 11.1 can perfectly price discriminate and produces y_2 units of output. The monopolist
  a Would be maximizing profits
  b Would set the same price for all units
  c Would make a profit equal to AB times y_2
  d Would be making zero profit
  e Would do both **a** and **c**

7 The marginal revenue at y_0 in Figure 11.2 is
  a 5
  b 0
  c 3
  d 10
  e 7

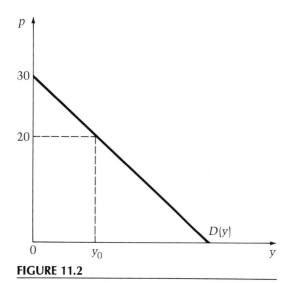

FIGURE 11.2

To answer questions **8** and **9**, consider the following information. The demand facing a monopolist is $y = 100 - (p/2)$. Marginal costs are constant at 40.

8 If the monopolist is not able to practice price discrimination, the profit-maximizing price for the monopolist is
  a 120
  b 60
  c 80
  d 40
  e None of the above

9 If the monopolist is able to perfectly price discriminate, then the price set for the *marginal* unit of output will be
  a 120
  b 60
  c 80
  d 40
  e None of the above

10 A theater has monopoly rights over first-run motion pictures. The monopolist knows that the price elasticities of demand for movies by adults and by children are 2 and 4, respectively. Then, if the monopolist charges different prices for adults and children, the profit-maximizing price for an adult ticket will be
  a Two times the price of a child's ticket
  b One-half the price of a child's ticket
  c One and one-half times the price of a child's ticket
  d One-fifteenth the price of a child's ticket
  e None of the above

True-False

11 The efficiency loss under perfect price discrimination is larger than under either pure monopoly or ordinary price discrimination.

12 The allocation of resources in a monopolistic industry is inefficient because the monopolist makes excessive profits, and it can be improved by taking away these profits.

13 A monopolist is currently producing at the minimum of its average cost curve at a quantity of 150 and total costs of $300. The firm faces a linear demand given by $p = 5 - 0.01y$. This monopolist is maximizing its profits.

14 A profit-maximizing monopolist facing no entry threat will operate on the elastic portion of the market demand curve.

15 Starting at some long-run equilibrium, if the demand for a monopoly's product falls, the price will fall more in the long run than in the short run.

16 If a particular regulated industry is characterized by rates of return on capital invested in the industry in excess of the price of capital, then one can conclude that the allocation of resources in this industry is efficient.

17 Even if an industry has IRTS over the entire range of output, the sum of the producers' and the consumers' surplus will be maximized by pricing at marginal costs.

18 Since monopoly is a "bad" thing for consumers but a "good" thing for producers, on balance we cannot be sure that monopoly is responsible for any loss in economic efficiency.

19 The higher the price elasticity of demand (in absolute value) for a product by a particular group of individuals, the lower will be the price set by a profit-maximizing, price-discriminating monopolist.

Short Problems

20 Suppose that the government declares a monopolist with declining long-run average and marginal costs to be a public utility and decrees that it must serve all who are willing to buy at an established price. The price provides the monopolist with a "fair return"; that is, a normal rate of return on capital. Show this output and price diagrammatically. Why is this output level not economically efficient?

21 The total revenue TR(y) earned by a monopolist as a function of the firm's output is given by TR(y) = $100y - y^2$. The total costs TC(y) as a function of output are TC(y) = $10 + 6y$. Current production of the monopolist is $y = 50$. Is the firm maximizing profits? If not, can you suggest an alternative objective that is being satisfied?

22 If the marginal revenue for a good X is negative, what is true of the price elasticity of demand? Explain.

23 Policymakers often argue for the "rationalization" of industries (that is, for there to be one or a few big firms instead of many small ones) in order to take full advantage of economies of scale. With what types of demand and cost conditions is this most likely to be a valid argument?

24 What two conditions are necessary for a monopolist to be able to successfully practice ordinary price discrimination?

25 A good costs $5 and the own-price elasticity is -0.2. What is the marginal revenue?

26 A doctor in a small town faces the following demand curve for her services and the long-run cost conditions illustrated in Figure 11.3.

a If the doctor is a monopolist in the town but is unable to price discriminate, will she be willing to practice in this town? Why or why not?

b What are the price and quantity of services that maximize the consumers' plus producers' surplus? Using the information provided in Figure 11.3, would the town, *as a whole*, be better off with the presence of the doctor? Why or why not? Algebraically determine the net surplus from the doctor's services. How might the town convince the doctor to stay in the town so that everyone is made better off?

27 The only racquetball club in town faces a

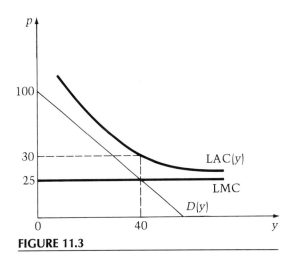

FIGURE 11.3

set of potential members, each of whom has a demand function

$$p = 5 - 0.1y$$

where y is the number of court bookings demanded per month and p is the price per booking (in dollars). The marginal costs of providing a unit of court bookings are constant and equal to $2. The club charges a fixed entry fee, which each buyer must pay to make bookings, and also charges for each booking. Assuming no income effects on the demand for the commodity, determine the entry fee that will be set.

28 In the 1960s, IBM practiced a policy of leasing its computers to customers only if the customers purchased all their computer cards from IBM. The price of the cards was set at a level exceeding the marginal cost of production (that is, the competitive price). This practice of forcing consumers to purchase a second item for the privilege of buying some other good is called **tying**. In the 1970s, the Justice Department charged IBM with tying to lessen competition.

  a Why do you think this tying arrangement was profitable for IBM?

  b In Chapter 5, we found that the optimal pricing strategy for a monopolist selling two complementary goods, one being a durable good and the other a variable input (e.g., computers and cards, or cameras and film), is to set the price of the variable good equal to its marginal cost of production and to charge a price for the durable good equal to consumer surplus. Why didn't IBM follow this pricing strategy?

Long Problems

29 Commodity X is produced by a profit-maximizing firm that has a monopoly both in its domestic market and in a foreign market. This firm charges different prices for its domestic market (p_d) and its foreign market (p_f), where $p_d > p_f$. The firm's marginal cost curve is positively sloped for all output.

  a Illustrate the monopolist's optimum price.

  b Suppose that the government introduces a consumer subsidy of $1 per unit that is paid only on units of X sold in the domestic market and not on foreign units. Analyze the effects of this subsidy on the domestic and foreign prices, total revenue from sales abroad and at home, total production costs, and total profits. Explain.

30 Suppose that a U.S. firm enjoys a monopoly in the domestic market for baseballs under the protection of high import duties, which effectively prevent imports. The world market for baseballs is competitive, and the world price is lower than the price charged by the domestic monopolist. If the import duty is removed, forcing the U.S. firm to lower its price to the world level, what effect will this have on the purchase of baseballs by people in the United States and the production of baseballs by U.S. firms? Explain carefully.

31 A monopoly that provides electricity in a small town has two plants for generating electricity. The short-run marginal costs of supplying electricity from each plant are as follows:

Plant 1: $SMC_1 = 15$

Plant 2: $SMC_2 = \dfrac{y_2 + 19}{2}$

where y_1 and y_2 are units of output in plants 1 and 2, respectively. (Each unit is 1000 kilowatt-hours.) The monopolist faces the following market demand curve:

$$p = 40 - \frac{y}{2}$$

where $y = y_1 + y_2$. Find the short-run profit-maximizing price and quantities produced by each plant.

32 Bell Canada (BC) is a supplier of telephone services. In the long run, the marginal cost of providing telephone services is zero, but there is a fixed installation cost of $30 per individual. An individual's demand curve for the telephone services is described by

$$y = 100 - 100p$$

where y is the number of message units and p is the price per message unit.

  a If price is set at the profit-maximizing level, can the firm cover its costs? Explain, using a diagram.

  b If the firm cannot cover costs in **a**, does this mean that telephone service is not socially worthwhile? Explain.

*c Suppose that BC offers "blocks" with the pricing schedule shown in the table.

Number of Message Units	Average Cost to Consumer ($)
0	0
20	0.80
40	0.60
60	0.40

Why would BC follow such a pricing schedule? Would increasing the number of blocks (beyond 60 units) increase profits? Explain carefully.

33 A theater has a monopoly on the rights to show movies in the town of Moosejaw. For its feature film of the week, it faces the following demands:

Adults: $p_a = 16 - y_a$

Children: $p_c = 10 - \dfrac{y_c}{2}$

where p_a is the price per adult ticket, p_c is the price per child ticket, y_a is the quantity of adult tickets purchased and sold, and y_c is the quantity of child tickets purchased and sold. The marginal costs of printing and selling the tickets are

$$MC(y) = \frac{y}{3}$$

and

$$TC(y) = \frac{y^2}{6}$$

where $y = y_a + y_c$.

a The monopolist can practice ordinary price discrimination. Determine the equilibrium prices and quantities for adults and children.

b Now suppose that the monopolist is banned from practicing price discrimination. Determine the equilibrium price and quantity in this case.

c Has there been an increase in the economic efficiency (or social welfare) due to the law against price discrimination in **b**? Why or why not?

34 Suppose that the government decides to levy a tax on producers of good Y. The amount of the

tax levied on each firm is $5000 per year, *regardless of the output produced by the firm.*

a What would be the effect of this tax on firm output, industry output, and price of Y in the long run if the LAC(y) curve for each firm is U-shaped and if good Y is produced in a competitive market by firms with identical cost conditions? Illustrate your answer.

b What would be the effect of this tax, as in **a**, but with good Y produced by a monopolist? Illustrate your answer.

c Is part or all of the tax passed onto the consumer in the form of higher prices? Explain and comment on the change in consumers' burden of the tax as the market becomes more competitive.

35 Assume that the author of a book receives a royalty equal to 25% of the total revenue from selling the book. The profit-maximizing publisher pays this royalty and all other costs of producing the book and is allowed to be the only supplier of the book and to set the price. The demand curve for the book remains the same every year. Marginal costs of production are constant.

a If the author and publisher were to agree to abolish this 25% royalty and replace it with a fixed annual payment equal to the total annual income that the author was receiving from the royalty, would the price of the book be affected? If so, how? Would the publisher's profits be affected? If so, how? Explain.

b If fixed annual payments are a Pareto improvement over royalties, why are royalties often used?

36 A city is considering building a bridge to an island that is almost inaccessible. The city has estimated that the demand for crossing the bridge would be given by

$$p = 25 - 0.5y$$

where p is the price and y the number of trips per year. In the long run, the marginal cost of providing bridge crossings is zero, but the costs of maintaining the toll booth are $500 per year, regardless of the number of crossings.

a Would the monopolist provide the bridge without government assistance?

b Is the bridge socially worthwhile to build? Explain.

c Suppose that the government pays the monopolist a subsidy of $K per bridge crossing, *just* sufficient to induce the monopolist to provide the bridge. Show the effects of this subsidy in your diagram in **a**.

d Now suppose that, instead of the subsidy of $K per bridge crossing, the government pays the monopoly an annual lump sum grant of $G. The amount of this grant is independent of the traffic across the bridge and is *just* sufficient to induce the monopoly to provide the bridge. Explain the effects of this grant with reference to your diagram.

*e Are the two ways of providing assistance to the monopolist equally costly to the government? Explain. Determine the total subsidy paid by the government in each case.

f Suppose that instead of providing a subsidy, the government permits the monopolist to practice ordinary price discrimination, charging different prices to different consumers. How might the monopolist successfully do this?

Answers to Chapter 11

Case Studies

A Ordinary price discrimination.

B The chemical company was trying to separate its market by preventing arbitrage, or resale, between the two groups of customers. If the powder sold to construction firms did not contain arsenic, then dentists could purchase the powder from construction workers at a lower price than that charged by the manufacturer.

C No, dentists have a more inelastic demand, which allows the chemical manufacturer to charge them a higher price. Dentists require a much smaller amount of the powder than construction companies, and the cost of the plastic powder is therefore only a small part of the dentist's total costs. As a result, it is not worthwhile for dentists to find substitutes for the powder.

D The necessary conditions for ordinary price discrimination are satisfied in this case. First, resale among different groups is impossible; second, the groups have different demand elasticities.

E The chemical company may hold a patent over the production of this specific plastic compound. Alternatively, the chemical firm may hold some market power as a result of an aggressive management style that has enabled the company to deter entry of other potential rivals.

Multiple-Choice

1 a	2 c	3 d	4 b	5 e
6 a	7 d	8 a	9 d	10 c

True-False

11 F	12 F	13 T	14 T	15 F
16 F	17 T	18 F	19 T	

Short Problems

20 At point A in Figure A11.1, the firm earns a normal rate of return. Output is not economically efficient because $p > LMC(y)$.

21 No. If profits were maximized, then the quantity produced would equate $MR(y) = 100 - 2y$ and $MC = 6$; that is, $y = 47$. Since $y = 50$, the firm is not maximizing profits; $y = 50$ is consistent with *total revenue* maximization where $MR(y) = 0$.

22 If $MR(y) < 0$, the absolute value of the price

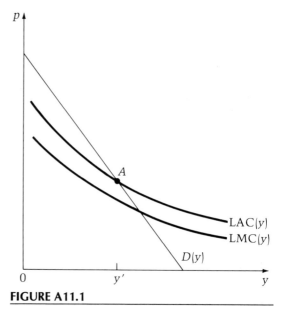

FIGURE A11.1

elasticity is less than 1 because $MR(y) = D(y)(1 - 1/\eta)$.

23 Rationalization may be a useful policy when the production technology is characterized by significant economies of scale and when demand is sufficiently small that only a few firms can satisfy demand when operating at the efficient average cost. For example, in Figure A11.2, three firms are operating at 10 units of output. One firm operating at 30 units of output would have lower average costs.

24 For a firm to successfully practice price discrimination, it must be able to segment the market in such a way that there can be no resale of the goods among groups and that the groups have different price elasticities of demand.

25 Because $MR = p[1 - (1/n)]$, $MR = -20$ for $p = 5$ and $\eta = 0.2$.

26 a No, she cannot cover her costs at *any* output level.

   b The combination of $p = \$25$ and $y = 40$ maximizes consumers' plus producers' surplus. The town would be better off because total surplus, equal to 1500 [the area under the demand and above the LMC(y)], would exceed total costs, equal to 1200. The doctor would stay in the town if she were allowed to perfectly price discriminate.

27 The monopolist will set a price per booking equal to the marginal cost, that is, $2; 30 bookings will be made. The fee equals consumer surplus at this price and quantity: $(5 - 2)30/2 = 45$.

28 a This was a way for IBM to price discriminate without having to identify the more inelastic users. If larger users have more inelastic demands, then by forcing customers to buy cards at the monopoly price, IBM is effectively charging a higher price for the "package" to customers with more inelastic demands.

   b The pricing strategy in Chapter 5 is profit-maximizing given identical customers. If customers have different demands for the joint product and IBM is unable to price discriminate explicitly on the computer (that is, charge different prices for the computer, based on individuals' consumer surplus), then the "indirect" price discrimination strategy followed by IBM may be profit-maximizing. To see this, consider Figure A11.3, in which a high and a low demand of two representative consumers are illustrated. If the price of cards is set equal to the marginal cost (assumed to be zero) and the computer price is set equal to the consumer surplus under the *low* demand, then total profits are $2 \times A0B$. Alternatively, if price p^* is charged for the cards and Ap^*D for the computer, then low-demand customers will pay $A0ED$ for the package, which is less than $A0B$, whereas high-demand cus-

FIGURE A11.2

FIGURE A11.3

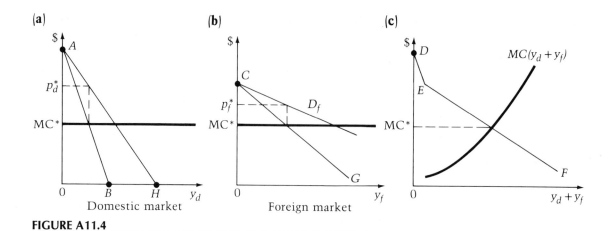

FIGURE A11.4

tomers will pay *AOFGD* for the package, which is greater than *AOB*. This strategy leaves the monopolist with larger profits.

Long Problems

29 a Figure A11.4*a* shows the domestic market, A11.4*b* the foreign market, and A11.4*c* the horizontal summation of the two marginal revenue curves *AB* and *CG* (or the "grand" marginal revenue curve *DEF*) and the marginal cost curve. Equate the marginal cost with the grand marginal revenue curve. Let MC* be the intersection of the two curves. Then, set MC* equal to the marginal revenues from the two markets. Since the domestic demand is more inelastic, the price in the domestic market, p_d^*, will be higher than in the foreign market, p_f^*.

b Domestic demand and the corresponding marginal revenue curve will increase by $1 at every quantity (marginal revenue is *A'B'* in Figure A11.5). This results in a shift in the grand marginal revenue curve to *D'E'F'* as shown in Figure A11.5*c*. As indicated in the figure, this reduces output and increases price in the foreign sector to y_f' and p_f', and increases both quantity and price in the domestic sector to y_d' and p_d' as shown in the figure. Total revenue from sales abroad will fall because the price has increased along the elastic part of the demand curve; however, the increase in profits from the domestic sector more than compensates for this decline, resulting in larger total profits.

30 Under the tariff, the monopolist sets *p** and *y** as shown in Figure A11.6. Now consider two

FIGURE A11.5

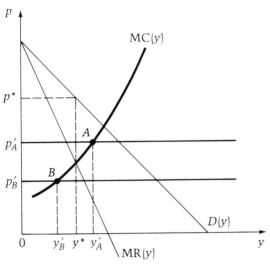

FIGURE A11.6

alternative possibilities for the world price level, p'_A and p'_B. If the world price is p'_A, then the production of baseballs by U.S. firms increases to y'_A when the tariff is removed because the new marginal revenue curve intersects the marginal cost curve to the right of the monopoly output. Alternatively, if p'_B is the world price, then marginal revenue intersects the marginal cost to the left of the monopoly output, and U.S. production of baseballs declines to y'_B.

31 The horizontal summation of the marginal cost curves is shown in Figure A11.7. At any given output level, if marginal costs are lower in one plant than in the next, the profit-maximizing monopolist will shift production to the first

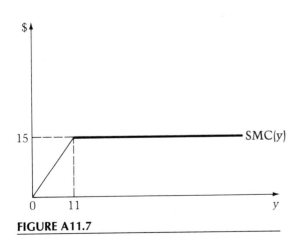

FIGURE A11.7

plant to lower total costs. As shown in the figure, this implies that plant 2 will be used for the first 11 units of output and plant 1 for the rest of the output. That is, equating SMC_1 with SMC_2 gives

$$15 = \frac{y_2}{2} + \frac{19}{2}$$

or

$$y_2 = 11 \qquad (1)$$

To find total output y and, therefore, the output produced in plant 1, y_1, the monopolist equates marginal revenue to marginal cost in each plant (which equals 15). That is,

$$40 - y = 15$$

or

$$y = 25 \qquad (2)$$

Equations (1) and (2) together imply that $y_1 = 14$, $y_2 = 11$, and $p = 27.5$.

32 a Rewriting the demand curve gives $p = 1 - 0.01y$ and $MR(y) = 1 - 0.02y$. Since marginal costs are zero, the monopolist maximizes profits (or minimizes losses) where $MR(y) = 0$; that is, at $1 - 0.02y = 0$ or $y = 50$. Price at this quantity is $p = 0.5$. Total revenues are $25; hence, the firm cannot cover its costs, as shown in Figure A11.8.

b The telephone service is socially worthwhile because the total surplus at the efficient

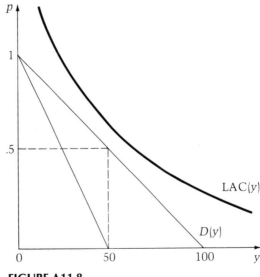

FIGURE A11.8

price $p = 0$ is 50 (area under demand curve), which exceeds the installation costs.

c BC is practicing block price discrimination. BC would increase blocks beyond $y = 60$ only if the marginal cost of doing so (zero in this case) would be less than the additional revenue. To find the additional revenue, the marginal revenue must be determined. The marginal revenue is found by calculating the change in total revenue with the change in output (total revenue = average revenue × output).

Total Revenue	y	Marginal Revenue
0	0	
16	20	$\frac{16}{20} = 0.8$
24	40	$\frac{8}{20} = 0.4$
24	60	$\frac{0}{20} = 0$

Note that marginal revenue equals marginal cost at $y = 60$. No more blocks will be offered.

33 a To determine the solution under ordinary price discrimination, one must horizontally add the marginal revenue curves from the two markets. The marginal revenue curves are

$$MR_a = 16 - 2y_a \quad \text{and} \quad MR_c = 10 - y_c$$

Rewrite the marginal revenue curves with quantity on the right-hand side:

$$y_a = 8 - \tfrac{1}{2} MR_a \qquad y_c = 10 - MR_c$$

Adding the two curves and setting $y_a + y_b = y$ gives a grand marginal revenue curve

$$MR(y) = 12 - \tfrac{2}{3} y$$

Setting $MR(y) = MC(y)$ gives $y = 12$. At this quantity, $MC = 4$. Marginal cost is set equal to the marginal revenues in each of the markets to determine the sales in each market: $y_a = 6$ and $y_c = 6$. Prices in each market are determined by substituting the quantities into the respective demand curves: $p_a = \$10$ and $p_c = \$7$.

b The nondiscriminating monopolist will set $MR(y)$ (the grand marginal revenue curve) with marginal cost. As in **a**, $y = 12$. The price is determined by substituting y into the grand demand curve (the horizontal summation of the two demand curves) $p = 12 - y/3$; hence, $p = \$8$. So,

$y_a = 8$ and $y_c = 4$. (Note that this price is between the two prices under price discrimination.)

c *Under discrimination:*

$$\text{consumer surplus (adults)} = \left(\frac{1}{2}\right)(6)(6) = 18$$

$$\text{consumer surplus (children)} = \left(\frac{1}{2}\right)(3)(6) = 9$$

$$\text{profits to firms} = \text{revenues} - \text{costs}$$

$$= [(10)(6) + (7)(6)]$$
$$- \frac{(12)(12)}{6}$$
$$= 102 - 24 = 78$$

Therefore, total surplus = $18 + 9 + 78 = 105$.
Without discrimination:

$$\text{consumer surplus (adults)} = \left(\frac{1}{2}\right)(8)(8) = 32$$

$$\text{consumer surplus (children)} = \left(\frac{1}{2}\right)(2)(4) = 4$$

$$\text{profits} = (8)(12)$$
$$- \frac{(12)(12)}{6} = 72$$

Therefore, total surplus = $32 + 4 + 72 = 108$. Efficiency increases if price discrimination is not allowed, though it should be noted that adults gain and children lose.

34 a When the lump-sum tax is imposed, the average total cost curve slides up the marginal cost curve as shown in Figure A11.9a. In the short run, $p < SAC(y)$, so some firms are forced to exit the industry and total industry supply falls. In the long run, price increases to p' (see figure), where firms' profits are zero. The number of firms in the industry is smaller; firm output increases from y^* to y'; industry output falls.

b For a monopolist, price would not change because the marginal cost curve is not affected by a lump-sum tax, as shown in Figure A11.9b. Although the monopolist is still making positive profits, the size of these profits has fallen.

c Under competition, consumers bear the entire burden of the tax in the long run; under monopoly, producers do. This is because a lump-sum tax does not change the marginal conditions for profit maximization by a monopolist but does effect the entry-exit decisions of competitive firms.

(a)

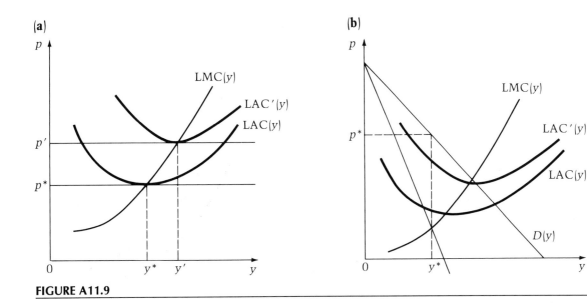

FIGURE A11.9

(b)

35 a Under the original agreement, in which the author is paid 25% of revenues, the publisher faces the pivoted demand curve $a'b$ in Figure A11.10. Marginal revenue of this demand $a'c$ is set equal to marginal costs at quantity y'; the price of the book is p'. Under the lump-sum payment scheme, the marginal revenue of the market demand ac is now relevant. The average total costs — AC(y) in the figure — by the average lump-sum payment, but marginal costs are not

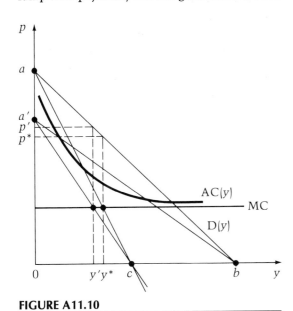

FIGURE A11.10

affected. Marginal revenue equals marginal costs at y^*; the price of the book is p^*. In this scheme, the price is lower, output is higher. The publisher is indeed better off because total industry profits have increased (marginal revenue of the market demand equals marginal costs), but the publisher pays the author the same amount as under the old scheme. Hence, the publisher pockets the increase in industry profits.

b Royalties may be used when the demand for the book is uncertain. The author and publisher share the risks under a royalty arrangement, whereas the publisher would bear all the risks under the lump-sum scheme.

36 a The monopolist would set $\text{MR}(y) = \text{MC}(y)$ at $y = 25$ and $p = 12.5$. Since profits, equal to $25 \times 12.5 = 312.5$, are less than the costs, the bridge would not be built by the monopolist.

b The bridge would be socially worthwhile to build because the total maximum profits (at $p = \text{MC} = 0$) would be 625, which exceeds the costs of 500.

c A subsidy of K per unit is illustrated by an upward parallel shift in the demand curve by K in Figure A11.11a. The K just sufficient to cover costs is at the point where the demand curve is tangent to the average total costs.

d A lump-sum grant is illustrated by a downward shift in the average cost curve in Figure A11.11b. The grant G just sufficient for revenues

(a)

(b)

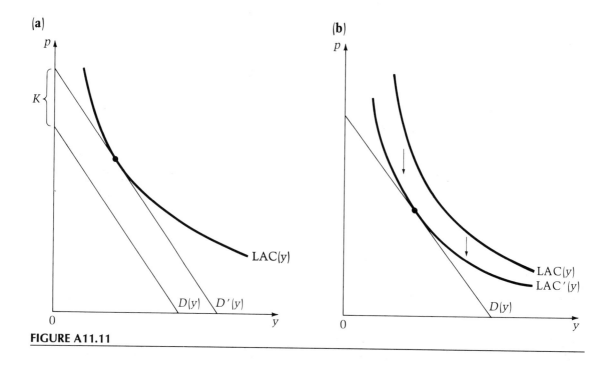

FIGURE A11.11

to cover costs is at the point where the average cost is tangent to the demand curve.

*e For the per-unit subsidy in **c**, K must satisfy

$$[p(K) + K]y(K) - 500 = 0 \qquad (3)$$

where $p(K)$ and $y(K)$ are the profit-maximizing price and output, given K. To find $y(K)$ and $p(K)$, $MR = 25 + K - y$ is set equal to $MC = 0$: $25 - y + K = 0$, which yields $y = 25 + K$. Substituting this expression for y into the demand curve gives $p = 12.5 - 0.5K$. Further substitution of these values into the profit function in Equation (3)

yields $K = 6.62$. Given this value of K, $y = 31.62$ and $p = 9.19$. The total payment by the government is $Ky = 6.62 \times (31.62) = 209.32$. The grant G, which just covers costs, is given by the costs (500) minus the maximum achievable profits without assistance (312.5); that is, $G = 187.5$. Hence, the grant program is less costly than the per-unit subsidy.

f The monopolist could try to capture some of consumer surplus by charging a higher price to inelastic users and a lower price to elastic users, if they could be identified. Total revenue from each group would increase.

12

UNDIFFERENTIATED OLIGOPOLY

Chapter Summary

Interdependence of Oligopolists

The "theory" of **oligopoly** does not have quite the elegant simplicity of the theories of monopoly and perfect competition. When one considers the definition of oligopoly—competition among the few—the reason for the relative complexity of oligopoly models becomes evident. In monopoly, only one firm, unthreatened by entry, produces in the market; in competition, many small firms produce, and no one firm perceives itself as capable of affecting market conditions. An oligopoly involves more than one firm, but not so many that a firm's actions can go unnoticed by its rivals. It is this **interdependence** among rivals' actions that distinguishes oligopoly from the other two market structures.

How should we model that interdependence? How do firms think in the real world? Does a firm believe that its rival will not react to its pricing strategy? At the other extreme, does it think that its rival will follow its every action? Does that behavior change if one firm is established in the market and the other firm is a new entrant in the market? And what exactly do firms choose: price, quantity, advertising, or something else?

Short-Run Models

These questions suggest some of the many aspects, absent from monopoly and competition, that one must consider when modeling an oligopolistic market. Two short-run models of **noncooperative** behavior—the **Cournot** and **Bertrand** models—differ in the choice variable of the firms. Cournot firms choose quantity; Bertrand firms choose price. In both cases, a **Nash equilibrium** is found in which each firm's strategy is profit-maximizing given the other firm's strategy, that is, firms are **individually rational**. As the number of firms increases in the Cournot model, the competitive solution is reached; however, in the Bertrand model, the equilibrium, characterized by price equals marginal cost, is invariant to the number of firms.

If firms were to behave **cooperatively** and collude on their choice of quantity and price, the best they could achieve would be the monopoly solution. If the profits were equally divided, all firms in the market would be better off than in either the Cournot or Bertrand noncooperative solution (assuming identical cost conditions for the firms). This collusive arrangement is **collectively rational** but individually irrational in that each firm has the incentive to cheat by producing more output than allotted under collusion or by shaving its price.

A well-known example of this conflict between individual and collective rationality is the **prisoners' dilemma game**. If the games played by noncooperative agents were repeated, and the agents were to devise **credible punishments** providing sufficient disincentives to cheat, then the collusive solution could be both individually and collectively rational.

Endogenous Market Structure

When market structure becomes endogenous — that is, when the number of firms is no longer fixed — the models of oligopoly become more complicated and fascinating. Under the assumptions of Cournot behavior and of knowledge of the "rules of the game" by all existing and potential firms in the industry, market structure is easily endogenized in this model through the introduction of **setup costs**, costs required to enter the market. From the perspective of an **established firm** in the market, set-up costs are **sunk** and have no effect on the firms' profit-making decisions. However, from the point of view of the **potential entrant**, the setup costs are avoidable by not entering and hence are important to the firm's entry decision. Moreover, the nature of the oligopoly behavior, if entry occurs, affects the decision to enter: The more cooperative the oligopoly is after entry, the more attractive entry will be. For example, in the case of Bertrand behavior, a "second" firm will never find entry profitable for positive setup costs; hence, monopoly is always predicted to arise.

Strategic Behavior

The established firm can be more aggressive and can behave strategically in such a way that a potential rival will not find entry profitable. Sylos and Labini suggest one way: An established firm can set a **limit output**; that is, the smallest value of industry output such that there is no profitable output level that the entrant can produce. The limit output, though possibly exceeding the monopoly output, may be profitable for the established firm to produce if it is entry-deterring. Although the Sylos postulate is instructive in strategic behavior by established firms, it is based on the unattractive assumption that the potential entrants take as given the current output of the established firm as an indication of the future output that will be produced by the established firm. This threat is not necessarily **credible**; that is, if the entrant *actually* enters despite the established firm's **threat**, the established firm may find a different output choice more profitable.

This brings us to recent developments in the economics literature. If an established firm makes high profits over a period of time, it follows that some barriers to entry must be in place protecting these profits. Structural features such as economies of scale and large research costs provide **natural barriers**; alternatively, incumbent firms can take deliberate actions to prohibit entry. Spence distinguishes between two types of actions. First, a firm may want to **position** itself prior to the entry of a rival in a way that will make its threats credible. For example, to indicate that it will produce more output if entry occurs, the firm may purchase additional equipment or carry excess inventories; or to show it will fight a price war, the firm may incur some expenditures on advertising specific to a price war before the war is actually fought. Second, firms can also **react** to rivals after entry occurs.

Key Words

Bertrand model	Nash equilibrium
Best response function	Noncooperative
Collusion	behavior
Cournot model	Oligopoly
Credible threats	Potential entrant
Dominant strategy	Prisoners' dilemma
Duopoly	game
Established firm	Profit matrix
Individual versus col-	Reacting versus
lective rationality	positioning
Limit-output model	Setup costs
No-entry condition	Sunk costs

Case Study: The Stability of OPEC

The oil cartel OPEC sells oil in the world oil market along with many smaller firms and oil-producing countries. A reasonable approximation of actual behavior by the smaller and fringe firms in this market is that they take the price set by OPEC and do not believe that their production of oil can have a large effect on the price. Figure 12.1 shows the costs and demand conditions for this oil market. MC_f is the horizontal summation of the fringe firms' supply curves, MC_c is the marginal cost curve of the cartel, and $D(y)$ is the market demand.

A Under the assumption that OPEC is a profit-maximizing cartel, indicate the price that OPEC will set and the resulting output shares by the

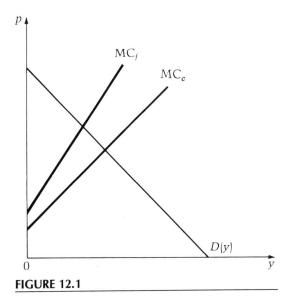

FIGURE 12.1

cartel and the fringe firms. (*Hint*: OPEC will want to take the fringe's reactions to its price announcements into account in choosing price. To do this, OPEC will subtract the output that the fringe firms will be willing to produce at every price and then will set its price using the "residual" demand that remains.)

B Given your solution in **A**, what might have been the reason for OPEC's surprise in 1976 when it discovered that the demand for oil was not as price-inelastic as had been thought?

C If the cost curves in the figure are short-run curves, what would you expect to happen in the long run if OPEC continued to set price at the short-run profit-maximizing level you found in **A**?

D In some industries, collusive aggreements among firms in the industry are stable; that is, they last for a long time. OPEC, for example, was formed in the early 1960s, dominated the oil market in the 1970s, and persisted as a strong cartel, until its recent problems began in 1985. Other collusive arrangements — for example, in the copper market — have had histories of instability. What factors contribute to the stability (or instability) of a cartel?

Exercises

Multiple-Choice

Choose the correct answer to each question. There is only one correct answer to each question.

1 The payoff matrix in Figure 12.2 gives the profits from spending either $1000 or $2000 on advertising to firms A and B, net of costs. The first number in each cell is the payoff to firm A, and the second number is the payoff to firm B, in thousands of dollars. The Nash equilibrium to this game is

   a Firm A will spend $1000 and firm B will spend $2000 on advertising.

   b Both firms will spend $2000 on advertising.

   c Both firms will spend $1000 on advertising.

   d Neither firm will advertise at all.

   e None of the above.

2 Two firms behave as Cournot duopolists in the market for soft drinks. The firms face identical constant marginal costs of c and a market demand $p = a - by$. In equilibrium,

   a The two firms will produce indentical quantities equal to $a/3b$.

Firm B

	$1000	$2000
$1000	10, 10	1, 15
$2000	15, 1	3, 3

Firm A

FIGURE 12.2

b The market price in this case will exceed the market price if the two firms colluded.

c The industry output will equal two-thirds the market demand at $p = c$.

d The market price will be $a/3$.

e None of the above.

3 As the number of firms in a Cournot oligopoly gets large,

a Output produced by each firm increases.

b Industry output increases, and price falls to the competitive level.

c The market price approaches the collusive price.

d The oligopolists behave in a more collectively rational manner.

e None of the above.

4 In the limit-output model,

a An entrant can be deterred from entering the market even if it faces the identical costs faced by the established firm.

b An entrant can be deterred from entering the market if output by the established firm is sufficiently high.

c An entrant responds to the residual demand, which is the market demand remaining after subtracting the established firm's output.

d All the above.

e Only **b** and **c**.

5 For a Bertrand oligopoly,

a The equilibrium price is equal to the monopoly price.

b The equilibrium price exceeds the price set by Cournot duopolists, assuming identical market conditions.

c The equilibrium concept is based on collectively rational behavior.

d The equilibrium price equals the competitive price.

e None of the above.

6 Figure 12.3 shows an entrant firm's long-run average cost curve and the market demand. Under the Sylos postulate, if the established firm sets an output level equal to $\bar{y}$,

a The potential entrant will enter the market between output levels y_1 and y_2.

b The potential entrant will not enter the market because the long-run average cost exceeds the residual demand at every quantity.

c The potential entrant will enter the mar-

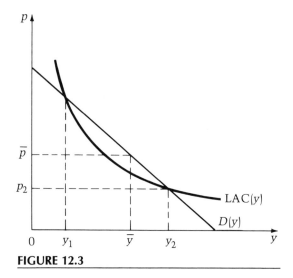

FIGURE 12.3

ket because the entrant does not believe the established firm will continue to produce $\bar{y}$.

d The potential entrant will enter the market and price will fall to p_2.

e None of the above.

To answer questions **7** and **8**, consider Figure 12.4, which shows the reaction functions of two Cournot firms. Each firm has marginal costs equal to 0; market demand is $p = 1 - y$.

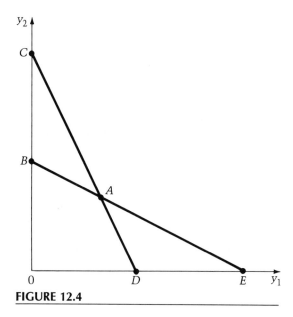

FIGURE 12.4

7 In Figure 12.4,

   a Firm 1's reaction function is CD; firm 2's reaction function is BE.

   b Firm 1's reaction function is BE; firm 2's reaction function is CD.

   c Distances $0B$ and $0D$ equal the monopoly output, $y = \frac{1}{2}$.

   d Both **a** and **c**.

   e Both **b** and **c**.

8 Suppose that only firm 2's marginal costs increase to $\frac{1}{4}$. Then, which of the following will occur?

   a Firm 2's reaction curve will shift downward.

   b Firm 1's reaction curve will shift upward.

   c The new equilibrium set of outputs (y_1^*, y_2^*) will lie along CD, with $y_2^* < y_1^*$.

   d Both **a** and **c**.

   e Both **b** and **c**.

*9 For a Cournot oligopoly with n firms facing constant marginal costs c and market demand $p = a - by$, the equilibrium price will be

   a $(a + cn)/(n + 1)$

   b $(a - c)n/b(n + 1)$

   c c

   d $a/2$

   e None of the above

True-False

10 Industry output in a duopoly model of Cournot behavior exceeds the industry output under collusive behavior.

11 The larger the setup costs faced by the entrant, the larger will be the limit output chosen by the established firm in the Sylos model.

12 The more firms that produce in a Cournot oligopoly, the larger is the industry output.

13 If firms in a Cournot oligopoly collude, the incentives to cheat increase as the number of cartel members increases.

14 The equilibrium price in a Bertrand oligopoly falls as the number of firms increases.

15 The larger the setup costs of entering a Cournot oligopoly, the larger will be the number of firms in long-run equilibrium.

16 If the setup costs of entering a Cournot oli-

gopoly must be incurred by new entrants, then established firms may make economic profits in long-run equilibrium.

17 The incentive to collude is greater among Bertrand oligopolists than among Cournot oligopolists, everything else held constant.

18 Bertrand pricing behavior and positive setup costs are sufficient to deter potential entrants from a market in which only one firm currently produces and earns monopoly profits.

19 The Nash equilibrium concept is a collectively rational concept.

Short Problems

20 Until 1924, the delivered price of steel in the United States was the base price in Pittsburgh plus freight costs from Pittsburgh to the customer's location. The Pittsburgh-plus-freight price would be quoted by any steel manufacturer, regardless of that particular manufacturer's location. This is called *basing-point pricing*; that is, the strategy of setting delivered prices by firms with plants in different locations equal to some common "base" price (f.o.b.) plus transport costs from *one* location. Why would firms be willing to adopt such a pricing practice?

21 Suppose that a ban on advertising is imposed in the cigarette industry, which we assume to consist of two firms. Show, using a simple game-theoretical model, how this policy may result in higher equilibrium profits for the two firms.

22 Suppose that two firms in the same market tacitly agree to share the market. Show that this agreement results in the collusive outcome when the firms' cost curves are identical.

23 Suppose that a firm in an oligopolistic industry faces the kinked demand curve for its product shown in Figure 12.5, where p^* is the current equilibrium price in the industry.

   a Why might the firm believe that its demand curve has this shape?

   b Explain why the price of the commodity may stay constant even if input prices, and therefore costs, change.

24 The International Air Transport Associa-

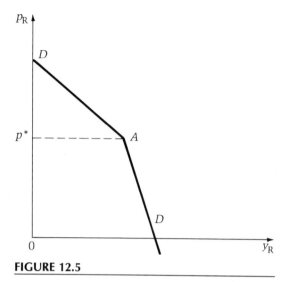

FIGURE 12.5

tion (IATA), a trade association consisting of most of the world's international airlines, sets the rates for international routes. Two basic fare levels are set by the IATA for its members to follow: regular and excursion fares. All member airlines of the IATA that fly the same route on a regularly scheduled basis are required to charge the same fares. Because IATA members cannot compete with each other in prices, many IATA member airlines offer tourist travel packages to attract customers. Offered at some price set by the airline, a travel package provides for all the needs of the tourist including the airline flight, hotel accommodation, vehicle rental, and sightseeing tours.

a Why is it in the interest of the airlines *as a group* to charge an identical price?

b Why do the IATA members offer the travel packages?

c Explain why IATA would want to check each package offered and have the right to veto any offerings.

Long Problems

25 Consider the following game. A firm, call it the established firm I, has a monopoly in the market for good Y. The demand curve for Y is given by $p = 50 - 0.5y$. The marginal costs of production from the current technology are constant and equal to 10. There are no fixed costs of production.

a Show that the monopoly profits that firm I will receive if there is no entry are equal to $800.

b Now suppose that a substitute technology is available that can reduce the marginal production costs to $0. The costs of developing the technology are fixed at $550. (The firms cannot speed up development by spending more money.) Firm I and a potential entrant E are each deciding whether or not to develop the technology. If only firm I develops it, then the firm will discard the old technology and simply produce as a monopolist with the new technology. If only firm E develops it, then the firms will produce as Cournot duopolists, where firm I will have marginal costs $MC_I = 10$ and firm E will have marginal costs $MC_E = 0$. If both develop the technology, they will produce as Cournot duopolists, where both firms I and E will have marginal costs equal to 0. If no one develops it, the status quo discussed in **a** will occur. Show the following:

(1) The monopoly profits to firm I if *only* firm I develops the new technology are $700.

(2) The Cournot profits to firms I and E if *only* E develops the technology are $\pi_I = 200 and $\pi_E = 250.

(3) The Cournot profits to firms I and E if *both* firms develop the technology are $\pi_I = \pi_E = 5.56.

c Given the profits in **a** and **b**, construct a payoff matrix for firms I and E with strategies "develop" (D) and "do not develop" (N). Show that if both firms move simultaneously in this game, there is only one Nash equilibrium, in which only firm E develops the technology. Give an intuitive explanation for that result.

d Would your answer in **c** change if firm I could move first in the research game? Explain. Would your answer change if firm E could move first? Explain.

26 Two firms produce two products that are perfect substitutes for each other, but the costs of production are different for the two firms. The demand and cost conditions are described by

$$p = 100 - \frac{(y_1 + y_2)}{2}$$

and

$$MC_1 = 19 \qquad MC_2 = y_2$$

where p is the market price, y_1 is the quantity

produced by firm 1, y_2 is the quantity produced by firm 2, MC_1 is the marginal cost of production by firm 1, and MC_2 is the marginal cost of production by firm 2.

a Derive the quantity reaction function for each firm on the assumption of Cournot behavior (that is, each firm maximizes its profits with respect to quantity, given its rival's output). Determine the equilibrium quantities for each firm and the market price.

b What will happen to industry output and price if the two firms maximize joint profits rather than behave as Cournot duopolists? Determine the equilibrium price and quantity in the collusive case.

27 Suppose that an industry is characterized by the inverse demand function

$$p = 1 - y$$

and zero variable costs. Firms in the industry reach a Cournot–Nash equilibrium in quantities.

a Find the equilibrium price, profits per firm, if there are
  (1) Two firms
  (2) Three firms
  (3) N firms

b Suppose that variable costs are still zero, but each firm incurs a setup cost of 0.05. Repeat (1), (2), and (3) from **a**. If there is free entry into the market, what will be the long-run equilibrium number of firms?

c Suppose each firm believes that if it produces in this market, it will sell $1/N$ of total output. Under this assumption, what will be the long-run equilibrium number of firms? Compare this answer with the one in **b**.

*28 An established firm in the market for widgets faces the following demand and cost conditions.

$$P = 100 - \frac{y}{2}$$

$$MC_1 = 40$$

where p is the price and y is the quantity demanded. A second firm is considering entering this market. If this firm enters, it can produce only with a production technology that has constant marginal costs,

$$MC_2 = 40$$

If both firms produce in the market, they will behave as Cournot duopolists.

a Find the Sylos limit output when setup costs of entry equal $450.

b Will the incumbent have the incentive to set the limit output to deter entry?

*29 Mac N. Ro, Inc., has a monopoly in the production of tennis shoes. The marginal cost of producing tennis shoes is $18. Mac Ltd., however, does not have the facilities for selling the shoes to consumers, so it sells them wholesale to a firm that, in turn, sells the shoes to consumers in a monopoly retail market. The retail firm faces marginal costs equal to the wholesale price of the shoes, p_w, plus marginal retail costs of $10. The consumer demand for tennis shoes is given by $p = 100 - y$.

a Determine the wholesale and retail prices and the market output.

b Show that Mac Ltd. could increase profits by vertically integrating forward into the retail business. That is, it would produce and sell the shoes, incurring a total marginal cost of $28.

c Can you think of an alternative to vertical integration that would yield the same profits?

Answers to Chapter 12

Case Study

A Figure A12.1 shows the market demand curve $D(y)$ and the marginal cost curves of the fringe MC_f, and of the cartel MC_c. At p_1 MC_f equals the market demand, and the fringe will supply the entire market; the cartel supplies 0. At p_2, the fringe supplies 0, so the cartel will satisfy the entire market. The residual demand for the cartel is dd'. The marginal revenue of the residual demand is set equal to the marginal costs of the cartel, MC_c. The profit-maximizing quantity of the cartel is y_d^*, and the price is set from the residual demand at p^*. The fringe equates p^* with MC_f and produces y_f^* output.

B OPEC may have calculated the elasticity from the market demand rather than the residual demand.

C If the fringe firms were making a profit at p^*, more firms would try to enter, through increased production, exploration of new reserves, or de-

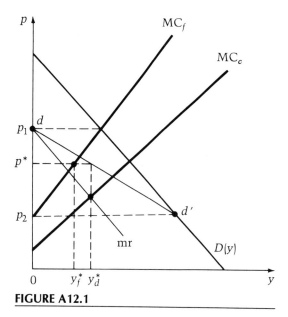

FIGURE A12.1

velopment of substitutes for oil. If this entry is successful, MC_f will shift to the right, and the residual demand of the cartel will shift inward, pushing the price down.

D A cartel will be more stable the fewer the firms in the cartel because cheaters can be more easily detected. Stability of the cartel is also more likely if entry barriers into the market are high. If supply from firms not in the cartel can respond quickly to increases in the cartel price, the cartel will be unstable. Where there are fixed supplies of resources, for example, fewer entrants will be able to enter the market and put downward pressure on price. The more there is to lose by cheating on the cartel, the less likely there will be cheating. The fewer substitutes that exist for the good, the less elastic the demand and the more stable the cartel.

Multiple Choice

1 b	**2 c**	**3 b**	**4 d**	**5 d**
6 b	**7 d**	**8 d**	***9 a**	

True-False

10 T	**11 F**	**12 T**	**13 T**	**14 F**
15 F	**16 T**	**17 T**	**18 T**	**19 F**

Short Problems

20 This practice is a collusive agreement by firms. Without this agreement, firms would compete in prices. Joint profits are higher under this agreement. This strategy may not be individually rational, however, because firms will have an incentive to lower the price below the collusive price for nearby customers.

21 Assume two things: (1) Profits to both firms using the strategy of no advertising are higher than those using an advertising strategy when both firms adopt the same strategy. (2) Each firm has the incentive to advertise, regardless of the rival's action. The payoff matrix in Figure A12.2 satisfies these assumptions. Thus, in the absence of a ban, the Nash equilibrium will be for both firms to advertise. Hence, a ban can raise profits from (100, 100) to (200, 200).

22 In Figure A12.3, market demand is given by $D(y)$ and the corresponding marginal revenue is $MR(y)$; $mc(y)$ is the marginal cost of one firm, and $MC(y)$ is the horizontal summation of the two marginal cost curves. The collusive outcome is $MR(y) = MC(y)$, at market output y^* and price p^*. Each firm produces $\frac{1}{2}y^*$.

Under the market-sharing rule, each firm faces one-half the market demand or $d(y)$, which is identical to $MR(y)$. Each firm equates the marginal revenue of its demand $mr(y)$ to $mc(y)$ and sets the price p^* and output $\frac{1}{2}y^*$.

23 a The firm believes that any price decrease will be matched by rivals; hence, demand is more

	Firm 2	
	Advertise	Do not advertise
Advertise	100, 100	300, 50
Do not advertise	50, 300	200, 200

Firm 1

FIGURE A12.2

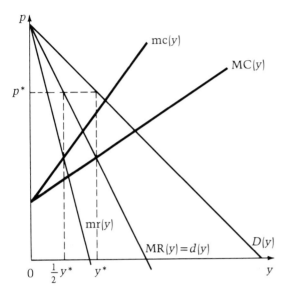

FIGURE A12.3

inelastic for price decreases. Furthermore, any price increases will not be matched; hence, demand is more elastic at higher prices.

b Because of the kink in the demand, the marginal revenue is discontinuous. Hence, $MC(y)$ can increase over a large range and $MR(y) = MC(y)$ at the same output level y^* and price p^*, as shown in Figure A12.4.

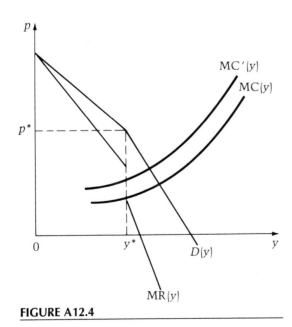

FIGURE A12.4

24 a Collusion results in larger profits for the group as a whole.

b The travel packages may be a way of disguising price cuts, or they may represent non-price competition.

c Since the travel packages may be a way of cheating on the collusive agreement, IATA's right of veto is a way to police the agreement.

Long Problems

25 a Monopoly price and quantity are found by equating MR_I and MC_I.

$$MR_I = 50 - y = 10 = MC_I \qquad so \qquad y = 40$$
$$p = 50 - 0.5 \times 40 = 30$$
$$\pi = (30 - 10)40 = \$800$$

b (1) If only firm I develops the technology,

$$MR_I = 50 - y = 0$$
$$y = 50$$
$$p = 50 - 0.5 \times 50 = 25$$
$$\pi = 50 \times 25 - 550 = 700$$

(2) Reaction functions are found for $MC_I = 10$ and $MC_E = 0$:

$$MR_I = 50 - 0.5y_E - y_I = 10$$

which implies that $y_I = 40 - 0.5y_E$ and

$$MR_E = 50 - 0.5y_I - y_E = 0$$

so

$$y_E = 50 - 0.5y_I$$

Substitute the second equation into the first:

$$y_I = 40 - 0.5(50 - 0.5y_I)$$

so

$$y_I = 20 \qquad y_E = 40$$
$$p = 50 - 0.5 \times 60 = 20$$
$$\pi_I = (20 - 10) \times 20 = 200$$
$$\pi_E = 20 \times 40 - 550 = 250$$

(3) If both develop the technology, then — from (2) — the reaction functions for the two firms are

$$y_I = 50 - 0.5y_E \qquad and \qquad y_E = 50 - 0.5y_I$$

Substitution of firm E's reaction function into firm I's yields

$$y_I = y_E = \frac{100}{3}, \qquad p = 50 - \frac{200}{6} = \frac{50}{3}$$

and

$$\pi_I = \pi_E = \left(\frac{50}{3}\right)\left(\frac{100}{3}\right) - 550 = 5.56$$

c The Nash equilibrium set of strategies is "develop" (D) for the entrant and "do not develop" (N) for the incumbent. As indicated in Figure A12.5, N is a dominant strategy for firm I: Whether firm E chooses D or N, firm I can do better by choosing N rather than D. For the entrant, D is a dominant strategy.

d If firm I could move first or firm E could move first, the answer in **c** would not change. Let firm I move first. It knows that whatever it does, firm E will choose D. Hence, firm I chooses the strategy with the larger payoff, N, and firm E follows with D. If firm E moves first, it knows that whatever it does, firm I will react by choosing N. Hence, firm E chooses the strategy with the largest payoff, D, and firm I follows with N.

26 a Each firm equates marginal revenue with its marginal cost.

Firm 1: $\quad 100 - \dfrac{y_2}{2} - y_1 = 19$, so

$$y_1 = 81 - \frac{1}{2}y_2$$

Firm 2: $\quad 100 - \dfrac{y_1}{2} - y_2 = y_2$, so

$$y_2 = 50 - \frac{1}{4}y_1$$

Substitute firm 2's reaction function into firm 1's reaction function:

$$y_1 = 81 - \left(\frac{1}{2}\right)\left(50 - \left(\frac{1}{4}\right)y_1\right)$$

$$= 56 + \frac{y_1}{8}$$

Solving for y_1 gives

$$y_1 = 64$$

Substitute $y_1 = 64$ into firm 2's reaction function:

$$y_2 = 50 - \frac{64}{4} = 34$$

Then, total output is $y = y_1 + y_2 = 98$, and market price is $p = 51$.

b If the two firms collude and maximize joint profits, they will allocate output to each firm so as to minimize total production costs. The horizontal summation of the marginal costs is shown in Figure A12.6. This problem is similar to a multiplant monopolist. That is, the two firms will choose output in each "plant" where $MC_1 = MC_2$ or

$$y_2 = 19 \qquad (1)$$

Total output is found by equating marginal revenue to the marginal cost of each firm. Since $MC_1 = MC_2 = 19$, total output is given by

	Entrant		
	D	N	
Incumbent D	5.56, 5.56	700, 0	5.56
N	200, 250	800, 0	200
	250	0	

FIGURE A12.5

FIGURE A12.6

$$100 - y = 19$$
$$y = 81 \qquad (2)$$

Equations (1) and (2) imply that $y_1 = 62$, $y_2 = 19$, and $p = 59.5$.

27 a (1) For two firms, the profit function for each firm (for example, firm 1) is $(1 - y_1 - y_2)y_1$. Firm 1's reaction function is given by

$$1 - y_2 - 2y_1 = 0 \qquad \text{so} \qquad y_1 = \frac{1}{2} - \frac{y_2}{2}$$

Similarly, firm 2's reaction function is

$$y_2 = \frac{1}{2} - \frac{y_1}{2}$$

Solving the two equations simultaneously for y_1 and y_2 gives

$$y_1 = y_2 = \frac{1}{3}$$
$$p = 1 - \frac{2}{3} = \frac{1}{3}$$
$$\pi_1 = \pi_2 = \frac{1}{9}$$

(2) For three firms, the reaction function of firm 1 is given by the condition

$$1 - y_2 - y_3 - 2y_1 = 0$$

Then the equations that are solved simultaneously for y_1, y_2, and y_3 are

$$y_1 = \frac{1}{2} - \frac{y_2}{2} - \frac{y_3}{2}$$
$$y_2 = \frac{1}{2} - \frac{y_1}{2} - \frac{y_3}{2}$$
$$y_3 = \frac{1}{2} - \frac{y_1}{2} - \frac{y_2}{2}$$

Solving the three equations gives

$$y_1 = y_2 = y_3 = \tfrac{1}{4}$$
$$p = 1 - \tfrac{3}{4} = \tfrac{1}{4}$$
$$\pi_i = \tfrac{1}{16}, \qquad i = 1, 2, 3$$

(3) For N firms, the reaction function for each firm (consider firm 1 again) is given by

$$1 - y_2 - y_3 - \cdots - y_N - 2y_1 = 0$$

But since the firms have identical costs, $y_1 = y_2 = \cdots = y_N$ in equilibrium, the profit-maximization condition can be written as

$$1 - (N + 1)y_i = 0$$

which implies that $y_i = 1/(N + 1)$, $i = 1, \ldots, N$

$$p = 1 - \frac{N}{N + 1} = \frac{1}{N + 1}$$
$$\pi_i = \left(\frac{1}{N + 1}\right)^2, \qquad i = 1, \ldots, N$$

b With setup costs, the price and quantities will be the same. However, profits will be smaller by 0.05. In the long-run, the number of firms will be such that

$$\left(\frac{1}{N + 1}\right)^2 - 0.05 = 0 \qquad \text{so} \qquad N = 3.47$$

Assuming that the number of firms must be an integer, $N = 3$.

c If each firm believes that it will sell $(1/N)$ of total output, then it will maximize

$$\pi = (1 - Ny)y - 0.05$$

where y is the output of a representative firm. Profit-maximization gives

$$1 - 2Ny = 0 \qquad p = 1 - \frac{1}{2} = \frac{1}{2}$$
$$y = \frac{1}{2N}$$

Note that the collusive output and price are reached. The reason is that each firm thinks rivals will do exactly the same thing, so they are able to collude tacitly and set the monopoly output. In the long run, firms will enter until

$$\pi = \frac{1}{4N} - 0.05 = 0 \qquad \text{so} \qquad N = 5$$

Note that more firms are attracted into the industry because monopoly profits rather than oligopoly profits are shared.

*28 a If the incumbent has y_1 units of output, then the reaction function for the entrant is

$$\text{MR}_2 = 100 - \frac{y_1}{2} - y_2 = 40$$

so

$$y_2 = 60 - \frac{y_1}{2}$$

If the second firm entered, total output in the industry would be

$$y = y_1 + y_2 = y_1 + 60 - \frac{y_1}{2} = 60 + \frac{y_1}{2}$$

Price can be written in terms of y_1 as

$$p = 100 - 0.5\left(60 + \frac{y_1}{2}\right) = 70 - \frac{y_1}{4}$$

and the profits to the entrant would be

$$\pi_2 = \left(30 - \frac{y_1}{4}\right)\left(60 - \frac{y_1}{2}\right) - F$$

where F is setup costs. Then, if $F = 450$, the condition for no entry is

$$\left(30 - \frac{y_1}{4}\right)\left(60 - \frac{y_1}{2}\right) = 450$$

so

$$1800 + \frac{y_1^2}{8} - 30y_1 = 450$$

Using the quadratic formula, we get

$$y_1 = 60$$

b Yes. The limit output happens to be the output that would be chosen by a monopolist, unthreatened by entry. In this case, entry is said to be blockaded.

*29 Given that the monopolist sets a wholesale price p_w, the retailer maximizes

$$\pi = (100 - y)y - (p_w + 10)y$$

Profits are maximized where

$$100 - 2y = p_w + 10, \quad \text{so}$$

$$p_w = 90 - 2y$$

This relationship gives the demand by the retailers for the shoes. Mac N. Ro, Inc., now maximizes

$$\pi = p_w y - 18y$$
$$= (90 - 2y)y - 18y$$

Profit-maximizing output and prices are

$$y = 18 \qquad p_w = 90 - 36 = \$54$$
$$p = 100 - 18 = \$82$$

Note that there are two markups: The manufacturer sets a price $36 higher than the marginal costs of $18, and the retailer sets a price $18 over its marginal costs of $54 + $10. The markup by the retailer lowers the manufacturer's profit. Manufacturer's profits are $36 \times 18 = \$648$.

b Mac N. Ro could do better integrating into the retail market. In this case, marginal costs would be $28. Then profits would be

$$\pi = (100 - y)y - 28y$$

Profit-maximization would occur where $MR(y) = MC(y)$ or

$$100 - 2y = 28 \quad \text{so} \quad y = 36 \qquad p = \$64$$

Profits would equal $1296.

c Alternatively, Mac could impose a ceiling of $64 on the retail price. By setting a wholesale price of $54 (the vertical integration price minus the retailer's average cost), Mac could earn the same profits as under vertical integration, whereas the retailer would only be able to cover costs.

13

PRODUCT DIFFERENTIATION

Chapter Summary

Differentiated Products

In the marketplace of the real world, consumers can choose among a variety of **differentiated products**. Buying a stereo can be a stressful and time-consuming occupation, given the range of available components. The variety of personal computers that flood the market turns a purchase decision into a complicated course on the semiconductor chip. Even choosing among ice cream flavors can be a complicated decision.

Why does product differentiation exist? The variety of products offered in the marketplace is a response to differences in consumer preferences. However, we do not observe every individual consuming exactly his or her favorite variety of a product. Product differentiation is limited by the producer **setup costs** required to develop a new product type. Which products will an entrepeneur choose to produce and how many products will be available? To answer these questions, we need to extend our previous models to allow for the endogenous choice of the number of goods and their characteristics. Two types of models have been developed in the economic literature for analyzing markets with differentiated products: the **Chamberlin model** and the **address model** of monopolistic competition.

Chamberlin Model of Generalized Competition

In the generalized competition model, or the Chamberlin model of **monopolistic competition**

for a large number of firms, product differentiation of a particular sort is introduced: **symmetric product differentiation**. That is, although each firm in a monopolistically competitive market offers a different product, the demands for the differentiated products are symmetric. At identical prices, all firms service the same number of customers. This symmetry assumption can be illustrated by an example in which consumer preferences are uniformly distributed over all the products: For 24 consumers and four products A, B, C, and D, six consumers prefer A, six prefer B, and so on, as their first choice; for each six-consumer group, two consumers prefer each remaining product as their second choice, and so on. In equilibrium, the *degree* of product differentiation is characterized by the number of firms in the market.

How is the equilibrium determined in a monopolistically competitive industry? To answer this question, it is useful to identify the demand curve faced by the firms. Given the symmetry restriction, each firm actually faces two demands: the symmetric demand curve of the firm when all rival firms' prices are held constant (the *dd* curve) and the firm demand when all firms' prices change simultaneously (the *DD* curve). The *dd* **curve** is *more elastic* than the *DD* **curve**. Moreover, the introduction of an additional product into the market shifts both the *dd* and the *DD* curves downward because the new product attracts $(1/n)$th of the customers.

The **Nash price equilibrium** of the monopolistically competitive model occurs where each firm's price choice maximizes profits, given the prices of rival firms. In the short run, the equilibrium prices for all firms will be identical and will satisfy the condition that the marginal revenue of the *dd* curve must equal the marginal cost at the price at which the *DD* and *dd* curves intersect. In the long run, another condition is added: Firms must make zero profits. Since a new entrant into the market captures $n/(n + 1)$ of the quantity produced by each of the established firms in the market, receiving almost the same profit as firms currently in the market for a large number of firms, profits must be zero in equilibrium. As in the Cournot and Bertrand models, the solution is **individually rational** but not **collectively rational**. Collusion would lead to a higher price. For a small number of firms, Chamberlin argued that firms will engage in **tacit collusion**.

In the Chamberlin model, the equilibrium price is **inefficient** because it exceeds marginal cost. Another potential inefficiency may arise in the number of products that are offered. When all products with additional surplus greater than the development costs are offered, the number of products is efficient.

Address Model of Spatial Competition

Often competition between products is localized; that is, each product competes only with the neighboring products. A neighboring product can have a literal interpretation (two movie theatres next door to each other compete) or a figurative one (Sugar Pops cereal competes with Marshmallow Krispies but not with Natural Granola cereal). The Chamberlin model of product differentiation would not be appropriate for analyzing such products because an entrant's demand function is not symmetric to the demand curves of the existent firms. A model of **spatial product differentiation**, called the **address model**, is needed.

In the address model, assumptions very similar to those of the Hotelling model are adopted: Consumers are evenly distributed along a geographical space, travel to a store is costly, and costs increase with distance traveled. A consumer is willing to patronize the product (or store) with the lowest price plus travel costs from his location. Each firm will choose a location and/or a price that maximize(s) profits, given its

rivals' choices. In the short run, the number of firms is fixed, so positive profits can be made in equilibrium.

In the long run, firms enter the market. Given that the entering firm must incur setup costs of development, we can determine the entry condition for long-run equilibrium. This condition indicates how far apart the firms can locate without having further entry take place. Because of the nonsymmetric product differentiation, firms can earn profits in this equilibrium, unlike in the Chamberlin model. Since supranormal profits are possible in the address model, established firms may practice a strategy of **product proliferation** in which they preempt potential entrants by locating their outlets in several places.

As in the Chamberlin model, the equilibrium price in the address model is inefficient. Moreover, the **efficiency of product diversity** can be assessed. The efficient number of outlets *minimizes* the total cost of supplying the products. The Nash equilibrium may be characterized by too much product diversity compared with the efficient solution.

Key Words

Address model	Localized competition
Chamberlin monopo-	model
listic competition	Market boundary
dd and *DD* curves	Nash price equilib-
Delivered price	rium
Differentiated prod-	Product diversity
uct	Product proliferation
Efficiency	Spatial product
Equity	differentiation
Generalized competi-	Symmetry assumption
tion model	Tacit collusion

Case Study: The Cereal Case

In 1972, the U.S. Federal Trade Commission (FTC) charged (but failed to convict) the four largest cereal producers — Kelloggs, General Foods, General Mills, and Quaker Oats — with a "shared monopoly" in which they colluded in product proliferation with a large number of cereal brands and engaged in intensive advertising.

In an interesting paper, Schmalensee (1978)[1] discusses the facts of the case and analyzes the economics of the government complaint. Some of the facts are that the top four companies had 85% of the market; between 1950 and 1970 the number of brands on the market increased from 25 to 80; before 1970 there was no significant entry from firms outside the market; after 1970 several outsiders successfully introduced natural cereals; and, only one entrant (Pet) was still in the market by the late 1970s.

A Why would the FTC be concerned with product proliferation of the cereal producers? How might a strategy of product proliferation be profitable?

B Might this behavior be consistent with a non-collusive oligopoly selling differentiated products?

Exercises

Multiple-Choice

Choose the correct answer to each question. There is only one correct answer to each question.

1 Good X is produced in an industry characterized by the Chamberlin model of monopolistic competition. Then, which of the following is true?

   a Since the firms face downward-sloping demands, they can make economic profits in the long run.

   b There are significant barriers to entry into the market for X.

   c Firms operate at excess capacity in the long run.

   d Only **b** and **c**.

   e None of the above.

2 In the Chamberlin model of monopolistic competition with large numbers, each firm believes that

   a If it lowers its price, all the rivals will lower their prices.

   b If it raises its price, all the rivals will raise their prices.

   c If it changes its price, none of the rivals will react by changing their prices.

   d Only **a** and **b**.

   e None of the above.

3 In the long-run equilibrium in the Chamberlin model with large numbers,

   a Economic profits are zero.

   b Price exceeds marginal cost.

   c The *DD* curve intersects the *dd* curve.

   d All the above.

   e Only **a** and **c**.

4 Figure 13.1 shows the *dd* and *DD* curves for a Chamberlin monopolistically competitive firm. The current price set by the firm is p^*. Which of the following is correct?

   a Some firms will want to leave the industry.

   b The firm will want to set marginal revenue of the *dd* curve equal to its marginal cost and lower its price.

   c Price p^* is the short-run equilibrium price but not the long-run equilibrium price because the firm is making economic profits.

   d Price p^* is neither a short-run equilibrium price nor a long-run equilibrium price.

   e Both **b** and **d**.

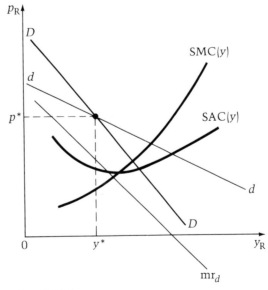

FIGURE 13.1

[1] R. Schmalensee (1978), "Entry Deterrence in the Ready-to-Eat Breakfast Cereal Industry," *Bell Journal of Economics*, Autumn, pp. 305–327.

5 If the demands for three goods X, Y, and Z are symmetric, then

a The number of people who prefer X to Y equals the number of people who prefer Y to Z.

b Among the individuals for whom X is the first choice, the number of people who prefer Y to Z equals the number of people who prefer Z to Y.

c The number of people for whom X is the first choice equals the sum of the number of people for whom Y is the first choice and the number of people for whom Z is the first choice.

d All the above.

e Only **a** and **b**.

To answer questions **6** and **7**, refer to Figure 13.2. Make the following assumptions: Firms A, B, and C are located at $-1, 0,$ and 1, respectively. Individuals are distributed evenly along a circle (of which only a segment is shown in the figure). Each customer demands only one unit of the good. The total price to the consumer is the price charged by the firm, p, plus the travel costs, assumed to be 1 per unit of distance.

6 What is true about the three firms in the market?

a If the prices charged by firms A and B are the same, then the market boundary between firms A and B is one-half the distance between the two firms, regardless of the price charged by C.

b The market area of firm B increases as its price relative to its rival's price increases.

c The price set by firm B will be lower than the prices set by firms A and C in equilibrium.

d The firms will not make short-run profits.

e None of the above.

7 In the long run, an entrant that takes the location and prices of the established firms as fixed will

a Face a demand curve symmetric to those of the established firms

b Underestimate the size of its potential profit by taking prices as given

c Want to locate halfway between firms A and B or between firms B and C, given that identical prices are set by firms A, B, and C

d Set a price for its product equal to marginal cost

e None of the above

True-False

8 In the long-run, firms in a Chamberlin model of monopolistic competition do not make monopoly profits. Therefore, this type of market structure is just as efficient as perfect competition.

9 Since all brands of cornflakes are made of essentially the same ingredients, they cannot be classified as differentiated products.

10 The symmetry assumption made in the Chamberlin model of monopolistic competition implies that if it pays one firm to decrease its price, then it pays all rival firms to decrease their prices.

11 If a new product is introduced in a market characterized by $n-1$ Chamberlin firms, then that product will attract $(1/n)$th of all customers in that market.

12 The dd curve faced by firms in a Chamberlin model of monopolistic competition is more inelastic at every price than is the DD curve along which all prices of all products change simultaneously.

13 The equilibrium price in the Chamberlin model of monopolistic competition is collectively rational but not individually rational.

14 In the address models of spatial competition, an entrant into the market faces a demand that is symmetric to the demand curves of the firms already in the market.

15 In a model of spatial competition in which firms are evenly distributed around the circumference of a circle, the short-run profits to each firm increase as the distance between firms increases, everything else held constant.

16 In a model of spatial competition, firms can make positive long-run economic profits because demands are not symmetric.

Firm A	Firm B	Firm C
-1	0	1

FIGURE 13.2

17 In both the Chamberlin model of monopolistic competition and the address models of spatial competition, the amount of product diversity is always efficient.

Short Problems

18 A study of the U.S. banking industry found that long-run average costs at current output levels as a percentage of efficient average costs were different for banks of different sizes. In particular, the smaller the size, the larger were long-run average costs relative to efficient average costs. These results show that banks of many different sizes can persist in the industry and that many operate at an average cost higher than the minimum of average costs. Do these facts imply that barriers to entry must be significant?

19 Good Y is produced in a market characterized by the Chamberlin model of monopolistic competition with free entry. If demand falls, can the price of Y be expected to fall in the long run? Does your conclusion depend on what happens to the slopes of the demand curves?

20 Give an intuitive explanation of why supranormal profits are not earned in the Chamberlin model of monopolistic competition, whereas in a model of spatially differentiated products, established firms can earn supranormal profits in the long run.

21 In a paper in *The Bell Journal of Economics* (Spring 1981), West tests the following hypothesis, established by Eaton and Lipsey: Under certain conditions, "It will always pay an existing firm to blockade entry by locating new plants in an expanding market at a time before it will pay a new firm to enter."[2] West collected 1978 data on supermarket locations from the Greater Vancouver Regional District of British Columbia. Safeway, Ltd., and Kelly Douglas & Company, Ltd., were two large companies in his data set, and all other firms were considered members of the competitive fringe. Through a statistical method, West showed that the process by which firms locate was consistent with the process

theoretically predicted by Eaton and Lipsey's locational model. Why would a large supermarket adopt a preemptive strategy in which it locates its stores sufficiently close to each other to make entry unprofitable? Does the established firm have to cluster its outlets until its profits, as well as those of the potential entrant, fall to zero? What implications does this behavior have for mom-and-pop grocery stores?

22 In the early 1980s, the Bertrand Report[3] on the major oil companies in Canada, subsidiaries of the United States and British oil companies, contended that the major oil companies had cost Canadians $6 million over the previous 5 years. One accusation was directed at the companies, marketing sector: Too many of their gasoline stations existed in particular locations, resulting in inefficiencies and, more important, in a deterrence to independent gasoline stations entering the market. Evaluate.

Long Problems

23 Assume that firms in a Chamberlin model face constant marginal production costs of c and a fixed entry cost equal to F.

    a Show the long-run equilibrium of a firm in this market on a diagram. Assume that the equilibrium price is $4.

    b The manufacturer of the product sold by the retail firms now stipulates that the product not be sold at any price below $5 and is able to enforce this policy of resale price maintenance. With the help of your diagram, analyze the possible long-run effects of this price restriction.

24 Good Y is produced in an industry characterized by Chamberlin monopolistically competitive firms with identical costs and identical demands. In the long run, each firm faces constant marginal costs of production and a license fee per year that equals F, regardless of the output level produced. The license fee is a payment to produce in the industry. Suppose that the license fee doubles. Show on a diagram the new long-run equilibrium for a representative firm.

25 Commodity Y is produced by Chamberlin firms in a constant-cost industry. Initially, in

[2] B. C. Eaton and R. G. Lipsey (1979), "The Theory of Market Preemption: The Persistence of Excess Capacity and Monopoly in Growing Spatial Markets." *Economica*, 46(May): 149–158.

[3] R. J. Bertrand (1981), *Canada's Oil Monopoly*, Toronto: James Lorimer.

long-run equilibrium, each firm produces 20 units of output per week. In this equilibrium, the Y-producing firms are spending $5 per unit of output on antipollution chemicals to satisfy government standards.

Dr. E. Mission has invented a device that would make the antipollution chemicals unnecessary. If she offers to supply the device to Y-producing firms at $100 per week per firm regardless of their level of output, will they accept her offer in the long run? Explain, using diagrams. (You do not need to show the new long-run equilibrium.)

26 Three Italian pizza parlors, A, B, and C, are equally spaced along a circular street of 90 equally spaced houses. (For example, firm A is at 0, firm B is at 30, and firm C is at 60.) One person lives in each house. The restaurants use the same pizza recipe and face the same production costs of $10 per pizza; only the locations are different. Customers patronize the restaurant with the lowest total price of a pizza: the price per pizza plus the transportation costs to the restaurant (equal to $1 per house that must be passed on the way to the restaurant). Each customer buys only one pizza per week, regardless of the price.

a Determine the demand curve facing firm B, given identical prices set by the competitors.

b Determine the equilibrium pizza price and quantity sold by each restaurant in the short run. For each firm, calculate the short-run profits earned by each restaurant and illustrate the market boundaries.

c Pizza parlors are a lucrative business on this street. Luigi, a chef at one of the pizza parlors, is thinking of quitting his job and opening up his own pizza parlor on the street. What is Luigi's demand function, given that the prices and locations of the established firms are fixed? Are these assumptions reasonable? Why or why not?

d If the setup costs of entering this market are $600, will Luigi enter, given your answer in **c**? Why or why not? What will be the profits of the established firms, given Luigi's decision?

Answers to Chapter 13

Case Study

1 A Brand proliferation in "cereal characteristic space" might be profitable if it deters entrants

from the market. By crowding the product space with a large number of sufficiently similar brands, new entrants would be unable to profitably introduce a new cereal. Hence, cereal producers would be able to preserve their monopoly power. For this reason, the FTC was concerned with the possibility of this strategic behavior. Moreover, this practice could be welfare decreasing if too many brands were introduced; that is, if the social benefits from an additional brand were less than the additional cost of providing it.

B Substitution of nonprice competition (introduction of new brands, advertising, etc.) for price competition is not unusual in concentrated, differentiated oligopolies. However, whether more brands were introduced or more advertising took place than would have been profit-maximizing in the absence of collusion was difficult to determine.

Multiple-Choice

1 c	**2** c	**3** d	**4** e
5 e	**6** e	**7** c	

True-False

8 F	**9** F	**10** T	**11** T	**12** F
13 F	**14** F	**15** T	**16** T	**17** F

Short Problems

18 If the industry is monopolistically competitive, then there are no barriers to entry. The empirical evidence suggests that the industry may be monopolistically competitive because the small and medium firms are operating with excess capacity.

19 Assume that the firms operate in a constant-cost industry; that is, a decrease or increase in industry output will not change the price of the factors used in production. If demand falls, the DD and dd curves shift to the left, losses are incurred, and some firms will drop out of the industry in the long run. This causes the DD and dd curves of the firms remaining in the industry to shift to the right until, once again, zero economic profits are earned. The equilibrium price will rise or fall depending on the price elasticity of the demand curves. For example, the equilibrium price may increase in the long run, as shown in

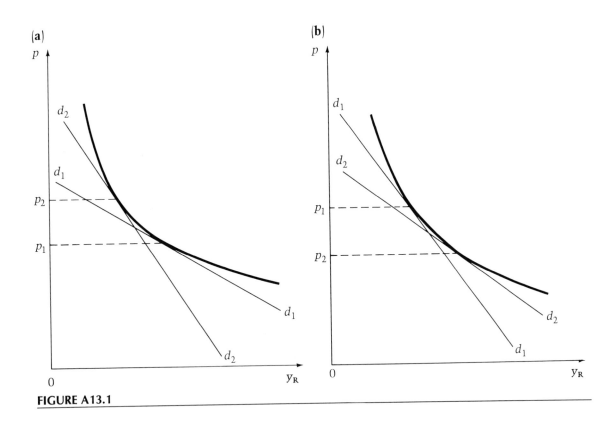

(a)

(b)

FIGURE A13.1

Figure A13.1*a*, or it may decrease in the long run, as shown in Figure A13.1*b*.

20 In the Chamberlin model of monopolistic competition, firm demands are symmetric. Hence, an entrant into the market can expect to take away some customers from every rival. In particular, it expects to sell $n/(n+1)$ of the output sold by the previous entrant. For a large number of firms, that quantity is nearly identical to that sold by the previous entrant; hence, if profits are being earned in the industry, entry will occur. In spatial competition, an entrant can expect to take business away from only the two closest neighbors. Therefore, if a firm enters at the same price as its closest neighbors, it can expect to sell only one-half of an established firm's output. Entry may not be profitable, even if the established firms are currently earning profits.

21 By preventing entry, the large supermarket would preserve its monopoly power. The established firm has to cluster its outlets close enough that if entry occurs, the entrant will make negative profits. This does not imply that the established firm must be making zero profits. Insofar

as mom-and-pop grocery stores serve the same customer group, it is possible that large supermarket chains can prevent entry by mom-and-pop stores.

22 As in problem **21**, the major oil companies may find strategic clustering of their gasoline stations profitable in certain areas if they can successfully deter entry by the independent gasoline stations.

Long Problems

23 a The long-run equilibrium price and output for a representative firm are $4 and y_R^*, shown in Figure A13.2*a*.

 b Suppose that a minimum price of $5 is set, as in Figure A13.2*b*. Then, because *all* firms must raise their prices to $5, each firm will move up its DD curve to point G and produce y_R' units of output. Hence, profits are made, so some firms will enter the industry. This will cause the DD curve to shift down until it intersects with the $LAC(y)$ curve at a price of $5 (point E). That is, at the new long-run equilibrium, shown by point E, each firm produces y_R'' and makes zero profits.

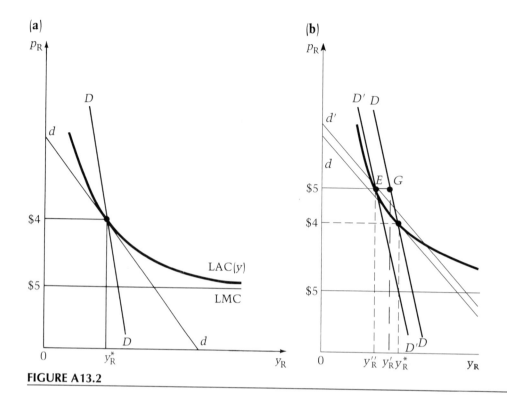

FIGURE A13.2

Note that because price is artificially constrained to $5, the LAC(y) curve is not tangent to the d'd' curve at the new equilibrium.

24 The initial equilibrium is at point A in Figure A13.3. If the license fee doubles, then the LAC(y) curve will slide up the LMC(y) curve to LAC'(y). Firms are making a loss and will want to exit from the industry. As they exit, the DD demand curve and the dd demand curve will shift to the right until the LAC(y) curve is tangent to the dd curve at the intersection of the two demand curves: for example, at point B in the figure.

25 The long-run equilibrium of a firm at 20 units of output and a price p_R^* is shown by point A in Figure A13.4. Under the $5 charge for antipollution chemicals, all the cost curves shift upward by $5 to LAC'(y) and LMC'(y). With Dr. E. Mission's invention, the original LAC(y) curve will slide up the original LMC(y) curve (because $5 per unit no longer has to be paid) to LAC''(y). At 20 units of output, the average charge for Dr. E. Mission's invention is $5. Hence, the LAC''(y) curve intersects LAC'(y) at 20 units of output and

FIGURE A13.3

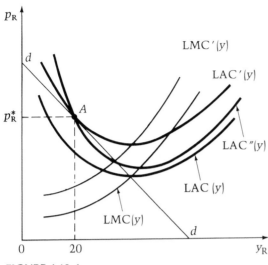

FIGURE A13.4

reaches its minimum when it intersects the $LMC(y)$ curve. Since the demand in the absence of Dr. E. Mission's invention, dd, lies above $LAC''(y)$ for some interval of output, the invention is profitable and firms will accept it.

26 a Let the price of pizza charged by firm B be p_b. Then the cost to an individual x' distance away from B is $p_b + x'$. If the individual buys from firm C instead, the cost of the pizza is $p' + 30 - x'$, where p' is the price charged by C. Then, the market boundary x' must satisfy

$$p_b + x' = p' + 30 - x'$$
$$x' = \frac{30 + p' - p_b}{2}$$

If pizza parlor A also charges p', then the market for firm B is $2x'$; hence, the quantity produced by B is $2x'$, or the demand curve for B is

$$y = 2x' = (30 + p' - p_b)$$

or

$$p_b = p' + 30 - y$$

b In the short-run, firm B will set marginal revenue equal to marginal cost ($= 10$) to get the profit-maximizing quantity and price:

$$p' + 30 - 2y = 10$$

or

$$y^* = \frac{p' + 20}{2}$$

The profit-maximizing y^* is substituted into the demand curve in **a** to determine the price set by firm B:

$$p_b = p' + 30 - \frac{p'}{2} - 10 = \frac{p' + 40}{2}$$

But since all firms are identical, the equilibrium price is

$$p^* = \frac{p^* + 40}{2} \Rightarrow p^* = 40$$

and

$$y^* = 30$$

Short-run profits of the established firms are given by

$$\pi_E = (p^* - 10)y^* = 30^2 = 900$$

The market boundaries for each firm are illustrated in Figure A13.5.

c Suppose that Luigi decides to locate between firms A and B. If both A and B are charging p^* for their pizzas, and x is the market boundary between Luigi and the two firms, then

$$p_L + x = p^* + 15 - x$$

so

$$x = \frac{p^* + 15 - p_L}{2}$$

where p_L is Luigi's price. Since Luigi's market is $2x$, his demand curve is

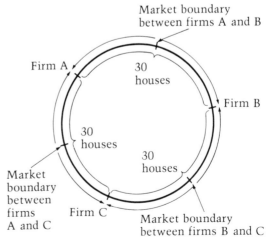

FIGURE A13.5

$$y_L = 2x = p^* + 15 - p_L$$

In **b**, we found that $p^* = 40$. Substituting this into Luigi's demand curve and rearranging it gives

$$y_L = 40 + 15 - p_L \quad \text{so} \quad p_L = 55 - y_L$$

Luigi's competitors are likely to respond to his entry into the market by changing their prices and/or locations. Hence, Luigi is overestimating his demand by holding prices and locations of his rivals constant.

d Luigi maximizes his postentry profits by equating marginal revenue of the demand to marginal cost. That is,

$$55 - 2y_L = 10 \quad \text{or} \quad y_L = 22.5$$

Profit-maximizing price is

$$p_L = 55 - 22.5 = 32.5$$

Profits to Luigi are

$$\pi_L = 22.5 \times 22.5 - K = 506.25 - K$$

where K is the entry cost. Since K is larger than 506.25, Luigi's profits would be less than zero, and so he will not enter the market. In this case, the established firms will earn profits of $\pi_E = 900 - K = 300$.

14

INPUT MARKETS AND THE ALLOCATION OF RESOURCES

Chapter Summary

Input and Output Markets

In the previous chapters about **output markets,** the role of **input markets** in determining the **allocation of scarce resources** toward competing uses was suppressed. Although the production relationship between inputs and outputs was identified for deriving the cost functions, input prices were held constant for the most part. We now turn to **input markets** to examine the firm's demand for inputs used in production. In this analysis, output markets, though still important, take a lesser role: Just as input prices "positioned" the firm's cost curve, the output price affects the value of an input, thereby positioning the demand curve for the input.

Perfectly Competitive Input Markets

First, we examine the **perfectly competitive** input market. Firms of all types may demand a particular input: for example, unskilled workers. The demanders may be, say, farmers in a competitive market or automobile producers with market power. As in the analysis of the output market, we derive the demand and supply of an input. For **primary** inputs such as labor and land, the suppliers are individuals, whereas firms are assumed to supply **intermediate** inputs. In all cases, demanders of inputs are assumed to be firms. The

perfectly competitive input market is based on familiar assumptions: **large numbers, perfect information, input homogeneity,** and **perfect mobility of resources.**

Input Supply

Many of the supply decisions made in input markets are analytically similar to those made in output markets; for example, the producer of an intermediate input sells this input to other firms. As long as the producer of the input is a profit maximizer, the supply of the input is derived in the same way as the firm's supply of some final good. When an individual sells primary inputs that are either nonrenewable or nonexhaustible, we usually assume for simplicity that the supply of the resource is perfectly price inelastic. Alternatively, if the primary input that the individual is selling is her own labor services, then the individual solves an income–leisure utility-maximization problem to determine how much time to devote to market activities.

Demand for One Variable Input

A profit-maximizing demander of an input will want to hire units of that input up to the point at which the additional revenue of the output produced by the input equals the money cost of the input, w. The additional revenue provided by the input is the extra output produced by the input times the marginal revenue of that output. The firm's demand for one input, referred to as the **short-run input demand**, can be derived from this relationship. Call the marginal revenue times marginal product the **marginal revenue product, MRP(z)**, and the average revenue times the marginal product the **average revenue product, ARP(z)**. The short-run demand curve for the firm is then defined by the MRP(z) curve below the ARP(z) because, for any wage above ARP(z), the firm is better off not to produce. The firm will choose z until **MRP(z) = w**. This rule is equivalent to the output rule **SMC(y) = MR(y)**.

Does this rule imply an efficient allocation of resources? To answer this question, we must determine how consumers value an additional unit of an input. Because the value to consumers of additional units of output is the output price, the value of an additional unit of the input is the **value of the marginal product**: price times the marginal product of that input. Hence, an efficient allocation of resources is characterized by **VMP(z) = w**. Because price equals marginal revenue for a competitive firm, perfect competition in both the input and output markets allocates resources efficiently, whereas a monopolist in the output market demands too few units of the input (and, hence, produces too little) since MRP(z) < VMP(z) for the monopolist.

Demand with Many Variable Inputs

The demand for an input when there are many variable inputs, referred to as the **long-run input demand**, is more elastic than the short-run input demand because of the increased flexibility in responding to changes in the price of an input in the long run. If the price of an input falls, the firm will substitute toward the input that has become relatively less expensive. As in consumer theory, the actual change in the quantity demanded of the input because of a change in its price can be decomposed into **substitution** and **output effects**. For both **normal** and **inferior** inputs, the quantity demanded of the input increases for a price decrease because of both substitution and output effects.

Equilibrium in the Input Market

The **aggregate demand for an input** is steeper than the horizontal summation of individual firms'

demands. This situation arises because the increase in the quantity demanded for the input due to a reduction in the input price results in larger production and hence a lower output price. This lower output price reduces the MRP(z) at every level of the input, and so the aggregate quantity demanded of the input is lower than the level implied by the horizontal summation of firms' demands. Equilibrium is found where the aggregate input demand curve intersects the input supply curve.

Monopsony

When only one purchaser of the input exists, there is a **monopsony**. The monopsonist sets the input price. When the supply curve of the input is positively sloped, the monopsonist must raise the input price to attract additional units of the input to the firm. Hence, the additional cost of hiring another unit of the input, the **marginal factor cost MFC(z)**, increases in z. The monopsonist maximizes profits by hiring units of the input up to the point at which the MFC(z) equals the MRP(z) at an input price that is below the MRP(z). Unless the monopsonist can find a way to perfectly discriminate in setting its input prices, this pricing rule will be inefficient.

Why do monopsonies come about? When the perfect-mobility assumption of perfect competition does not hold, a monopsony can arise. Individuals with very few employment opportunities, workers who would face large moving costs in changing jobs, or owners of inputs requiring large transportation costs are likely to face buyers with monopsony power. If the monopsonist can identify groups of workers with different supply curves, then it might engage in wage discrimination. In the case of two groups of workers, the monopsonist will minimize labor costs of a given number of workers by equating the MFC(z) of group 1 to the MFC(z) of group 2. The profit-maximizing number of workers is then found by equating the horizontal summation of the MFC(z) curves to the MRP(z). The more immobile the labor, the more successful the monopsonist will be in this wage-setting behavior. An additional source of monopsony power is associated with the demand for a highly specialized input.

Intertemporal Problems

Problems in nonrenewable resources and occupational choice require an **intertemporal** framework for anlysis. The owner of a **nonrenewable resource** (for example, oil) that is fixed in supply faces the following two-stage problem: First, he must allocate his resource over time so as to maximize the **discounted value** of his income stream (wealth). Second, the owner maximizes his utility subject to this **wealth** constraint. The **separation theorem** allows the resource owner's problem to be separated in this way when the rate of interest for borrowing equals the lending rate of interest. This important theorem enables us to analyze the first part of the two-stage problem — supply behavior — without reference to preferences.

In the nonrenewable-resource problem, resource owners will maximize the discounted value of their asset by supplying the resource on the market in the period with the highest discounted price (assuming zero production cost). In other words, as long as the discounted price is equal in all periods, or the "price rises at the rate of interest" — **Hotelling's law** — the resource owner will be willing to supply some of his resource in both periods. Indeed, the competitive equilibrium satisfies this law.

Key Words

Average revenue product (ARP)
Discounted value
Hotelling's law
Inferior inputs
Input markets
Intermediate inputs
Intertemporal problems
Long-run input demand
Marginal factor cost (MFC)
Marginal revenue product (MRP)
Monopsony

Nonexhaustible resources
Nonrenewable resources
Normal inputs
Primary input
Reservation salaries
Separation theory
Short-run input demand
Substitution and output effects
Value of the marginal product (VMP)
Wealth

Case Study: Do High Prices Mean We're Running Out of Minerals?

In an empirical study, Margaret Slade[1] estimated the price path of minerals over time. She noted that resource prices are observed to rise and fall over time and that the behavior of prices depends on the various components of resource costs. For example, the technological change to the use of large earth-moving equipment for strip mining ore bodies reduced mining costs in the first part of the twentieth century. She hypothesized that the price paths would be U-shaped and found strong support for this hypothesis in the prices of copper, iron, nickel, silver, and natural gas.

A Why would the price path of a mineral be U-shaped over time? In particular, what are the components of costs that would give rise to a U-shaped price path?

B Do rising prices reflect increasing scarcity of a mineral over time? Why or why not?

Exercises

Multiple Choice

Choose the correct answer to each question. There is only one correct answer to each question.

1 If a firm uses two inputs, input 1 and input 2, that are complementary in production, then the firm's long-run demand curve for input 1
 a Shifts down and to the left when the price of input 1 increases
 b Shifts down and to the left when the price of input 2 decreases
 c Is the marginal revenue product curve for input 1, given a fixed amount of input 2
 d Is flatter than the marginal revenue product curve of input 1
 e None of the above

2 Suppose that a firm in a perfectly competi-

[1] Margaret Slade (1982), "Trends in Natural-Resource Commodity Prices: An Analysis of the Time Domain," *Journal of Environmental Economics and Management*, 9: 122–137.

tive market maximizes profits while the price of the input is \$5 and the marginal product of the input is $\frac{1}{2}$ unit of output. Then, the price of the output must be

   a \$2.50
   b \$10
   c \$1
   d \$0.10
   e None of the above

3 The demand curve for an input Z will be more elastic in which of the following cases?

   a The more elastic are consumer demands for the goods produced with factor Z
   b The greater is the decline in the marginal productivity of Z
   c The more inelastic is the supply of factors of production complementary to factor Z
   d Only **a** and **b**
   e None of the above

4 A monopolist in the output market that is a competitive purchaser of labor is currently setting a price of \$100 per unit and hires labor at \$25 per worker, and the marginal worker produces 0.25 unit. To maximize profits, the monopolist should

   a Stay where it is
   b Hire more labor (and produce more output)
   c Hire less labor (and produce less output)
   d Reduce its output price
   e None of the above

5 A firm purchases labor from a perfectly competitive labor market and is a monopoly seller of its output. Currently, the firm is maximizing its profits at 60 units of output. It faces a demand curve for its product given by $p = 200 - y$. The marginal costs of hiring an additional worker are \$1200. Thus, the marginal productivity of the last worker hired must be

   a 20 units of Y
   b 15 units of Y
   c $8\frac{4}{7}$ units of Y
   d Not enough information to determine the marginal productivity
   e None of the above

6 If the value of the marginal product of labor exceeds the wage rate, then there is probably

   a A monopoly in the output market
   b A monopsony in the input market

   c Perfect competition in the input and output markets
   d Either **a** or **b**
   e None of the above

7 Which of the following is *not* an assumption of perfect competition in the input market?

   a All inputs used in production are homogeneous.
   b There are many input demanders and suppliers.
   c All demanders and suppliers of inputs have perfect information.
   d Inputs can be costlessly transported or relocated.
   e All the above are assumptions of the perfectly competitive model.

8 Suppose that at the prices of input 1 and input 2, w_1 and w_2, respectively, a firm's cost-minimizing combination of inputs for producing y_1 units of output is given by point A in Figure 14.1. Then if the price of input 1 increases to w'_1,

   a The firm will demand $z_1^A - z_1^B$ fewer units of the input as a result of the substitution effect.
   b The firm will demand fewer units of input 1 due to the output effect.
   c The marginal cost of production will shift upward if the input is either normal or inferior.
   d Input 1 must be an inferior input.
   e None of the above.

9 If the MRP of an input is $MRP(z) = 60 - z/2$ and the supply curve of the input is $S(z) = z/4$, then the wage rate set by a monopsonist is

   a 80
   b 15
   c 60
   d 30
   e None of the above

10 A perfectly wage-discriminating monopsonist who is also a (nondiscriminating) monopolist in the output market sets

   a $MRP(z) = MFC(z)$
   b $VMP(z) = MFC(z)$
   c $MRP(z) = w$
   d $VMP(z) = w$
   e None of the above

11 A certain exhaustible resource is supplied by a competitive industry. If the marginal extraction costs are zero, then the price of the resource in equilibrium must

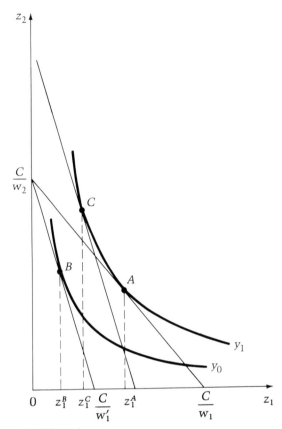

FIGURE 14.1

a Be constant over time

b Rise by r dollars per year, where r is the rate of interest

c Rise more slowly than the rate of interest

d Rise at the rate of interest

e None of the above

*12 A certain exhaustible resource is supplied by a competitive industry. If the marginal extraction cost is positive (but constant), then the price of the resource in equilibrium must

a Be constant over time

b Rise by r dollars per year, where r is the rate of interest

c Rise more slowly than the rate of interest

d Rise at the rate of interest

e None of the above

True-False

13 The more inelastic the supply of inputs of production complementary to an input Z, the more inelastic is the demand curve for Z.

14 The greater the costs of input Z as a percentage of total production costs, the more inelastic is the demand curve for Z.

15 If firms purchase an input Z up to the point at which the $MRP(z) = w$, then the allocation of resources is always efficient.

16 If only input Z is used in production by a monopolist, the condition $MRP(z) = w$ gives the profit-maximizing choice of input and, with the production function, gives the profit-maximizing choice of output.

17 The input employment condition for a price-taking firm in the input market that is also a price-taker in the output market is $VMP(z) = w$.

18 For a decrease in an input's price, both the substitution and output effects result in negatively sloped demand curve for the input, whether it is a normal or an inferior input.

19 A firm's short-run demand curve for an input is the $MRP(z)$ curve below the $ARP(z)$ curve.

20 A firm's long-run demand curve for an input is more price elastic than the firm's short-run demand curve for the input.

21 The aggregate input demand is flatter than the individual firm's demand curve for that input.

22 A firm that is a monopsonist in the input market and a monopolist in the output market and can perfectly wage discriminate in the input market and perfectly price discriminate in the output market will set $VMP(z) = w$.

23 The marginal cost to OPEC of recovering a barrel of oil is, say, $1 per barrel. If OPEC behaved like a perfect competitor instead of a monopolist, the world price of oil would be equal to the marginal cost, or $1 per barrel.

Short Problems

24 A monopsonist uses only labor to produce product Y, which she sells in a competitive market at a fixed price = 1. Her production and labor supply functions are $y = 6z - 3z^2 + 0.2z^3$ and $w = 6 + 3z$, respectively, where z is quantity of labor. Determine the values of z and w that maximize profits.

25 Show that the optimal condition for employment of input Z by a price-taking firm is equivalent to the optimal condition for production of output Y (which uses factor Z) for a price-taking firm.

26 Commodity X is produced by a perfectly competitive industry. In the short run, the only variable input in each industry is Z, also supplied in a competitive industry. With the aid of diagrams, derive the firm short-run demand curve for Z.

27 Why will the aggregate demand curve of firms in a competitive market for an input be less elastic than the summation of the demand curves of the separate firms? (Assume that firms are price-takers in the output markets.)

28 Suppose that a firm is a monopolist in the product market and a monopsonist in the labor market. Show that its choice of wage and employment level is not efficient.

29 Explain why the marginal revenue product for an input is steeper than the firm's long-run demand curve for the input.

30 If the marginal product of labor is $100/z_1$, the marginal product of capital is $50/z_2$, the wage is $5, the price of capital is $100, and the price of the product is $12, how much capital and labor will a perfectly competitive firm demand?

31 In many poorer countries of the world, petroleum workers are paid two or three times more for similar work than are workers in manufacturing. Why would you guess this to be true?

Long Problems

32 In the long run, a firm uses 10 units of labor (input 1) and 100 units of capital (input 2) at a price ratio of $w_1/w_2 = 10$. The firm's total costs are $C = \$1000$.

a What are the wage and rental prices? Illustrate the optimal choice of the firm on an isoquant-isocost diagram.

b Show the effect of a capital price increase on labor and capital when output is constant (substitution effect) and when costs are held constant.

c Compare the substitution and output effects of an increase in the price of an input with the substitution and income effects from consumer theory. Is the conditional input demand analogous to the compensated consumer demand? Is the unconditional input demand analogous to the ordinary consumer demand? Explain.

33 Assume that the market for a particular labor service is competitive. The supply curve of labor is given by

$$z_s = 800w$$

where z_s is the number of hours of labor supplied and w the hourly wage rate. The demand curve for labor is

$$z_d = 24,000 - 1600w$$

where z_d is the number of hours of labor demanded.

a What are the equilibrium wage and number of hours worked?

b Suppose that the government agrees to pay workers of this type one-third of the difference between $40 and the wage paid by employers for each hour worked; that is, the government pays a *supplement* over and above the wage the workers receive from their employers. Given this program, how many hours are worked, what wage rate is paid by employers, and how much do these workers receive in total for each hour worked?

c Assume that a typical worker of this type receives a wage rate of $6.25 per hour. Show on an income–leisure diagram the effect that the government program in **b** has on the individual's optimal choice of income and leisure, given this wage rate. Will all individuals of this type increase the number of hours that they are willing to work at a particular wage rate as a result of the government program? Why or why not?

34 Initially assume that the market for a particular labor service is competitive. The supply curve for labor is

$$z_s = 200 + 400w$$

and the demand curve for labor is

$$z_d = 1200 - 600w$$

where w is the wage rate per hour, z_s is the hours of labor supplied per day, and z_d is the hours of labor demanded per day.

a What are the competitive equilibrium wage rate and the number of hours worked?

b Consider one of the firms demanding labor in this market. Assume that this firm produces as a monopolist in the output market and faces demand $p = 90 - 2y$. Furthermore, the firm uses only labor and requires 10 hours of labor to produce 1 unit of output for all output. What will be the profit-maximizing number of labor hours z_d hired by this monopolist? What are the profit-maximizing price set and output produced by this monopolist?

35 Suppose that a firm's labor demand function (in thousands of worker hours) is of the form

$$z_d = 9 - 0.5w$$

and the supply function it faces is of the form

$$z_s = -6 + 2w$$

a Find the equilibrium z and w.

b Suppose that the government institutes a minimum hourly wage of $6.

(1) Find the new profit-maximizing level of w and z.

(2) How many individuals would like to work for the firm but cannot at the minimum wage?

c Suppose that, instead of instituting the minimum wage, the government agrees to pay the firm $3 per hour for each worker it employs. Calculate the new equilibrium w and z and calculate how much the subsidy costs the government.

36 Suppose that the owner of a nonrenewable resource is a monopolist. Initially assume that production costs of extracting the resource are negligible and the stock of the resource is fixed.

a Derive the variation on Hotelling's law that will determine the monopolist's allocation of the resource over time.

*b Suppose that the marginal extraction costs of the resource are c and that there are no fixed costs of production. Again, determine the variation on Hotelling's law for this case. Will the price in period 1 be higher or lower in this case relative to the zero-cost case in **a**? Explain.

Answers to Chapter 14

Case Study

A Costs of extraction will decrease over time due to technological change, increase over time due to declining grades of the ore, and increase over time due to the intertemporal effect (the opportunity cost of extracting the resource today instead of tomorrow). In the early stages of the life cycle of mineral extraction, the technological factor may dominate the declining grade and intertemporal effects, giving rise to a declining price path. Eventually, the price path rises as the high-quality ore is depleted and the intertemporal opportunity cost of extracting the resource increases.

B Rising prices often signal that the resource is running out. However, even if the resource is becoming more scarce, improvements in transporting, smelting, and refining the resource may reduce the price of the refined product. Moreover, market structure or the regulatory structure of the industry may be changing; for example, price controls kept the price of petroleum in the United States and Canada artificially low in the postwar period. Finally, substitutes for the resource may keep the price of the resource low.

Multiple-Choice

1 d	2 b	3 a	4 c	5 b	6 d
7 e	8 b	9 b	10 c	11 d	*12 c

True-False

13 T	14 F	15 F	16 T	17 T	18 T
19 T	20 T	21 F	22 T	23 F	

Short Problems

24 The monopsonist sets the value of the marginal product equal to the marginal factor cost, and VMP(z) is given by $p[MP(z)] = 6 - 6z + 0.6z^2$. The marginal factor cost is $6 + 6z$. Equating the two expressions gives

$$6 - 6z + 0.6z^2 = 6 + 6z$$
$$0.6z - 12 = 0$$
$$z = 20$$

The wage is found by substituting $z = 20$ into the labor supply:

$$w = 6 + 60 = 66$$

25 The profit-maximizing condition for employment of factor Z by a price-taking firm is $w = p[MP(z)]$, where w is the wage rate, p is the output price, and $MP(z)$ is the marginal product of the factor of production. Dividing both sides of the condition by $MP(z)$ gives

$$p = \frac{w}{MP(z)} = \frac{w}{(\Delta y / \Delta z)} = \frac{w \, \Delta z}{\Delta y} = \Delta C / \Delta y = MC(y)$$

26 Figure A14.1 shows a firm's marginal revenue product and the average revenue product curves for input Z. Given a wage rate w_1, the firm maximizes profits by setting $w_1 = VMP(z)$ at point A. If the wage rate exceeds $\overline{w}$, the maximum of the average revenue product curve, the firm will shut down on the short run because variable costs are not covered. Hence, BC, the $VMP(z)$ curve below $\overline{w}$, is the short-run demand curve for a firm in a perfectly competitive industry.

27 Let $D(z)$ in Figure A14.2 be the summation of the value of the marginal product curves (firm demand curves for the input) across all firms in the industry. At an input price of w^*, suppose that z^* units of the input are demanded by the industry. Now suppose that the price of the input

FIGURE A14.2

falls to w'. Each firm will want to hire more of the input until the $VMP(z)$ equals w'; in the aggregate, this increase in the demand for the input and the corresponding increase in the quantity of output supplied will lower the price of the output. Hence, the $VMP(z)$ will fall and the horizontal summation of the new $VMP(z)$ curves will be given by $D'(z)$. At w', only z' units of the input will be demanded; hence, points A and B are points on the aggregate demand.

28 A firm that is a monopolist in the output market and a monopsonist in the input market equates $MRP(z)$ with $MFC(z)$. The profit-maximizing choices of the wage and employment are given by w^* and z^*, respectively, in Figure A14.3. At this point, the value of an additional worker is given by $VMP(z^*)$, whereas the opportunity cost of this individual working is given by w^*. Hence, additional surplus could be realized by moving to point B, where the value of the marginal product from an additional worker equals the opportunity cost of that worker. The shaded area represents the loss in surplus from the monopolist-monopsonist.

29 In Figure A14.4, the $MRP_1(\overline{z}_2)$ and $MRP_1(z_2')$ curves are the marginal revenue products of input 1 when input 2 is held at $\overline{z}_2$ and z_2', for $z_2' > \overline{z}_2$, respectively. The two inputs are assumed to be complements in production; hence, a higher value of z_2 increases the marginal prod-

FIGURE A14.1

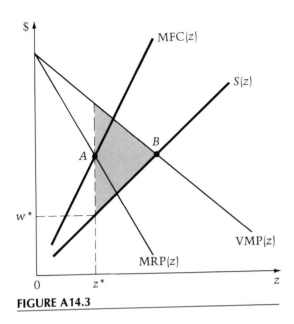

FIGURE A14.3

uct of z_1 at every input level. Suppose initially that $\bar{z}_2$ and $\bar{z}_1$ are employed when the price of z_1 is $\bar{w}_1$. A decline in w_1 to w_1' increases the quantity demanded of z_1 and, because the inputs are complements in production, increases the demand for z_2. This results in an increase in the marginal product of z_1. At a price of w_1', z_1' and z_2' units of the two inputs will be demanded. Points A and B are the firm's long-run demand curve for input 1.

30 A perfectly competitive firm will equate the value of the marginal product of labor to the price of labor and the value of the marginal product of capital to the price of capital; that is,

$$\frac{12 \times 100}{z_1} = 5 \quad \text{and} \quad \frac{12 \times 50}{z_2} = 100$$

Hence, $z_1^* = 240$ and $z_2^* = 6$.

31 If workers are paid the value of their marginal product, then petroleum workers would receive higher wages than manufacturing workers because the price (value) of petroleum is higher than the prices of manufacturing products.

Long Problems

32 a The isocost curve is given by

$$1000 = w_2\left(\frac{w_1}{w_2} \times z_1 + z_2\right)$$
$$= w_2(10 \times 10 + 100)$$

and so

$$w_2 = 5 \quad \text{and} \quad w_1 = 50$$

Figure A14.5 illustrates the firm's labor–capital choice. Note that the firm is, in the long run, denoted by a tangency of the isocost and isoquant curves.

b Figure A14.6 illustrates the increase in the

FIGURE A14.4

FIGURE A14.5

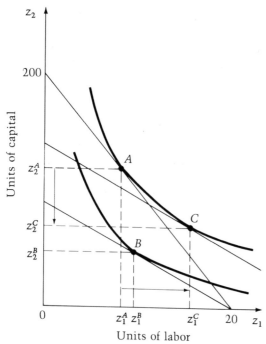

FIGURE A14.6

constant; along a firm's demand for an input, total costs are *not* constant.

33 a The equilibrium wage rate and number of hours worked are found by equating the supply with demand.

$$800w = 24{,}000 - 1600w$$

so

$$w = \$10, \qquad z_1 = 800 \times 10 = 8000$$

b The government pays $(40 - w_1)/3$, where w_1 is the wage paid by the employer. Hence, workers receive $w_2 = w_1 + (40 - w_1)/3 = 40/3 + 2w_1/3$. Then, substituting w_1 (the wage paid by the employer) into the demand curve for labor and w_2 (the wage received by workers) into the supply curve for labor and equating the new demand and supply curves gives

$$800 \left(\frac{40}{3} + \frac{2w_1}{3} \right) = 24{,}000 - 1600w_1$$

Thus, $w_1 = 6.25/\text{hour}$ and $w_2 = 40/3 + 2 \times 6.25/3 = \$17.50$. Substituting w_2 into labor supply gives

$$z_1 = 800 \times 17.50 = 14{,}000$$

c When the individual receives a wage of $\$6.25$ per hour, his income line is given by AB in Figure A14.7. The utility-maximizing bundle

price of capital by a pivot inward of the isocost curve. The substitution effect of A to C results in a decline in input 2 but an increase in input 1. When total costs are constant, the price increase changes the input bundle from A to B: Input 2 falls and input 1 increases (in this case).

c As in consumer theory for two goods, the substitution effect for an increase in the price of an input results in a substitution away from that input and in favor of the lower cost one. In consumer theory, the compensated demand curve is analogous to the conditional demand in producer theory in that both measure only the substitution effect. However, such comparisons of the ordinary consumer demand and a firm's unconditional demand for an input *cannot be made*. To understand this, recall that the consumer's problem is to maximize utility subject to income. This is analogous to *only* the first-stage of the firm's problem: output maximization subject to costs. To find a firm's input demand, a second stage must be solved. In the second stage, the firm chooses the cost-output combination that maximizes profits. In summary, along an ordinary demand, the consumer's money income *is*

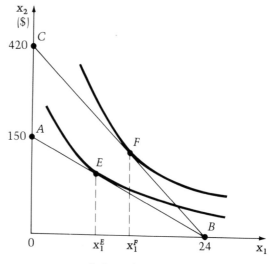

Leisure hours per day

FIGURE A14.7

chosen by the individual is point E. Under the government program, his wage increases to $17.50/hour, and the budget line pivots to CB; so the individual chooses point F. As indicated, not all individuals will work more under the government program. The reason is that the income effect from the wage increase outweighs the substitution effect.

34 a The competitive equilibrium wage rate and number of hours worked are found by equating supply and demand:

$$200 + 400w = 1200 - 600w$$
$$1000w = 1000$$
$$w^* = 1$$

and so

$$z^* = 600$$

b The monopolist sets the MRP of labor equal to the wage rate. The marginal revenue is $MR = 90 - 4y$, and the marginal product is 0.1; hence, $MRP = (90 - 4y)(0.1) = 9 - 0.4y$. Setting $MRP = 1$ (since $w = 1$ from problem **a**) gives $9 - 0.4y = 1$. This implies

$$y = 20, \quad p = 90 - 40 = 50, \quad z_d = 200$$

35 a The profit-maximizing z and w for the monopsonist (the firm is a monopsonist because it faces an upward-sloping supply curve of labor) are found by equating demand and the MFC. Rewriting the supply curve gives

$$w = 3 + \frac{z}{2} \quad \text{and} \quad MFC(z) = 3 + z$$

Rewriting the demand curve gives

$$w = 18 - 2z$$

Equating $MFC(z)$ and the labor demand gives

$$3 + z = 18 - 2z$$

so

$$z = 5, \quad w = 3 + \frac{5}{2} = 5.5$$

b (1) If the minimum hourly wage is set at 6, then the $MFC(z)$ of the monopsonist equals 6 up to the supply curve; then at $z = 6$, the $MFC(z) = 3 + z$ as before. Setting the demand equal to the new $MFC(z)$ gives $18 - 2z = 6$; so $z = 6$.

(2) Substitute $w = 6$ into labor supply: $z =$

$-6 + (2 \times 6) = 6$ individuals would like to work at wage of $6, and exactly 6 are hired.

c If the government pays the firm $3 for every unit of labor hired, then the demand for labor will shift upward. That is, the wage the firms are willing to pay at every quantity of labor is $3 higher or

$$w = 18 - 2z + 3 = 21 - 2z$$

Equating the new demand to $MFC(z)$ gives

$$21 - 2z = 3 + z$$

so

$$z = 6, \quad w = 3 + \frac{z}{2} = 6$$

That is, the same solution is reached as in **b**, but the government pays $3(6) = $18. The policies in **b** and **c** are illustrated in Figure A14.8. Initial demand is $D(z)$; demand with subsidy is $D'(z)$.

36 a To solve this problem, we must consider the marginal benefits and costs to the monopolist of extracting an *additional* unit of the resource today rather than tomorrow. The monopolist who extracts an additional unit of the resource today receives the marginal revenue MR_1 from that unit, *not* the price. If, instead, the monopo-

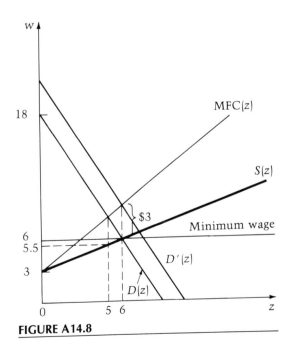

FIGURE A14.8

list postpones production of that unit until to-morrow, she will receive the marginal revenue in period 2 (MR_2). To compare the two returns, we *discount* MR_2 by the rate of interest i. Then the monopolist is indifferent between extracting the resource today or tomorrow if

$$MR_1 = \frac{MR_2}{1 + i}$$

*b The same argument applies in this case, except that the marginal revenue received in each period is decreased by the marginal extraction costs c. Then the variation in Hotelling's law is

$$MR_1 - c = \frac{MR_2 - c}{1 + i}$$

To determine whether the initial price increases for positive c, suppose initially that the rule in **a** holds (marginal revenue rises at the rate of interest). But if this is the case, the rule stated for positive marginal costs will *not* hold because marginal extraction costs today, c, exceed tomorrow's *discounted* extraction costs, $c/(1 + i)$. The monopolist will want to postpone some production into the future; hence, today's price will increase relative to the case with zero extraction costs.

15

EFFICIENCY AND THE ALLOCATION OF RESOURCES: A GENERAL EQUILIBRIUM APPROACH

Chapter Summary

General Equilibrium

The efficiency of the general equilibrium of the economy is the focus of this chapter. We require that the allocation of resources in a general equilibrium be Pareto-efficient; that is, there is no reallocation that can make some people better off without making one or more people worse off. The leading actors in this drama of the economy are individuals: the people who own the inputs and for whom the goods are made. Firms play a background role as the mechanism by which inputs are transformed into output; however, the *owners* of firms are important in our analysis because they are individuals in this economy.

An Exchange Economy

In an **exchange economy,** there is no production; goods are merely traded and consumed. Consider, for example, an island on which there are two goods and two consumers. An **Edgeworth box diagram** shows all the possible allocations for the inhabitants of the island. Given that each consumer has smooth and convex indifference curves and that both goods are essential, then any point at which the indifference curves are tangent to each other (that is, the marginal rate of substitution between the two goods is identical for both consumers) is a Pareto-optimal allocation. The set of such Pareto-optimal allocations forms the **contract curve;** if the allocation lies off the contract curve, consumers can agree to exchange goods in a mutually beneficial manner.

So far, we have not placed any structure on the mechanism by which resources are allocated; it may be prices as in a capitalist economy or it may be a centralized authority as in a planned economy. We have merely indicated what the final allocation must look like for the economy to be efficient. Because our focus so far has been the price system, it seems fitting to ask whether the allocation of resources under the price system will satisfy the efficiency criteria.

Given the initial allocation of goods between the two individuals and markets for both goods, these individuals will be willing to trade if their MRSs are not equal. For some prices announced by the Walrasian auctioneer, the level of consumption of each good is the solution to a constrained utility-maximization problem in which each individual sets MRS $= p_1/p_2$. When markets clear (that is, when demand equals supply in each market), the **competitive equilibrium** is realized. **Walras's law** states that if at some p_1/p_2, demand equals supply in one market, then demand must equal supply in the second market; hence, p_1/p_2 is the competitive equilibrium price. Since all consumers face the same prices, all MRSs are equal; hence, there is no reallocation that would yield a Pareto improvement.

General Equilibrium with Production

Suppose that not only are there two individuals consuming two goods but also that each of these goods is produced by a fixed number of firms using two inputs and a CRTS technology. Given some simplifying assumptions, there are three necessary and sufficient conditions to achieve efficiency in the general equilibrium with production. Each condition is necessary in the sense that if *one* is not satisfied, efficiency is not achieved; they are sufficient in the sense that if *all* are satisfied, the equilibrium is a Pareto-optimal allocation.

The first condition, introduced in the exchange economy, is that there be **efficiency in consumption**. This requires that the MRS between the two goods must be identical for the two consumers, thus implying that the allocation of goods produced is Pareto optimal for all. The second condition is **efficiency in production**; that is, the marginal rates of technical substitution between the two inputs must be identical for all firms. This condition implies that the bundle of goods being produced is on the **production possibilities frontier**. Production and consumption are brought together in the third condition of **efficiency in product mix**; that is, the **marginal rate of transformation (MRT)** in the production of the two goods must equal the MRS in the consumption of the two goods.

Perfectly Competitive General Equilibrium with Production

Once again, let us ask whether the allocation of resources under the price system satisfies the efficiency criteria. The first condition of Pareto ef-

ficiency in consumption is satisfied in exactly the same manner as it is in an exchange economy. The competitive equilibrium is realized when all markets clear and consumers face the same prices, thus implying equality of their MRSs.

Next we consider production. In a perfectly competitive market, each firm minimizes its costs of production by equating its MRTS with the input price ratio w_1/w_2, where this price ratio clears the market. Because all firms are price takers in a competitive market, the MRTSs are equal across firms; hence, the second condition of Pareto efficiency is satisfied.

Perfectly competitive firms maximize profits. This implies that firms selling products 1 and 2 set the value of the marginal product of an input equal to the price of the input. Then, for goods 1 and 2, $p_1/p_2 = MP_2/MP_1 = MRT$. Because consumers set MRS $= p_1/p_2$, this implies that MRS = MRT. Hence, the third condition of Pareto efficiency is satisfied: In a competitive equilibrium, the allocation of resources is Pareto efficient.

Welfare Economics

The **first theorem of welfare economics** assures us that given the appropriate assumptions, a competitive equilibrium is efficient. That is, if all markets are competitive and there are no taxes, subsidies, or externalities, then the allocation of resources is efficient. But what happens if one (or more) of those requirements does not hold? For example, suppose that there is a monopoly in one good and competition in the other. In this case, the third condition of Pareto efficiency (MRS = MRT) will not be satisfied in that consumers will want more of the monopoly good, but the monopolist won't produce it. A tax on a good will also violate the product-mix condition in that consumers will be willing to give up more of the untaxed good for the taxed good at the margin than is necessary in production.

When labor is one of the primary inputs in the model and leisure is one of the goods, the three efficiency conditions are preserved, and the competitive equilibrium is again efficient. As in the case of a sales tax or a monopoly in the goods market, an income tax or a monopsony in the labor market will create an inefficiency in the general equilibrium.

The **second theorem of welfare economics** states that for any given Pareto-optimal allocation of goods that is obtainable in the model, there exists a distribution of ownership of inputs such that the given allocation is the competitive equilibrium allocation associated with the input allocation. Thus, to achieve **equity**, there must be some redistribution of the ownership of inputs. However, to achieve **efficiency**, all that is required is that competitive markets are used.

Key Words

Contract curve	First theorem of
Edgeworth box dia-	welfare economics
gram	General equilibrium
Efficiency	Marginal rate of
Efficiency in con-	transformation
sumption	Pareto efficiency
Efficiency in produc-	Production possibili-
tion	ties frontier
Efficiency in product	Second theorem of
mix	welfare economics
Equity	Sources of inefficiency
Exchange economy	Walras's law

Case Study: The United States – Canada Free-Trade Agreement

The United States and Canada are important trade partners. Approximately 80 percent of Canadian exports go to the United States, and 60 percent of Canadian imports come from the United States. This flow of goods and services across the border has been limited to some extent by the mutual imposition of tariffs and nontariff trade barriers. Many of these trade barriers will be eliminated as a result of the recently signed United States – Canada free-trade agreement, which came into effect in 1989. Proponents and opponents of the free-trade agreement are divided across industry lines; for example, the textiles and brewing industries in Canada oppose the free-trade agreement, arguing that they will not be able to compete with large American producers. In contrast, the minerals and fishing industries in Canada are relieved to see the disappearance of trade barriers.

A Is the allocation of resources under trade bar-

riers Pareto efficient? If not, why do you think trade barriers were imposed in the first place?

B Is the allocation of resources under free trade Pareto efficient? If so, why do you think there are so many groups against the free-trade agreement?

Exercises

Multiple-Choice

Choose the correct answer to each question. There is only one correct answer to each question.

1 Firms A and B produce canoes and windsurfers. Firm A's MRT is 1 canoe for 10 windsurfers, and firm B's MRT is 1 canoe for 20 windsurfers. Which of the following is correct?

  a The allocation of resources is efficient.

  b Total output could be increased if A specialized in canoes and B in windsurfers.

  c Total output could be increased if A stopped producing altogether.

  d Firm B's actual production of windsurfers must be twice that of A.

  e None of the above.

2 Which of these conditions is *not* a necessary condition for Pareto efficiency in a general equilibrium?

  a The marginal rates of substitution between two goods must be the same for all individuals consuming those goods.

  b The marginal rate of transformation between two goods must be equal to the marginal rates of substitution for all individuals consuming those goods.

  c The marginal rates of technical substitution between inputs must be equal for all goods that use those inputs in production.

  d Production must take place on the production possibilities frontier.

  e All the above are conditions of Pareto efficiency.

3 Suppose that Jovita prefers apples to oranges considerably more than does Chin and that Jovita and Chin face the same prices of apples and oranges. Define the MRS of apples for oranges as the amount of apples that an individual is willing to give up to get an additional orange. Then, at the utility-maximizing bundles of oranges and apples, which is true?

a Jovita's MRS of apples for oranges exceeds Chin's MRS of apples for oranges.

b Jovita will definitely consume more than her endowment of oranges.

c Jovita's MRS of apples for oranges equals Chin's MRS of apples for oranges.

d Both **b** and **c**.

e None of the above.

Use Figure 15.1 to answer questions **4** and **5**.

4 Mary has an initial endowment of 2 apples and 8 oranges; Tom's initial endowment is 8 apples and 2 oranges. Which of the following is true?

a Mary and Tom will not want to trade because they are each maximizing their utility.

b If Mary traded some of her oranges for some of Tom's apples, both Mary and Tom could be better off.

c If Mary traded some of her apples for some of Tom's oranges, both Mary and Tom could be better off.

d Mary's MRS of apples for oranges equals Tom's MRS of apples for oranges at point *E*.

e None of the above.

5 After trading takes place from the initial endowment *E*, the new allocation will be

a Anywhere along curve *CC'*

b Along *SS'*

c Characterized by a lower MRS of apples for oranges for Mary than for Tom

d All the above

e Only **b** and **c**

6 The MRT for goods A and B is

a The ratio of the marginal products of the two inputs used in the production of *either* good A or B

b The ratio of the marginal products of an input used in the production of goods A and B

c The slope of the isoquants for goods A and B along the contract curve

d Both **b** and **c**

e None of the above

To answer questions **7** and **8**, refer to Figure 15.2, which shows the production possibilities curve for food and clothing. The combination of the two goods being produced in the economy is given by point *E*. The distribution of food and clothing between the two individuals in the economy is described by point *C*.

7 The allocation of resources toward the production of 100 units of food and 200 units of clothing is

a A Pareto-efficient mix of outputs if the slope of the production possibilities curve (PPC) at *E* equals the slope of the indifference curves at *C*

b Inefficient if the slope of the PPC exceeds the slope of the indifference curves (too much food is being produced)

c Inefficient if the slope of the PPC is less

FIGURE 15.1

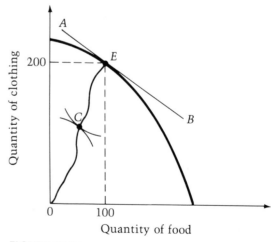

FIGURE 15.2

than the slope of the indifference curves (too little food is being produced)

d Pareto efficient in production because the marginal rates of technical substitution between inputs are equal in the production of the two goods

e All the above

8 If all markets are competitive; if there are no distortions, taxes, or subsidies in the system; and if point E is the mix of ouputs produced in the general equilibrium; then which is correct?

a The slope of AB is the ratio of the price of clothing to the price of food.

b The ratio of the price of food to the price of clothing is given by the slope of the indifference curves at point C.

c A change in the initial endowment of inputs to the two individuals will not change the competitive equilibrium.

d The slope of the PPC equals the ratio of the input prices.

e None of the above.

9 Goods 1 and 2 are produced in competitive markets. A tax on good 1 results in an inefficient allocation of resources because of which of the following?

a The MRSs between good 1 and good 2 are not equal for all individuals.

b The MRTSs between the inputs used in the production of good 1 and good 2 are not equal.

c The MRSs between good 1 and good 2 are not equal to the ratio of the output prices.

d The MRSs between good 1 and good 2 are not equal to the MRT between goods 1 and 2.

e Both **c** and **d**.

10 Suppose that a perfectly competitive economy is operating on the production possibilities frontier with good 2 on the vertical axis and good 1 on the horizontal axis. If the marginal product of labor in the production of good 1 is 5 and the marginal product of labor in the production of good 2 is $\frac{1}{2}$, then which of the following is correct?

a The MRT is 10 units of good 2 for 1 unit of good 1.

b The MP of capital in the production of good 2 must be one-tenth the MP of capital in the production of good 1.

c The marginal cost of good 1 is 10 times the marginal cost of good 2.

d The MRT cannot be determined without knowing the marginal product of capital in the production of good 1 and good 2.

e None of the above.

11 In a perfectly competitive economy, with utility-maximizing individuals and profit-maximizing firms, the equilibrium prices of goods 1 and 2 are $5 and $10, respectively. Then,

a The MP of labor used in the production of good 2 must be two times the MP of labor used in the production of good 1.

b The MRTS between inputs in the production of good 1 must be $\frac{1}{2}$.

c The production of good 1 must be twice that of good 2.

d The marginal cost of good 1 is one-half the marginal cost of good 2.

e None of the above.

True-False

12 If good Y is produced by polluting firms in a competitive industry, then the efficiency of the economy can be improved by imposing an excise tax on good Y, provided that no distortions exist elsewhere in the system.

13 The slope of the isoquants at 100 units of good 1 and 200 units of good 2 along a contract curve of production equals the slope of the production possibilities curves at output levels $x_1 = 100$ and $x_2 = 200$.

14 The MRT between goods 1 and 2 equals the ratio of the marginal products of an input used to produce those two goods.

15 A price-discriminating monopolist does not minimize the costs of producing output.

16 Suppose that each individual has a downward-sloping demand curve for good Y produced by a monopolist. The monopolist is able to perfectly price discriminate and charge a different price for every unit purchased by every individual. This price-discriminating behavior results in an inefficient allocation of resources.

17 The condition for Pareto efficiency in consumption says that the MRS between two goods must equal the ratio of the prices of the two goods.

18 If a subsidy is placed on food purchases, then in a general competitive equilibrium with no other distortions, too much food will be produced and purchased from an efficiency point of view.

Short Problems

19 Evaluate this statement with a diagram: If there is a sales tax on consumer good 1 but not on other goods, then too few resources will be allocated to production of good 1 from an efficiency point of view.

20 a What is the condition for Pareto efficiency in exchange?

b Using a numerical example, give your intuition for the condition in **a**.

c Show that the Pareto condition in **a** is satisfied under perfect competition.

21 Give your intuition for the Pareto condition that the MRT between two goods must equal each consumer's MRS between those two goods.

22 Consider an economy with only one distortion: a monopsony in a particular input market. Discuss how the allocation of resources in this economy is inefficient. Discuss how Pareto efficiency might be achieved if a union were formed.

Long Problems

23 State the Pareto conditions for an economically efficient allocation of resources. Briefly describe the meaning of each condition. Then show whether *each* of the following market situations provides an economically efficient allocation of resources.

a Perfect competition

b A duopoly in the market for good 1; competition in the market for good 2

c A subsidy on each unit of food purchased

24 A million years ago, only two kinds of goods, wild boar and berries, were available. Two individuals, Ayla and Durc, lived in a particular forest and had no access to neighboring tribes. Ayla has the usual negatively sloped, convex indifference curves. Durc, however, likes only wild boar, but any berries he acquires can be cost-

lessly fed to the snakes in the forest. There are 10 pounds of wild boar and 10 bushels of berries in the forest. Each individual is endowed with 5 units of each commodity.

a Show the initial situation in an Edgeworth box diagram.

b Show the set of all Pareto-efficient outcomes of trade.

c If Durc and Ayla end up at a Pareto-efficient allocation after a trade, will Durc be left with some of the berries? Explain, using a diagram.

25 Consider an economy with no production. The economy is endowed with 50 bushels of alfalfa a and 50 bushels of barley b. Two individuals, Mary and Larry, live in this economy and have the usual convex, negatively sloped indifference curves. Larry has an initial endowment $(a, b) = (50, 0)$, and Mary has an initial endowment $(a, b) = (0, 50)$. This initial endowment is not on the contract curve. At the initial endowment, Larry's and Mary's marginal rates of substitution of b for a are, respectively, 2 and 5. (Define the MRS of b and for a as $|\Delta b / \Delta a|$.)

a If Mary offers a trade whereby she would give Larry 3 of her barley for 1 of his alfalfa, would Larry accept the trade? Why or why not? Illustrate your answer. Show, on the same diagram, the set of efficient trades these individuals would rationally make.

b Now introduce prices. One of the points on the set of efficient trades you illustrated in your diagram will be a competitive equilibrium. Show such a point and illustrate the equilibrium price ratio p_a / p_b.

26 Consider an economy with no production. The economy is endowed with 100 bushels of alfalfa a and 100 bushels of barley b. Two individuals, Tom and Harry, live in this economy. Tom has an initial endowment of $(a, b) = (80, 40)$ and Harry has an initial endowment of $(a, b) = (20, 60)$.

a Use a carefully labeled Edgeworth box diagram to illustrate the initial endowment. Label the initial endowment A. Assume that the initial endowment is not on the contract curve.

b Show, on the same diagram as in **a**, the set of efficient trades these individuals could rationally make. Next find a trade that makes them both better off and label this point B. State how much each person is giving up and receiving in the movement from A to B. What important condition of Pareto efficiency is satisfied at B?

c We know that one of the points in the set of efficient trades you found in **b** is a competitive equilibrium. Show this point on a diagram by deriving the "offer curves" for Tom and Harry. That is, at every price ratio, find the amounts of A and B that maximize each consumer's utility, given the price line. The point at which the two offer curves intersect identifies the competitive equilibrium price ratio.

*27 Consider an individual who consumes both goods 1 and 2 and produces goods 1 and 2 with two factors of production: land and labor. He has a fixed endowment of both inputs.

a Show on a diagram his equilibrium when he cannot trade.

b Show on a diagram his equilibrium when he can trade at fixed prices p_1 and p_2 with an individual in another country who produces and consumes good 1 and good 2.

*28 Review problem **26c** in this chapter. Now suppose that Tom acts like a monopolist in that he sets the relative price of alfalfa to barley. Show the relative price that Tom will set by drawing the relevant budget line through the initial endowment and indicating the final trade that will take place. How does this price ratio compare with the competitive equilibrium price ratio found in problem **26c**?

Answers to Chapter 15

Case Study

A No. Suppose that the market for lumber in the United States and Canada starts out as perfectly competitive. Now suppose that the United States places a tariff on every unit of lumber imported from Canada. The tariff will artificially increase the price of lumber in the United States. Consider a representative consumer in the United States and one in Canada. The U.S. consumer equates his MRS of other goods for lumber to the ratio of the tariff-inflated price of lumber and the price of other goods. The Canadian consumer will equate her MRS of other goods for lumber to a lower price ratio (because the price of lumber in Canada will simply equal the marginal cost of production). Hence, the MRSs will not be

equal and, for a given product mix, too little lumber will be consumed in the United States. Moreover, the product mix is inefficient in that U.S. consumers are willing to give up more of other goods to get additional lumber than need be given up in production in Canada. Gains from trade could be realized if the trade barriers were removed.

Tariff barriers may be imposed for several reasons: (1) To protect infant industries—that is, industries that need protection from foreign competition to get started; (2) to affect the terms of trade when a country is large; (3) in response to strong lobbying pressure by a few groups when the benefits from trade barriers are concentrated among a few but the costs are dispersed over many. Recent research indicates that when markets are imperfectly competitive, there may be strategic benefits from unilateral trade restrictions.

B In an economy with no taxes, subsidies, or externalities, free trade will achieve an efficient allocation of resources. Although efficient, there may be resistance on equity grounds. The distributional effects in moving from a situation of trade barriers to one of free trade may be significant. Several studies indicate that free trade will result in large employment shifts, workers will need to retrain for new jobs, and many companies will not survive the increased competition. Both efficiency and equity should be considered in a careful evaluation of government policies.

Multiple-Choice

1 b	**2** e	**3** c	**4** b	**5** b	**6** b
7 e	**8** b	**9** d	**10** b	**11** d	

True-False

12 T	**13** F	**14** T	**15** F
16 F	**17** F	**18** T	

Short Problems

19 If there is a tax on a good, a wedge between the price and the marginal cost of production will exist. Under a tax, $p_1 > w/MP_1$ (or MC_1); so $p_1/p_2 > MP_2/MP_1 = MRT$ (the tradeoff between good 1 and good 2 in production). Each individual will equate his MRS of good 2 for good 1 to

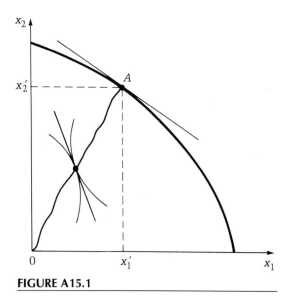

FIGURE A15.1

at the same level of utility. The MRT is the amount of good 2 that must be given up in production to release sufficient inputs to produce another unit of good 1. For example, if the MRS is greater than the MRT, the individual is willing to give up more good 2 than is necessary to get another good 1; hence, less good 2 and more good 1 should be produced and consumed. As this happens, the MRS falls and the MRT increases.

22 Assume that the monopsonist of an input Z is a competitor in the output market. The monopsonist will set the value of the marginal product equal to the MFC of Z. If the monopsonist produces good Y, then $p[MP(z)] = MFC(z)$. This creates a wedge between the value of an additional unit of Z and the opportunity costs of using Z, as shown in Figure A15.2 by AB. An inefficient amount of other inputs will be used in lieu of Z. If a labor union can increase the wage rate to w^*, the supply curve of the input faced by the monopsonist will be perfectly elastic, and the value of the marginal product will equal the opportunity cost, as indicated by point C in the figure.

the ratio of prices p_1/p_2; hence, MRS > MRT, implying that too little good 1 is produced, as shown in Figure A15.1. Note that the slope of the production possibilities frontier is less than the slope of the indifference curves in the final allocation.

20 a The MRSs between any two goods must be equal for all individuals consuming those two goods.

  b Suppose that goods 1 and 2 are being consumed by individuals 1 and 2. Individual 1 has an MRS of good 2 for good 1 equal to 5; individual 2 has an MRS of good 2 for good 1 equal to 1. That is, individual 1 is willing to trade up to 5 units of good 2 to get 1 more unit of good 1, whereas individual 2 is willing to give up the 1 unit of good 1 for 1 unit of good 2. A possible trade, acceptable to both individuals, would be for individual 1 to give between 1 and 5 units of good 2 for a unit of good 1. Trading will continue until the MRSs are equal.

  c This condition is satisfied under perfect competition. At the utility-maximizing bundle of goods, each individual's MRS equals p_1/p_2. Since all individuals are price takers, the ratio of prices is the same for all individuals; hence, the MRSs are equal.

21 The MRS of good 2 for good 1 represents the amount of good 2 that an individual is willing to give up to get another unit of good 1 and remain

Long Problems

23 The efficiency conditions are
  (1) $MRS_A = MRS_B$ for all goods 1 and 2 and all consumers A and B.

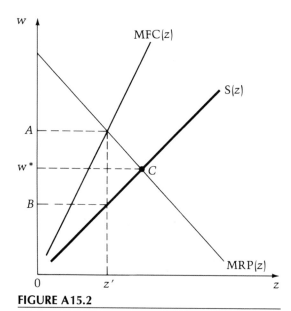

FIGURE A15.2

(2) $MRTS_1 = MRTS_2$ for all inputs 1 and 2 and all goods 1 and 2.

(3) $MRS = MRT$ for all goods 1 and 2 and all individuals.

a Consider each of the efficiency conditions. (1) Since every individual equates his MRS between every pair of goods to the ratio of prices of those two goods and since everyone faces the same prices, the MRS between those two goods must be the same for all individuals. (2) Since producers using two inputs, such as input 1 and input 2, equate the MRTS between those inputs to the ratio of prices for those inputs, and all firms face the same input prices, the MRTS between those two inputs must be the same for all firms. (3) The MRT between two goods 1 and 2 is defined as the ratio of the marginal product of an input, such as input 1, in the production of good 2 divided by the marginal product for that input in the production of good 1. All producers of good 1 and good 2 satisfy $w_1 = p_1 MP_1^1$ and $w_1 = p_2 MP_1^2$, respectively, so $MP_1^2/MP_1^1 = MRT = p_1/p_2$. Since $MRS = p_1/p_2$, the MRT equals the MRS in a competitive economy.

b Duopolists in a market for good 1 set the marginal revenue product of an input equal to the price of the input. In a competitive market for good 2, firms set the value of the marginal product of the same input equal to the price of the input. Then, $p_1 MP_1^1 > w_1$ in the good 1 market and $p_2 MP_1^2 = w_1$ in the good 2 market. Taking the ratio of the two conditions gives $MRT = MP_1^2/MP_1^1 < p_1/p_2 = MRS$. Hence, the condition for efficiency in product mix is violated.

c If a subsidy of s per unit is placed on food, then individuals are effectively facing a food price of $p_f - s$. They will set the MRS of other goods, good 2, for food equal to $(p_f - s)/p_2$. For profit-maximizing firms, $MRT = p_f/p_2$. Hence, $MRS < MRT$, and too much food is produced and consumed in the economy.

24 a The initial endowment is given by E in Figure A15.3, where Ayla's convex indifference curve intersects Durc's straight-line indifference curves. Since Durc does not like berries and can throw them away, increasing the bushels of berries does not increase his utility, for a given amount of wild boar.

b Given that Durc and Ayla start at E, they will trade within the shaded lens. The Pareto-efficient points that can be achieved are given by

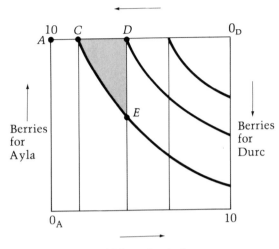

FIGURE A15.3

CD in Figure A15.3. Note that the indifference curves are not necessarily tangent at the corner solution. Nevertheless, along CD, Durc's indifference curve is the highest one that can be achieved given Ayla's indifference curves, and Ayla's is the highest indifference curve given Durc's indifference curve.

c Durc will not be left with any berries after a Pareto-efficient point. It is easy to see that Ayla can increase her utility by taking the berries that Durc wanted to throw away.

25 Figure A15.4 illustrates the initial endowment E.

a Since Mary is willing to trade at most 5 barley for 1 alfalfa and Larry needs only 2 barley for 1 alfalfa to keep him at the same utility level, the trade could take place. This trade is indicated by point F. An efficient set of trades will lie on the curves SS', along which $MRS_M = MRS_L$, where MRS_M and MRS_L are Mary's and Larry's marginal rates of substitution of barley for alfalfa, respectively.

b If the price ratio p_a/p_b is introduced, then line ED represents the budget constraint that passes through the initial endowment. The competitive equilibrium is point G on SS', where $MRS_M = p_a/p_b = MRS_L$.

26 a The initial endowment is indicated in Figure A15.5 by point A.

FIGURE A15.4

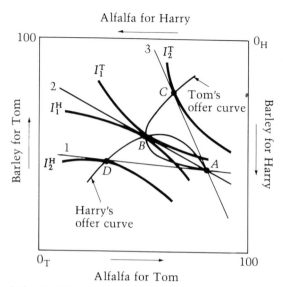

FIGURE A15.6

b The set of efficient trades is given by CD in Figure A15.5. A trade in which both are better off is given by B. In moving from A to B, Tom gives up 30 alfalfa; Harry receives 30 alfalfa. Tom receives 15 barley; Harry gives up 15 barley. The Pareto condition that is satisfied is that the MRS_T of alfalfa for barley equals the MRS_H of alfalfa for barley.

c The offer curves are found by letting the price ratio increase; three price lines are denoted by 1, 2, and 3 in Figure A15.6. When the price line is 1, Tom chooses point A; for price line 2, he moves to B; for price line 3, he chooses C. Harry's

responses to the three price ratios are D, B, and A, respectively; hence, Tom's offer curve is given by ABC, and Harry's offer curve is given by ABD. The competitive equilibrium price ratio is given by price line 2 through the intersection of the two offer curves, point B in the figure. At B, $MRS_T = MRS_H = p_a/p_b$.

*27 a When an individual cannot trade, she will maximize her utility subject to the production possibilities frontier at point A in Figure A15.7.

FIGURE A15.5

FIGURE A15.7

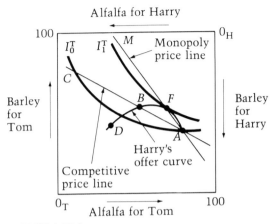

FIGURE A15.8

and good 2 given by point D, where the MRT equals the ratio of prices, but now can maximize her utility subject to the budget constraint and reach a higher utility level at E. That is, she can import $(x_1' - x_1^*)$ from the other country and export $x_2^* - x_2'$.

*28 If Tom is a monopolist, he will want to set the price p_a/p_b that will maximize his utility. The initial endowment A and *Harry's* offer curve are illustrated in Figure A15.8. Harry's offer curve ABD represents Harry's reaction to announced prices and, hence, is a constraint on Tom's maximization problem. Tom will choose the bundle on his highest indifference curve, tangent to ABD; this bundle is denoted by point F. The ratio of monopoly prices is given by the slope of the price line MA. This price ratio will be higher than the competitive ratio of prices (the slope of AC); that is, as a price setter, Tom will set a high (relative) price for alfalfa, the good that he wants to sell.

b The individual who can trade at fixed prices p_1 and p_2 faces a budget constraint given by the line BC, where the slope of $BC = p_1/p_2$. The individual will produce those amounts of good 1

16

THE DISTRIBUTION OF INCOME

Chapter Summary

Efficiency Versus Distribution

Two important questions should be asked about all economic problems. Is the **allocation** of resources toward competing ends **efficient**? Is the **distribution** of the product "just"? We have devoted considerable space to the discussion of efficiency, and, thanks to Pareto, we have reached some important and sometimes surprising conclusions about the ability of markets to allocate resources efficiently. Economists have less expertise on the issue of distribution. Nevertheless, the economist should not stop at the conclusion that markets are efficient without evaluating the distribution of output among individuals.

Productivity Principle

Two philosophical principles of **distributive justice** have been put forth: the **productivity principle** and the **redistributionist principle**. The productivity principle simply suggests that individuals should receive the part of the pie that they produced. When markets are perfectly competitive, each individual is paid her value of the marginal product, and the entire product is exhausted by this distribution. In a sense, the productivity principle justifies the distributional outcome of the competitive market model.

Then why is this principle not widely accepted by economists? If the supply of workers increases, the equilibrium wage as well as the total wage paid to workers falls, when the demand is inelastic. Although labor works as hard, its reward falls under this rule. Rather than being just, this outcome simply reflects the fact that *markets reward scarcity*. Rather than being rewarded the fruits of our labor, the market rewards us according to the scarcity of our talents relative to society's endowment of resources.

Redistributionist Principle

The redistributionist principle says that **equity is** a critical component of justice. Kenneth Arrow, a proponent of this principle, argues that an ethical standard of justice must be impersonal. To illustrate the concept of impersonal judgment, an "original position" is introduced. In this position, each individual knows all the possible conditions he *can* have in society but does not know the actual position he *will* have. Given the symmetry and risk aversion, philosopher John Rawls argued that individuals will desire an insurance contract that leads to a more equal distribution of income.

If a redistributionist position is accepted as the **normative** objective in society, economists can analyze whether or not a particular policy will achieve this objective. Three such policies are considered: minimum wage, income maintenance programs, and income and rent taxes.

Minimum Wage

The effectiveness of a **minimum wage** in redistributing income to low-wage earners depends on the structure of the labor market. For a perfectly competitive labor market, the minimum wage will benefit individuals who can hold onto their jobs but will result in unemployment and underemployment and possibly a lower total income to other workers. However, a moderate minimum wage makes a monopsonist's MFC of hiring labor constant, encouraging the monopsonist to hire more workers at the higher minimum wage. If the minimum wage is set too high, the monopsonist may choose to hire less labor. Analysis of the minimum wage gives insight into the effects of unions in redistributing income to workers through wage floors.

Wage floors can be analyzed in a **two-sector** model: a unionized and a nonunionized sector. Unlike a competitive equilibrium, a wage floor in the unionized sector will result in **underemployment** in the sense that labor is not allocated to its most productive use: Too few workers in the unionized sector and too many in the nonunionized sector will be hired compared with the efficient allocation. Moreover, workers will join the union until the expected union wage (the union wage times the proportion of time each member works) equals the wage in the nonunionized sector. In equilibrium, there will be **unemployment**: More union members will be competing for the limited number of jobs in the unionized sector than will be hired.

Income Transfers and Taxes

A policy of **utility maintenance** that would provide an unconditional income transfer that leaves all individuals at some minimum standard of living is impossible to implement because utility is not cardinal. In practice, welfare programs may **transfer income**, which is conditional on the individual's income. If the individual's income exceeds some target income level, no subsidy is received; otherwise, the individual receives the target income less the income earned. Individuals who would work in the absence of this program may choose not to (or choose not to report

the income) and receive the target income. To avoid this disincentive problem, the **negative income tax**, which is based on an *unconditional* income transfer and a **proportional tax rate**, has been proposed. Because everyone receives the subsidy, the work disincentives *may be* less severe and the government's cost *may be* reduced.

Of course, none of these schemes is free. The government must find ways to collect revenues to pay for such programs. Various taxation mechanisms are possible. A **lump-sum tax** is efficient, but it does not achieve redistribution unless the lump-sum tax is an **economic rent tax** — that is, payment to a factor above its reservation price. **Income taxes** are a natural redistribution policy; however, as with most other policies, it creates inefficiency. Under an income tax, the marginal rate of substitution of income for leisure diverges from the competitive wage rate. If income is actually economic rent, then the efficiency loss may be small.

For some policies, redistribution is consistent with efficiency (for example, minimum wage in monopsonistic labor markets), whereas many redistribution policies create inefficiency. Although economists do not have the expertise to determine which redistributional principle "should" be followed, they can identify policies that will achieve the desired normative objective and point out possible conflicts between efficiency and equity.

Key Words

Distributive justice
Equity
Income tax
Income transfers
Lump-sum tax
Minimum wage
Negative income tax (NIT)
Productivity principle
Redistributionist principle
Two-sector models
Underemployment
Unemployment
Utility maintenance mechanism
Wage floor

Case Study: Incentives to Work Under Welfare Programs

Many opponents of the current welfare program in the United States argue that welfare programs discourage individuals from working. Even welfare recipients complain that they have a disincentive to work under the current program. They point out that a recipient who takes a job that pays a low initial income during a training period will be cut off from all welfare payments and, at least initially, will be worse off. We analyze this and alternative welfare programs in this case study.

A Use an indifference curve diagram to show the optimum of a worker who is free to work as many hours as she likes at an hourly wage rate of $8. She has no nonwage income. The government introduces a welfare program that pays $50 per day to anyone who is unemployed. (The payment is cut off if she works even a little.) Will she stop working or will she continue to work under the welfare program? Support your conclusion with an indifference curve diagram.

B An alternative social security scheme is proposed that also pays $50 per day to anyone who is totally unemployed but that allows partial payments to people who are not totally unemployed. Under this scheme, the $50 payment is reduced by $1 for every $2 that the recipient earns. Will an individual who did not work under the original scheme do some work and thus cost the government less if this scheme is adopted? Explain, using diagrams.

C The government is worried about the incentive effects of the welfare program in **A** on the hours worked and so considers a program in which the government subsidizes a worker's wage instead of paying the $50 grant. In particular, the government would supplement the worker's current wage in such a way as to leave a worker at the same level of utility as under the $50 payment plan in **A**. Show on a diagram how high the wage would have to be to reach the utility level in **A**. Does the worker work more under this program than he would in **A**? Do you think this is a good policy?

Exercises

Multiple-Choice

Choose the correct answer to each question. There is only one correct answer to each question.

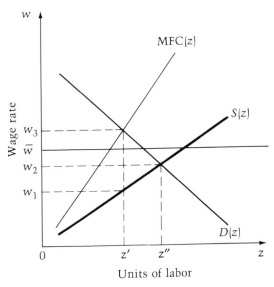

FIGURE 16.1

Figure 16.1 applies to question **1** and **2**.

1 A monopsonist in the labor market illustrated by Figure 16.1 will do which of the following?

    a Set wage w_3 and hire z' units of labor
    b Set wage w_1 and hire z' units of labor
    c Set wage w_2 and hire z'' units of labor
    d Use an efficient mix of labor and other inputs in production
    e None of the above

2 If a minimum wage of $\overline{w}$ is imposed in the labor market, then
    a The monopsonist will hire fewer than z' workers.
    b The monopsonist will use an efficient mix of labor and other inputs in production.
    c The monopsonist will hire between z' and z'' workers.
    d There will be no excess supply of labor at the wage set by the monopsonist.
    e None of the above.

3 When a union of formerly competitive workers forces a monopsonist to push up the wage, the number of workers employed will
    a Rise
    b Remain unchanged
    c Fall
    d May do any of the above, depending on

the extent to which the wage is raised above the monopsonistic level

4 The productivity principle asserts that

a Economic equity is served best when all people receive goods in accordance with their needs.

b Economic equity is served best when all people receive goods in equal amounts.

c Economic equity is served best when all people receive goods in accordance with hours worked.

d Economic equity is served best when all people receive goods in accordance with their marginal product.

e None of the above.

5 The productivity principle implies that

a The total product is equal to the sum of the payments to all inputs.

b Inputs are paid according to the product they produce.

c If all markets are competitive, then the allocation of resources is both efficient and equitable.

d All the above.

e Only **a** and **b**.

To solve problems **6** and **7**, refer to Figure 16.2, which shows two individual's income lines and indifference curves. The income line in the absence of any government programs is *AB*; under a negative income tax, the income line is *BCD*.

6 Under the negative income tax (NIT),

a The government will receive positive tax revenues of *EF* from the individual in Figure 16.2*a*.

b The government will pay a net subsidy of *BC* to the individual in Figure 16.2*b*.

c The government will receive positive tax revenues of *GH* from an individual in Figure 16.2*b*.

d Both **a** and **b**.

e None of the above.

7 According to the figure,

a Leisure is a normal good for the person in Figure 16.2*b* but an inferior good for the person in Figure 16.2*a*.

b If either individual had been maximizing utility at x_1^* before the NIT was imposed, then that individual would receive a positive subsidy from the government under the NIT.

c Both individuals will take more leisure under the NIT.

d Both **a** and **c**.

e None of the above.

True-False

8 In a monopsonistic labor market, the imposition of a minimum wage rate above the unconstrained monopsony wage rate must produce an excess of labor supplied over labor demanded at the minimum-wage level.

(a)

(b)

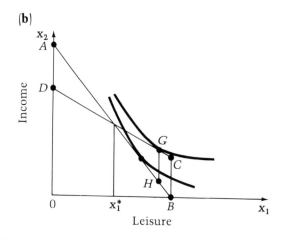

FIGURE 16.2

9 If all markets are perfectly competitive, then the allocation of resources will satisfy the productivity principle.

10 If the market for economists is competitive and the demand for economists is inelastic, then an increase in the supply of economists will increase the collective reward paid to all economists.

11 If an economy adheres to "marginal productivity ethics," then the market reward to an individual will always increase as the amount of work by the individual increases.

12 In a competitive market, resources are allocated to those uses in which the value of the marginal product is the greatest.

13 The redistributionist principle argues that inequality is justified only if it makes everyone better off.

14 A minimum wage that is effectively imposed above the current wage set in the market always results in excess supply of labor.

15 An unconditional income transfer requires less money to raise an individual's utility to some target level than would an income transfer conditional on the recipient's income.

16 A redistributionist would prefer a progressive tax over an unconditional tax as a mechanism for collecting government revenues.

Short Problems

17 Show how the monopsony model might predict increased employment from imposition of minimum-wage law.

18 Graphically show the maximum loss in surplus that the imposition of a minimum wage might cause in a perfectly competitive economy with homogeneous labor and a given labor demand curve. Explain why the loss can vary and on what it depends.

19 Some economists argue that the productivity principle is a justification for the distribution of income that results from a market (or capitalistic) economy but does not provide an ethical principle of justice. Discuss their argument.

20 Two people have the winning lottery number for a $500,000 jackpot. The winner of the jackpot will be determined by the flip of a coin. However, the two individuals can decide before the coin is flipped what proportion of the $500,000 the winner of the coin flip should receive. If the two individuals are risk-averse, what proportion of the jackpot will they decide to give to the winner of the coin toss?

21 Suppose that an individual consumes two commodities, *leisure* and *all other goods*, and receives income only from working at a wage rate of $100 per week. Assume that the individual chooses to consume 30 weeks of leisure and $2200 of all other goods.

Now suppose that the government proposes an NIT of the following form. The individual who makes less than $4000 per year will *receive* one-half the difference between $4000 and the income the individual earns per year. The individual who makes more than $4000 per year will *pay* one-half the difference between what he makes and $4000.

Show on a graph the effect of this tax on the individual's utility-maximizing bundle of leisure and all other goods. Does the individual work more or less as a result of the NIT?

22 Suppose that the government gives everyone an unconditional income transfer S and imposes an income tax on earned income. Define M^* to be the income at which the income-leisure constraints, under this program and in its absence, intersect. Show that an individual with income less than M^* will always choose more leisure under this negative income tax, if leisure is a normal good.

Long Problems

23 Consider a profit-maximizing firm that is a monopolist in the market for its product Y and a competitor in the market for a particular type of labor Z. The firm's only variable input is Z, and the price of Z is w^*.

  a Using a diagram, explain this firm's profit-maximizing choice of output in the market for Y; on another diagram, explain its profit-maximizing choice in the market for Z.

  b Suppose that a minimum-wage law is introduced, under which the minimum wage is higher than the rate that the firm had been paying. Using both of your diagrams, analyze the consequences of this minimum-wage law in the labor market and in the Y market.

c Suppose that this particular labor is demanded by both the monopolist and by firms in a competitive market. Furthermore, suppose that the minimum wage is imposed only in the monopoly sector. Using diagrams, show how this minimum wage can result in unemployment in the monopoly sector under the assumptions of inelastic labor supply and perfectly mobile labor.

24 Consider the market for a particular labor service. Assume that the labor market is monopsonistic. The derived demand curve for labor by the monopsony is

$$z_d = 10 - \frac{1}{2}w$$

The supply curve of labor is

$$z_s = w + 4$$

where w is the wage rate per hour, z is the hundreds of hours of labor supplied per day, and z_d is the hundreds of hours of labor demanded per day.

a Show that the monopsonist will set a wage equal to $2 per hour. Determine the number of labor-hours hired by the monopsonist.

b Now suppose that a minimum-wage law is introduced, under which the minimum wage rate is $4 per hour. With the help of a diagram, analyze the consequences of this minimum wage law in this labor market. Calculate the number of labor hours that will be employed under this law.

25 The government has imposed a minimum wage that is higher than the wage that a particular university pays its student employees. Two students disagree about the effect this will have on student employment. One student opposes the minimum wage on the grounds that though the students who can get jobs will be better off, many more students will want to work than the university will pay at the minimum wage. Moreover, she argues that total employment will probably fall.

a Use a diagram to explain the economic reasoning behind this argument. Assume, for the moment, that the first student is correct.

b The other student argues that the university keeps wages at low levels because it knows that if it pays one student more, it will have to pay all students more. The minimum wage will limit the university's power to control wages. This means that the university will hire more labor at a higher wage. Use diagrams and economic theory to explain this argument, now assuming that the second student is correct.

26 The labor supply function for workers in a union is given by $w = 5 + 3z_s$, and the demand for its services are given by $w = 40 - 2z_d$. What wage will the union set if

a It tries to maximize the total income of its workers

b It maximizes the surplus of workers in excess of their opportunity costs of working

*27 A monopsonist employs some domestic workers and some foreign workers. The supply curves are such that it is profitable to pay a lower wage rate for foreign labor than for domestic labor.

a Use diagrams to explain the monopsonist's profit-maximizing choice.

b Now the government imposes a quota on employment of foreign workers, which does not allow the monopsonist to employ as many foreign workers as before. With the aid of your diagrams, analyze the effects of this policy.

Answers to Chapter 16

Case Study

A Whether the individual will continue to work or not depends on the shape of her indifference curves. It is possible that an individual will stop working, as indicated in Figure A16.1. The individual initially chooses point A; under the welfare program, the individual moves to point B and takes 24 hours of leisure. (However, if the individual's indifference curves were flatter, she might continue to work despite the offer of $50.)

B The welfare scheme with partial payment is given by the income line CDBE in Figure A16.2. Note that above $100 in earnings, the individual receives no government assistance. The individual is shown to take less leisure under this program (point G) than under the program in **A**

FIGURE A16.1

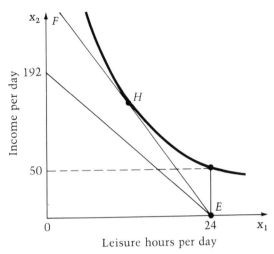

FIGURE A16.3

(point B). (However, if the individual's indifference curve were very steep, she might decide to take 24 hours of leisure.)

C Consider an individual who would not work at all under the program in **A**. If the government supplements the individual's wage to leave him on the same indifference curve, the new income line would be given by *FE*, as in Figure A16.3. The individual would then choose bundle *H*. The

problem with this policy is that individuals who would not work under the current program (in **A**) would have to be identified to qualify for the wage subsidy.

Multiple-Choice

1 b	**2** c	**3** d	**4** d
5 d	**6** a	**7** b	

True-False

8 F	**9** T	**10** F	**11** F	**12** T
13 F	**14** F	**15** T	**16** T	

Short Problems

17 The demand curve for labor and the supply curve for labor faced by a monopsonist are shown in Figure A16.4. The monopsonist equates the marginal factor cost to the demand curve for labor and sets a wage rate equal to w^*. If the wage is increased to $\overline{w}$ through minimum-wage legislation, the marginal factor cost curve would become *ABCE*. The monopsonist sets the demand equal to the new MFC and hires $\overline{z} > z^*$ units of labor.

18 In the absence of a minimum wage, the equilibrium wage and employment would be w^* and z^*, as in Figure A16.5. If a minimum wage is set at $\overline{w}$, then $\overline{z}_d$ units of labor will be hired. Since the

FIGURE A16.2

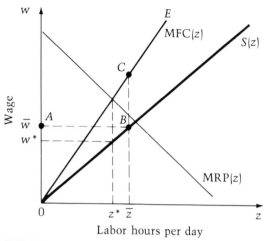

FIGURE A16.4

marginal value of another worker, $\overline{w}$, exceeds the opportunity cost of the marginal worker, there is a loss in surplus, given by the shaded area. The loss can vary, depending on the slope of the supply and demand curves.

19 The productivity principle states that income should be distributed to individuals according to the product produced by the individual. Since individuals are paid the value of their marginal products in a competitive market, income is distributed precisely in this manner. However, this method of distribution can lead to economic inequalities that are ethically unaccep-

table. For example, this method awards scarcity: The less there is of a factor, the greater is its reward, even if it is not putting forth more effort in the production of goods and services in the economy.

20 One-half. Each individual would rather give up one-half of the winnings rather than take the chance of getting zero.

21 If leisure is a normal good (or not highly inferior), the individual will work fewer hours under the NIT, as in Figure A16.6. Under the NIT, the individual's income line is given by CD. The income line in the absence of the NIT is AB. The individual chooses bundle E in the absence of the NIT and bundle F under the NIT. In the figure, the NIT increases leisure as a result of both a substitution effect — the opportunity cost of leisure has fallen — and an income effect.

22 Figure A16.7 shows this negative income tax. The government guarantee of S and the income tax shift the budget line AB upward and decrease the slope, so the final income line faced by the individual is CB'. If the individual chose point D before the imposition of this tax — that is, if his income was below M^* — then he will choose a point such as E with more leisure. This can be seen by identifying the substitution and income effects of this program. The substitution effect increases leisure from x_1^D to x_1' and, because leisure is normal, the income effect increases it to x_1^E.

FIGURE A16.5

FIGURE A16.6

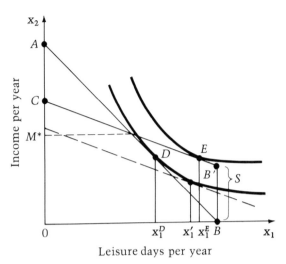

FIGURE A16.7

produces y^*. In the input market, the profit-max-imizing labor choice z^* satisfies $MRP(z) = w^*$. Of course, z^* is that amount of labor required to produce y^*.

b Under the minimum wage, the firm faces a per-unit labor cost of $\overline{w}$. As indicated in Figure A16.8b, the MRP of labor equals $\overline{w}$ at $\overline{z}$. The increase in labor costs shifts the marginal cost curve upward to $MC'(y)$. Marginal cost equals marginal revenue at $\overline{y}$ units of output.

c Individuals will allocate themselves to the two sectors until the wage rate earned in the competitive sector w_c equals the *expected* wage in the monopoly sector; that is, $w_c = \overline{w}\overline{z}/z_m$, where $\overline{z}$ is the number of individuals hired in the monopoly sector at $\overline{w}$ and z_m is the total number of individuals looking for work in that sector. In Figure A16.9, quadrant I shows the labor demand of the monopolist as a function of the *expected* wage; in quadrant II is the *aggregate* labor demand of the competitive firms; quadrant III gives the labor supply curve constraint; and quadrant IV projects z_m onto the first quadrant. In equilibrium, $\dot{z}_c$ individuals are hired in the competitive market at a wage $\dot{w}$; $\overline{z}$ individuals are hired in the

Long Problems

23 a The product market is shown in Figure A16.8a, and the firm's profit-maximizing input choice is shown in Figure A16.8b. In the output market, the firm equates $MC(y)$ with $MR(y)$ and

FIGURE A16.8

FIGURE A16.9

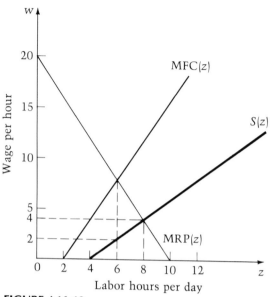

FIGURE A16.10

monopoly sector at $\overline{w}$; and $\dot{z}_m - \overline{z}$ unemployed individuals are in the monopoly sector.

24 a The monopsonist sets the MFC(z) equal to the MRP of labor. Rewrite the demand and supply curves for z as follows:

$$w_d = 20 - 2z \qquad w_s = z - 4$$

The marginal factor cost is MFC(z) = $2z - 4$. Equating MFC(z) = MRP(z) gives

$$20 - 2z = 2z - 4 \qquad \text{and} \qquad w = 6 - 4 = 2$$
$$z = 6$$

b Given a wage rate of $4 per hour, the monopsonist will set the MRP(z) equal to $4 and hire $20 - 2z = 4$, or $z = 8$ workers. The equilibrium wage and employment before and after the imposition of the minimum wage are shown in Figure A16.10. Note that $4 is the competitive equilibrium wage rate.

25 a The first student thinks that the labor market is either competitive, as in Figure A16.11a, or the university is a monopsonist and

FIGURE A16.11

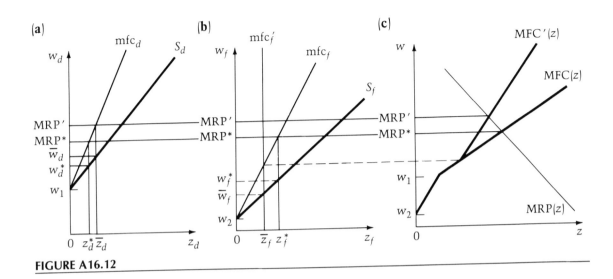

FIGURE A16.12

the minimum wage is considerably higher than the monopsony wage shown in Figure A16.11b. In both cases, labor employment drops from z^* to z_d, and the number of students willing to work at the new wage is z_s.

b This student thinks that the university is a monopsony. Given the current monopsony wage at w^*, the minimum wage $\overline{w}$ induces the employer to hire z' units of labor, where $z' > z^*$. The marginal factor cost changes from MFC(z) to $\overline{w}BCE$ because of the minimum wage, as shown in Figure A16.11c.

26 a Workers are "suppliers" or "producers" of labor services, so they maximize their income by maximizing revenues from sales of their labor services. The marginal revenue of the demand for labor is $MR = 40 - 4z$; hence, $MR = 0$ where $40 - 4z = 0$ or $z = 10$ and $w = 40 - 2z = 20$.

b To maximize the "profit" from selling labor, the MR of the demand is set equal to the opportunity cost of labor; that is, $40 - 4z = 5 +$

$3z$. Thus, $z = 5$ and $w = 40 - 2(5) = 30$. Note that the wage is determined from the demand curve.

27 a The respective supply curves of domestic and foreign workers are illustrated in Figure A16.12a and b. The marginal factor costs mfc_d and mfc_f are horizontally summed to give MFC(z) in Figure A16.12c. MFC(z) is set equal to MRP(z). This value of the marginal worker, MRP, is set equal to the marginal factor costs in the domestic and foreign labor markets. Thus, z_d^* domestic workers and z_f^* foreign workers are hired at respective wages of w_d^* and w_f^*.

b If a quota is employed on foreign workers, as shown by $\overline{z}_f$ in Figure A16.12b, then the summation of the MFC curves, MFC'(z), has a steeper slope beyond $\overline{z}_f$ foreign workers. Now, MRP(z) = MFC'(z) at MRP', fewer foreign workers are hired $(\overline{z}_f)$ at a lower wage $\overline{w}_f$, and more domestic workers are hired $(\overline{z}_d)$ at a higher wage $\overline{w}_d$.

17

EXTERNALITIES AND PUBLIC GOODS

Chapter Summary

Taxonomy of Externalities

When one individual's consumption of a good affects the utility of another individual, the first person imposes an **externality** on the second person. Whether the externality is positive (providing a beautiful flower garden for passersby to enjoy) or negative (talking in class while the more conscientious students are trying to hear an intriguing lecture on microeconomics), the presence of the externality will prevent the allocation of resources under a competitive market from being efficient. In this case, the **recipient** of the externality is affected by the **carrier** (the externality) imposed by the **source**. If not forced to internalize the costs or benefits from the externality imposed on others, the source will provide too little of the good that generates a **positive externality**; in the case of a **negative externality**, the source provides too much of the good.

In addition to there being "good" and "bad" carriers, there are several varieties of externalities. A **consumption–consumption** externality occurs when consumers are both the source and the recipient; for example, a smoker, sitting next to a table of nonsmokers at a restaurant. Externalities for which producers are both the source and the recipient are of the **production–production** variety; for example, a steel mill pollutes a river that is used downstream by a farming commu-

nity. For **consumption–production** externalities, consumers impose an externality on producers; for example, teenagers playing loud music outside a concert hall. The familiar industrial air pollution accidents are of the **producer-consumer** type.

Remedies for Externalities

How can the source be encouraged to decrease production of negative externalities and to increase positive externalities? There are three possibilities. First, the source and the recipient can enter into **private negotiations**. If the two parties recognize their interdependence, they may be able to reach a mutually beneficial solution, whereby the recipient pays the source to increase the amount of a positive carrier or decrease a negative externality. A second remedy is **internalization**, whereby a third party identifies a gain to be had from intervening between the source and recipients; examples are restaurants providing smoking and nonsmoking sections and the rise of the shopping center to internalize the benefits to specialized retailers from large department stores. Finally, **government intervention** may be the only feasible remedy to the allocational distortion.

Under governmental intervention, there are three possible **public policies**. First, the government can create **property rights**. If the government gives property rights to a polluting firm that dumps sewage into a river that is used downstream for agriculture, then the farmers must bribe the firm not to pollute; if the property rights are reversed, then the firm must pay the farmers for the right to pollute. Although the assignment of property rights will affect the **distributional** consequences, all final outcomes resulting from any assignment will be efficient: The government can simply leave the determination of the payment schemes to the individuals. A second policy is **public regulation** based on a **cost-benefit analysis**. For example, to dissuade a negative carrier from smoking, a **tax** may be placed on cigarette sales, or **regulatory standards** may be imposed on the amount of pollutants that can be emitted from automobiles or industrial plants. If the process of collecting information and enforcing standards is too costly relative to the benefits generated, the government may simply opt for no **intervention**.

When the number of sources and recipients is large, contact is infrequent, and the resource is common property, the government may choose to regulate. To identify the regulatory targets, the government needs detailed information, in contrast to a private solution, so that it can make a **cost-benefit analysis**. In the example of the polluting firm and the farmers, the benefits from generating the externality equal the maximum amount the firm is willing to pay to be able to pollute. The costs are described by the minimum amount of income that would be necessary to pay the farmers to make them as well off as in a pollution-free environment. Maximization of benefits less costs yields the optimal amount of pollution. At this optimal solution, the marginal social benefit is just equal to the marginal social cost of the externality.

Public Goods

Public goods have positive externalities for the entire community. A public good is **nonrivalrous**; that is, my consumption of the good does not preclude someone else from consuming it and vice versa. If, in addition to being nonrivalrous, the good is **nonexcludable** (that is, no one can be denied access to it), like Halley's comet, then it is a **pure public good**.

The problem with public goods, especially pure public goods, is that they will not be pro-

duced by a profit-seeking firm. If no one can be denied access, no entrepreneur, no matter how clever, could convince individuals to pay for the good, hence, it must be provided by a public authority. Certainly, this is the case for pure public goods such as defense and advertising-free TV stations. (The intriguing exception to this rule for pure public good is commercial TV broadcasting, supplied by private firms. But when the good is redefined as the *excludable* and *rivalrous* service of time to advertise to a captive audience, the presence of private firms in this market becomes evident.)

How much of the good will public agencies provide? As for any other externality, the government must undertake a cost-benefit analysis. The marginal cost is simply the real resource costs of providing the service. The marginal social benefit is the **sum of marginal values** of the public good by all users of the public good; that is, the **vertical summation** of individual demand curves for the public good. There is one catch. If the tax to pay for the public good is proportional to consumers' revealed value, then self-interested consumers will attempt to **free-ride** by underestimating the true value of the project. If the tax bill is independent of the project and the project is undertaken as long as the sum of announced valuations exceeds the project's costs, then each individual with positive valuation will announce a sufficiently large valuation to ensure that the project will be undertaken, regardless of the announcements by the other consumers. Similarly, if individuals split equally the cost of the project, then publicly announced valuations will not be truthful.

Key Words

Carrier
Cost-benefit analysis
Default option
Exclusive rights
Free-rider problem
Government intervention
Internalization
Nonexcludable goods
Nonrivalrous goods
Positive and negative externalities

Preference revelation mechanisms
Privately negotiated solutions
Property rights
Public goods
Recipient
Regulatory standards
Source

Case Study: Should Information Be Given Away?

Information is a public good. Your knowledge of a mathematical formula does not prevent another individual from being able to "consume" that mathematical formula. Similarly for an invention: A computer whiz who discovers a supercomputer can try to keep that information secret, but the inventor's "consumption" of the information on that invention does not destroy the information. If the cost of transmitting the information were zero, the *social* marginal cost of sharing the information would be zero. Hence, as long as someone benefits from acquiring that information, an efficient allocation of the information involves sharing the information with others. Even if that information were costly to acquire at the time of the discovery, those costs are "sunk" and are therefore irrelevant to the information transfer decision.

A What effect would the imposition of the socially optimal rule for information transfer have on the rate of technological progress? Explain.

B One way of encouraging research is through the legal mechanism of patents. A patent gives private property rights to an inventor for 17 years. Even if this legal protection solves the research problem, will the *use* of the information be efficient? Why or why not?

C Can you think of a scheme that would encourage the socially optimal level of research and use of the innovation? Discuss possible problems with your scheme.

Exercises

Multiple-Choice

Choose the correct answer to each question. There is only one correct answer to each question.

1 Consumers of public goods are likely to
  a Overstate their true preferences if they expect to be taxed in accordance with their marginal private benefit
  b Understate their true preferences if the tax is independent of the project and the project

is undertaken if the total announced valuations exceed the project costs
  c Understate their true preferences if they expect to be taxed in accordance with their marginal private benefits
  d Act in accordance with **a** and **b**
  e None of the above

2 Allison lives above a posh restaurant. Every night before retiring, she practices her trumpet. Because Allison is not very good, business in the restaurant drops every evening when she plays her trumpet. What kind of externality does Allison's trumpet playing represent?
  a Consumption–consumption.
  b Consumption–production.
  c Production–consumption.
  d Production–production.
  e Trumpet playing is not an externality.

Use Figure 17.1 for problems **3** and **4**. The marginal value curves of national defense for two representative consumers, Brian and George, are given by MN and MQ. The marginal cost of national defense is given by $MC(y)$.

3 The marginal social value of $\hat{y}$ units of public defense for these two individuals is
  a $0B$, the marginal value to the individual with the higher value
  b $0A$, the marginal value to the individual with the lower value

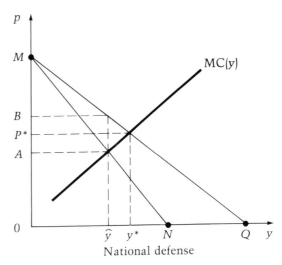

FIGURE 17.1

c $0P^*$
d $0B + 0A$
e None of the above

4 The optimal amount of the public good to provide, given the two individuals' marginal value curves, is

a The amount of national defense given by the intersection of the vertical summation of *MN* and *MQ* with MC (y)
b $0y^*$
c $0\hat{y}$
d The amount of national defense given by the intersection of the horizontal summation of *MN* and *MQ* with MC (y)
e None of the above

Refer to Figure 17.2 for problems **5** and **6**. Snowmobiles are noisy and impose unpleasant costs on cross-country skiers who like to get away from all the noise and the fast pace of city life. Figure 17.2 shows the total cost TC and total benefits TB of snowmobiles as a function of the number of snowmobiles purchased.

5 If the current number of snowmobiles is $\hat{y}$, then

a The optimal number of snowmobiles is being purchased.
b The TB of snowmobiles exceeds the TC of snowmobiles.
c The marginal benefit of an additional snowmobile is less than the marginal cost of an additional snowmobile.

FIGURE 17.2

d The TB of snowmobiles is less than the TC of snowmobiles.
e None of the above.

6 At y' snowmobiles,

a The government may want to impose a tax on snowmobiles to decrease their number.
b The government will want to give property rights to the cross-country skiers and allow the two parties to reach an agreement.
c The government may want to ban snowmobiles from certain areas.
d The government will not want to do anything (more than it already may be doing) because y' is the optimal number of snowmobiles.
e The government may want to adopt either **a**, **b**, or **c**.

7 In the absence of regulation and well-defined property rights,

a The quantity of a negative externality will be less than the optimal quantity.
b The quantity of a positive externality will be greater than the optimal quantity.
c The recipient of a negative externality may want to bribe the source to reduce the amount of the externality.
d The source of the positive externality may want to bribe the recipient to accept more of the externality.
e None of the above.

8 If the government undertakes a project when the sum of individuals' (A and B) valuations of the project, $v_a + v_b$, exceeds the cost of the project K, then the announced valuations of A and B, x_a and x_b, respectively, will be their true valuations of the project if

a Individual A pays $K/2$, and individual B pays $K/2$.
b Individuals A and B pay x_a and x_b, respectively.
c Individuals A and B pay an amount that is independent of their announced valuations of the project.
d None of the above.

True-False

9 If individual A provides a positive externality to individual B, then too little of the externality will be produced in the absence of a bribe.

10 A nonrivalrous good is one for which my consumption of the good does not preclude the possibility of anyone else benefiting from it.

11 A competitive market will produce too little of a pure public good.

12 The marginal social value curve for a public good is the horizontal summation of individual demand curves for the good.

13 If the total benefit of loud music equals the total cost of the music, then the optimal amount of loud music is being played.

14 The source of a negative externality may want to bribe the recipient to allow the source to produce more of the externality in the absence of property rights.

15 If property rights are assigned to the recipient of a negative externality, then the source of the externality may want to bribe the recipient to allow more of the externality to be produced.

16 The distributional consequences of negotiating over the production of a negative externality are independent of the assignment of property rights.

17 Profit-seeking firms have no incentive to produce nonrivalrous, nonexcludable goods.

Short Problems

18 Define a pure public good. What information would the government need to determine how much to produce of a public good? How would this information be used in making the decision? Comment on the problems a government might have in trying to get the information needed to make correct decisions on the provision of public goods.

19 Define an externaltity. Does the assignment of property rights provide a solution to the resource allocation problems posed by externalities? Explain.

20 Show graphically how overall economic efficiency can be increased by the presence of a strong union that achieves a wage rate above the equilibrium wage in its negotiations with a perfectly competitive industry that is creating negative externalities.

21 Determine whether or not the allocation of resources is Pareto efficient under each of the following situations:

a A polluting monopoly in the market for good 1 and nonpolluting competition in the market for good 2

b A public good

22 Discuss forms of government intervention that might be useful in combating a negative externality.

23 What is the rationale for requiring motorists to have drivers' licenses? Automobile insurance? Fastened seat belts?

Long Problems

24 Suppose that paved sidewalks are public goods. There are two people in the country, Mr. A and Ms. C. The marginal cost curve for paved sidewalks is given by $MC = 10 + 2y$.

a Describe the free-rider problem regarding the provision of nonrivalrous goods.

b Suppose that the true marginal value curve of A for paved sidewalks is given by

$$y_a = 50 - \frac{p}{2}$$

and the true marginal value curve of B for paved sidewalks is given by

$$y_b = 25 - p$$

Find the efficient quantity of paved sidewalks.

25 To reach a particular destination, an individual must cross a bridge. At present, no toll is charged. However, a commuter incurs time costs valued at $9 per hour. Suppose that the time it takes to travel across the bridge is a function of the flow of traffic across the bridge in one hour, x. Assume that for a flow of traffic less than 1000 cars per hour, it takes 15 minutes to cross the bridge, but for a flow of traffic greater than 1000 cars per hour, the average time for a commuter to travel that distance becomes $t = 0.00025x$, where t is measured in hours.

To reach the same destination, an alternative uncongested route can be taken. Suppose that an individual can reach the destination using this alternative route in $\frac{5}{6}$ of an hour. Because the value of an individual's time is $9, the time cost of this alternative route is $(\frac{5}{6})($9) = 7.50. There is no other cost of this route. Then, the maximum price (including time costs) that the individual will be willing to pay to cross the bridge is $7.50.

a What is the private (or average) commuting cost of an individual commuter crossing the bridge? What is the social (or marginal) commuting cost of an individual crossing the bridge? Why is the social cost greater than the marginal cost when more than 1000 cars cross in one hour?

b Compute the hourly traffic that will cross the bridge.

c Should a toll be charged? If so, what should it be? What would the new volume of traffic be?

26 Analyze an optimal tax system for firms in a polluting industry when the pollution damage takes the following forms:

a Pollution damage D (in dollars) increases in the firm's output y in the following way: $D = cy$, where c is a constant; the firm is in a purely competitive industry.

b Same as **a** but firm is a monopolist.

27 A city wants to clean up its pollution and so collects the following facts: Automobile traffic emits 20 tons annually, and industrial pollution is 15 tons. Evidence is that cleanup of automobile emissions (a) and industrial pollution (i) could be accomplished at the following costs:

$$C_a = \frac{y_a^2}{2} + 7$$

and

$$C_i = y_i^2 + 35$$

where y_a and y_i are automobile and industrial pollution reductions, respectively. Hence, $MC_a = y_a$ and $MC_i = 2y_i$.

a Mayor McKenna argues that *all* pollutants should be banned. Under what conditions would his proposal be economically efficient?

b Suppose that the benefits of pollutant reduction are

$$B = 0.25y^2 + 2y + 49 \quad (MB = 0.5y + 2)$$

where $y = y_a + y_i$. The mayor's adviser suggests an "equitable" solution. If automobile emissions are reduced by 16 units and factory emissions by 10 units, then the cleanup costs in each sector will be equal to 135. Total cleanup costs will be 270. Moreover, the benefits from cleaning up 26 units of pollution are 270. Criticize this analysis.

c What is the economically optimal level of cleanup from each source?

d Suggest a public policy mechanism for achieving this optimal level.

*28 In this problem, we show that a simple majority rule may not be a desirable mechanism for policy-making. Consider a community of three individuals: Perez, Wong, and Ashford. Three community projects are being considered, A, B, and C. The table indicates the preference ordering of each individual.

Rank	Perez	Wong	Ashford
1	A	C	B
2	B	A	C
3	C	B	A

Suppose that the community preferences are determined by a *majority voting rule*. For example, in comparing projects A and B, the community prefers A to B because two of the three individuals prefer A to B. Show that the community preferences are not transitive, even though individual preferences are.

Answers to Chapter 17

Case Study

A Without property rights over intellectual property, the rate of technological progress would decline. Inventors would be unwilling to invest in research activities if they could not collect the reward from their achievements.

B No. The inventor will have a monopoly over the invention and produce a suboptimal level of output from the invention.

C Designing an efficient scheme for encouraging innovation is very difficult. Through a contest, the government could allow firms to compete for certain projects. The winner (the one able to develop the project most cost effectively) would receive a lump-sum reward equal to the total surplus generated from his efforts. Then the invention would be made available to all firms. The problem with this approach is that it relies on the government to identify socially desirable projects and to calculate the size of the reward.

Multiple-Choice

1 c	2 b	3 d	4 a
5 c	6 d	7 c	8 d

True-False

9 T	10 T	11 T	12 F	13 F
14 F	15 T	16 F	17 T	

Short Problems

18 A pure public good is nonrivalrous in that my consumption does not preclude another person from consuming the good and is nonexcludable in that no one can be denied access to it. To determine how much of the public good to produce, the government would need to know the marginal valuation curves from all persons and the marginal cost of producing the public good. The optimal production of the public good would be that amount for which the marginal cost equals the vertical summation of all the marginal valuations. Individuals would not reveal their true marginal valuation of a public good if they thought they could have access to it when someone else paid for it.

19 An externality is a benefit that is received from or a cost that is imposed on an individual who acts in self-interest. To see the importance of property rights in solving the externality problem, consider the example of a steel mill producing pollution, a negative externality to a downstream farming community. If the farming community were given property rights to clean air, then the steel mill would have to pay for the right to pollute the air; if the steel mill were given property rights, the farming community would have to bribe the steel mill not to pollute.

20 Suppose that a competitive industry produces pollution. The marginal social cost of production is given by MSC(y) in Figure A17.1. However, the private firms worry only about the private costs (MPC(y)). In a competitive market, demand equals supply at y', p'. The efficient allocation of resources is where demand equals the MSC(y); that is, at y^*, p^*. If a union can raise the

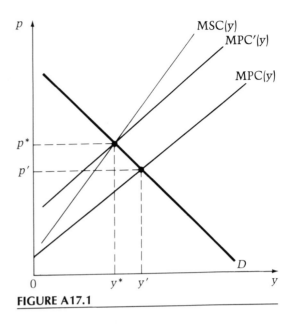

FIGURE A17.1

wage such that the marginal private costs increase to MPC$'(y)$, then the competitive market will produce the efficient output y^*.

21 a A polluting monopolist sets MR$_1$ = MC$_1$. Competitive firms set p_2 = MC$_2$. Then in the market allocation, MR$_1/p_2$ = MC$_1$/MC$_2$. If the market allocation were efficient, then it would satisfy p_1/p_2 = MSC$_1$/MC$_2$, where MSC$_1$ is the marginal social cost of producing good 1. Since p_1 > MR$_1$ but MSC$_1$ > MC$_1$, it is possible that the polluting monopolist is producing the efficient level of good 1, or less than or greater than the efficient level.

b Every individual consuming the public good sets her MRS of good 2 (other goods) for the public good, good 1, equal to the ratio of prices; hence, the market sets MRS = p_1/p_2 = MRT. However, for a Pareto-efficient allocation of resources, the *summation* of MRS across all individuals, ΣMRS, must equal the MRT. Since MRT in a competitive equilibrium is less than ΣMRS, too little of the public good is produced.

22 The government could give property rights to the recipients so that the recipients could charge the source of the externality. This would force the source to internalize the negative effects of the externality. Alternatively, the government could tax the source of the externality, but then the government would need detailed information about the costs of the externality. Finally, the government might bribe the source to get rid of the externality with a cleanup subsidy.

23 Individuals without drivers' licenses are a negative externality on other individuals. By requiring a driving license, the government can control the amount of this externality. Similarly, automobile insurance and seat belts are intended, in part, to protect individuals from poor driving by other individuals.

Long Problems

24 a If the individuals think that someone else will pay for the paved sidewalks, then no one will pay for them because everyone will believe that they can have them for nothing.
  b The efficient quantity of paved sidewalks is found by equating the vertical summation of the marginal benefit curves with the marginal cost curve. To find the vertical summation of the marginal value curves, rewrite the functions as

$$p_a = 100 - 2y_a \quad \text{and} \quad p_b = 25 - y_b$$

Then the vertical summation is MB $= 125 - 3y$. Equating with MC $= 10 + 2y$ gives $125 - 3y = 10 + 2y$, so $115 = 5y$ and $y = 23$.

25 a The private or average commuting cost (ACC) of an individual crossing the bridge is $(\frac{1}{4})(\$9) = \$2.25$ if the flow of traffic is less than 1000 cars per hour and $(0.00025x)(\$9) = \$0.00225x$ if the flow of traffic is greater than 1000 cars per hour. The social cost of an individual crossing the bridge is the change in the total cost due to an additional individual crossing the bridge; that is, the marginal commuting costs (MCC). Again, this is $2.25 when the flow of traffic is less than 1000 cars per hour. For a flow greater than 1000 cars per hour, total costs equal $(\$9)(0.00025x)x = \$0.00225x^2$. So, the marginal commuting costs are $0.0045x. In deciding whether or not to cross the bridge, an individual considers only her private costs. However, the social cost of an individual crossing the bridge includes not only the individual's costs, but also the costs from the negative externality of increased congestion that she imposes on everyone else.

  b The hourly traffic across the bridge is found by equating the demand price with the private

(average) commuting costs. Demand price $= (\frac{5}{6})(\$9) = \$7.50$. So, $\$7.50 = \$0.00225x$, from which $x = 3333$.

  c Yes, a toll should be charged. The efficient level of traffic is found by equating demand price with the marginal commuting cost; that is, $\$7.50 = 0.0045x$, which implies $x^* = 1666$. The toll that should be charged is the t that shifts the private (average) costs curve upward to intersect the demand at $x^* = 1666$. That is, t must satisfy $t + \$0.00225(1666) = \$7.50$, from which $t = 3.75$. The private and social solutions are illustrated in Figure A17.2.

26 a The private market equilibrium with pollution is shown by the intersection of demand and the marginal private cost curve, MPC(y), in Figure A17.3a. MSC(y) is higher than MPC(y) at every output. A tax equal to t^* on every unit of output (pollution) will shift MPC(y) to MPC'(y), and the efficient output is reached.

  b If the polluting firm is a monopolist, there are two problems: The monopolist produces too little output; but because MPC(y) rather than MSC(y) is used to determine output, too much output and therefore too much pollution may be produced. The two effects may offset each other by chance, as shown in Figure A17.3b. In this case, no action is necessary. Otherwise, if the monopoly effect dominates and too little output is produced, a control on monopoly prices might be instituted; if the pollution effect dominates, a tax on pollution may be imposed, as in Figure A17.3a.

FIGURE A17.2

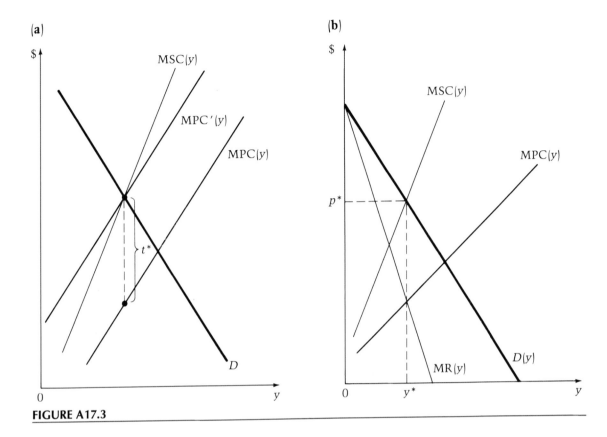

(a)

(b)

FIGURE A17.3

27 a If the marginal benefit from banning 20 tons of auto emissions equals the marginal costs MC_a, and if the marginal benefit from banning 15 tons of industrial pollution equals MC_i, the total cleanup would be efficient.

b The mayor wants to equate *total* benefits with *total* costs rather than marginal benefits with marginal costs.

c To find the optimal level of cleanup, equate the marginal benefits with the horizontal summation of marginal costs; the latter is found by rewriting MC_a and MC_i as $y_a = MC_a$ and $y_i = MC_i/2$. Then, $y = y_a + y_i = 3MC/2$, so $MC = 2y/3$. Equate with marginal benefit:

$$MB = \frac{y}{2} + 2 = \frac{2y}{3} = MC \qquad so \qquad y = 12$$

To find out how many of the 12 units will be automobile pollutants and how many will be industrial pollutants, set $MC = MC_a = MC_i$. At $y = 12$, $MC = 2 \times \frac{12}{3} = 8$. Then, $MC_a = 8$, so $y_a = 8$. $MC_i = 8$, so $y_i = 4$.

d To achieve the optimal level of pollution, a tax on emissions can be imposed.

*28 Compare projects A and B. Perez and Wong prefer A and B. By majority vote rule (MVR), the community prefers A to B. Compare B and C. Perez and Ashford prefer B to C. By MVR, the community prefers B to C. Compare C and A. Wong and Ashford prefer C to A. By MVR, the community prefers C to A. Hence, although individual preferences are transitive, MVR leads to intransitive community preferences: A is preferred to B, B is preferred to C, but C is preferred to A.